OVID
Amores
Metamorphoses

Selections
Second Edition

Charbra Adams Jestin
&
Phyllis B. Katz

Bolchazy-Carducci Publishers, Inc.
Wauconda, Illinois

Editor
Laurie Haight Keenan

Five New Illustrations
© Copyright 1998 Linda Larson

Maps
Charlene M. Hernandez and Benjamin J. Jansky

Cover Design and Typography
Charlene M. Hernandez

Cover Graphic
Aphrodite & Eros, Terracotta from Tanara, IVc BC
Seattle Museum of Art, Photo: R. Schoder, S.J.

Latin Text
The Latin text of *Amores* is from *P. Ovidi Nasonis: Amores, Medicamina Faciei Femineae,
Ars Amatoria, Remedia Amoris* (Oxford: Clarendon Press, 1994), E. J. Kenney, ed.,
by permission of Oxford University Press. The Latin text of *Metamorphoses* is from
Ovid, Vols. III and IV, *Metamorphoses,* The Loeb Classical Library (Cambridge: Harvard
University Press, 1984), G. P. Goold, ed., by permission of Harvard University Press.

Bolchazy-Carducci Publishers, Inc.
1000 Brown Street, Unit 101
Wauconda, Illinois 60084 USA

http://www.bolchazy.com

Printed in the United States of America
2007
by United Graphics

ISBN 978-0-86516-431-4

Library of Congress Cataloging-in-Publication Data

Ovid, 43 B.C.–17 or 18 A.D.
   [Amores. Selections]
   Ovid : Amores, Metamorphoses : selections / [edited by] Charbra Adams Jestin &
Phyllis B. Katz.—2nd ed.
      p.   cm.
   Text in Latin, with introd., notes, and vocabulary in English.
   Includes bibliographical references (p.).
   ISBN 0-86516-431-2 (alk. paper)
   1. Latin language—Readers. 2. Ovid, 43 B.C.-17 or 18 A.D.—Problems, exercises, etc.
3. Mythology, Classical—Poetry. 4. Metamorphosis—Poetry. 5. Love poetry, Latin.   I.
Jestin, Charbra Adams, 1951-   . II. Katz, Phyllis B., 1936-   . III. Ovid, 43 B.C.-17 or 18 A.D.
Metamorphoses. Selections. IV. Title.

PA2099.09J47 2000   00-023105
478.6'421—dc21

To Loftus and Arnie,
maritis optimis quibuscum
"concordes egimus annos"

ACKNOWLEDGMENTS

Without the help of many classicists, colleagues, friends, and other keen-eyed readers, this textbook could not have reached its present form. Initially a thesis written by C. A. Jestin for an M. A. degree in Classics granted by Wesleyan University, it first fell under the watchful eyes of Professors James O'Hara, advisor, and Michael Roberts, second reader, each of whom contributed pages of commentary and criticism. Their careful and ever-encouraging editing helped to shape the work in its earliest stages.

Margaret Graver of the Classics Department, Dartmouth College, read nearly every page of this manuscript. Her background in the teaching of Latin to high school, college, and university students gave her an ideal perspective for this textbook. Her careful and thoughtful editing of the Latin text, glossaries, and student questions and answers, helped us to clarify and refine material, and her insightful comments on the introductions to the passages were always helpful.

Claire Loiselle, Latin teacher at Avon High School, Avon, Connecticut, also read much of the text in manuscript. She contributed many important suggestions based on her knowledge as a classicist and as a highly regarded teacher of long experience.

Laurie Haight of Bolchazy-Carducci Publishers has shepherded this work throughout its preparation. She has encouraged us at every turn and willingly answered all of our questions, profound or tedious.

We wish to thank those reviewers of the first edition whose identifications of errors and sugestions for further explication have helped to improve the second edition of this textbook.

To all of these people we express our thanks for guiding us to the completion of this textbook. Their suggestions and advice have been indispensable to us. Whatever weaknesses remain are entirely our own.

A NOTE ON THE LATIN TEXT

The Latin text for the *Amores* has come from *P. Ovidi Nasonis: Amores, Medicamina Faciei Femineae, Ars Amatoria, Remedia Amoris*, edited by E. J. Kenney and published by Oxford University Press. Consonantal *u* has been changed to *v* and double quotation marks have replaced the single marks. The text of the *Metamorphoses* has been taken from the Loeb Classical Library, third edition, revised by G. P. Goold and published by Harvard University Press. Quotation marks have been adjusted to reflect stories told within stories and to signal the end of the selected passages from those stories. Line numbers throughout have been regularized to every fifth line.

CONTENTS

LIST OF MAPS

LIST OF ILLUSTRATIONS

A NOTE TO THE STUDENT

What is the appeal of Ovid's *Amores* and *Metamorphoses?* His collection of love poems, the *Amores*, are written with the wit and humor, and sometimes the regret, of one who has seen love at first hand. His epic story of transformations from creation to the reign of Augustus, the *Metamorphoses*, is the work of a consummate storyteller. Ovid speaks to us today through a voice as clear at the beginning of the third millennium as it was to his contemporaries on the eve of the first.

This book is organized to help you to read, comprehend, and enjoy the poetry of Ovid that constitutes the AP syllabus. The textbook begins with six of the *Amores*, each with an introduction that highlights the main theme of the poem and places it within the context of love elegy in general. Five selections from the *Metamorphoses* follow, each illustrating a different type of metamorphosis or change. The introductions to the selections place the characters and their metamorphoses in the larger context of the work.

Each page provides help with vocabulary, grammatical structures, and a variety of poetic devices. As the book progresses, however, the number of references pointing out the stylistic devices already noted in earlier passages decreases. We hope that by the end of the text you will have developed an eye and ear for picking up the more obvious ones on your own. A full vocabulary is provided at the back of the book as well as a list of all words occurring five or more times in the Latin text.

In addition there are questions and answers for every Latin passage to provide you with further help in translation. They are designed to help you to think critically about the Latin and will be most beneficial if you try to answer the questions on your own before looking at the answers. The appendices include explanations of metrical terms and figures of speech which also occur in the on-page glosses in small capital letters.

Ovid's language and style are not difficult. You should note, however, the following points as you begin to read his poetry:

- Latin poetry was written to be heard as well as to be read. You should practice reading each poem aloud and look for the ways by which the sound of words reinforces the meaning expressed.
- Your reading aloud will be enhanced by an understanding of the meters employed and the many possibilities the poet used to vary the metrical pattern so that a line moves faster or slower. Macrons are provided in the glossed vocabulary and in the full glossary at the end.
- Be aware of sound patterns such as alliteration, assonance, and onomatopoeia (see Appendix for definitions of these terms).
- Pay attention to nuances of word order; word order in poetry is often quite different from prose. Ovid is particularly fond of using chiastic and interlocked word order and uses the Golden Line with great effect (again see the Appendix for definitions of these terms).
- Some features of Ovid's language may be unfamiliar to you. For example, you will often find:
  ‣ the first person plural (we) in place of I
  ‣ the alternate form of the third person plural perfect active indicative (-*ere* in place of -*erunt*)
  ‣ a plural noun substituted for a singular such as *amores* for *amor*
  ‣ the perfect passive participle as an adjective
  ‣ the ablative alone without a preposition in phrases telling where or when
  ‣ many poetic lines enjambed—the syntactical meaning carried over from one line to the next (therefore you need to look for a full stop, i.e., a period, colon, or semi-colon, when you are translating to be sure that you are reading for a complete thought)
  ‣ the dative case used with compound verbs
  ‣ an abrupt shift from the past to the present tense (the historical present) for vividness
  ‣ an adjective in the third foot of the line paired with the noun at line end and
  ‣ the alternate -*is* accusative plural third declension ending

OVID'S LIFE AND WORKS

Publius Ovidius Naso was born in Sulmo, in the North of Italy, in 43 B.C., just a year after the assassination of Julius Caesar. The Battle of Actium, which would strengthen the power of Octavian, Caesar's grandnephew and avenger, occurred twelve years after Ovid's birth, and Ovid approached adulthood while Octavian consolidated his authority.

Through skillful manipulation, Octavian secured complete loyalty and favor from the Senate. When in 27 B.C. he voluntarily "relinquished" all military power, he was rewarded with the responsibility of administering Gaul, Spain, Syria, and Egypt, and was granted the honorary title Augustus, by which he was known thereafter. Augustus maintained the allegiance of the Roman citizenry through his persuasive influence and great wealth: his authority became absolute, although he fostered the illusion that Rome was governed by the *Senatus Populusque Romanus.*

Augustus brought peace to Rome after years of civil strife. He instituted many public works projects and restored traditional gods and religious practices. To counteract the ostentation of the new and wealthy Rome, he tried to inculcate a simple lifestyle, offering his own as an example. He also established laws with very severe penalties against adultery and with rewards for those who married and produced children. Augustus banished his own daughter, Julia, in 2 B.C., for her repeated scandalous affairs.

At the same time, Augustus did much to encourage the arts. He drew young and promising poets, among them Vergil and Horace, into his sphere of influence, encouraging them to write works that would glorify Rome. Although Vergil and Horace maintained their independent voices and their integrity as poets, they did serve Augustus's political and cultural ambitions. Ovid felt no such compelling allegiance, writing with an independence, even an irreverence, which his older colleagues did not dare to display openly; it was

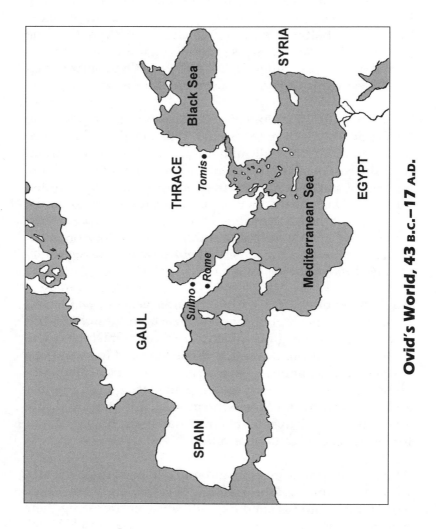

Ovid's World, 43 B.C.–17 A.D.

these independent and iconoclastic works which were, in part, responsible for Ovid's permanent banishment from Rome.

Born into an equestrian family, Ovid received a traditional upper class education that readied him for an active political life. He was sent to Rome to study rhetoric with the great orators of his day. Nevertheless, Ovid preferred poetry to speechmaking. He traveled and began a political career, but abandoned it in 24 B.C. against the advice of his father; in an autobiographical poem written in exile, the poet confesses that everything he wrote turned to poetry.

Ovid wrote his first major collection of poems, the *Amores*, at the age of twenty. In choosing to write love elegy, he was working within a long tradition; his predecessors included Tibullus and Propertius, Gallus, whose poetry has been lost, and, to some extent, Catullus. While still working on the *Amores*, Ovid began the *Heroides*, a series of elegiac love letters written by great female characters from mythology. Ovid blends here for the first time the genres of elegy, epic, and tragedy, a mingling that anticipates his rhetorical strategy in the *Metamorphoses*. From elegy, Ovid turned to tragedy and produced a version of the *Medea*, which has not survived.

In his mid-thirties, Ovid returned to his former theme of love in a series of didactic or instructional works devoted exclusively to this motif. The *Medicamina Faciei* is a treatise on the use of cosmetics. The *Ars Amatoria* is a manual of three books of instructions for male and female lovers; two books advise men on how to attract and keep women; a third advises women on attracting men. This irreverent, provocative poem is a kind of satire of Augustus's official, legislated morality, and may have been one of the causes of Ovid's exile. At age forty-three he wrote the *Remedia Amoris*, a handbook that tells readers how to combat love and cure themselves of this passion.

During all this time, Ovid was also working on his *Metamorphoses*, and from the ages of forty-three to fifty he devoted himself almost exclusively to this work. His fifteen-book poem of nearly 12,000 lines switches smoothly from epic to elegy when the subject matter warrants. As he reached the end of this work, Ovid embarked on a new project, the *Fasti,* a poem in twelve books, each treating a calendar month and explaining contemporary indigenous religious practices by giving the historical precedents for them. This poem would certainly have appealed to Augustus; it was incomplete, however, when Ovid was banished in 8 A.D.

After banishment from Rome at the age of fifty, Ovid spent the remainder of his days cut off from family and friends in the remote Thracian city of Tomis on the west shore of the Black Sea. Here he was isolated from all the civilization that had nourished and sustained him. We do not know the exact cause of his banishment; the poet himself speaks of a *carmen* and an *error* in one of the poems in the *Tristia,* poems he wrote during his banishment, in the hope that they would move Augustus to recall him. The *carmen* is almost certainly the *Ars Amatoria;* the *error* may be connected with the banishment of Augustus's daughter, but there is no indisputable evidence for either cause. In addition to the *Tristia,* poems that chronicle the poet's grim life in Tomis, Ovid wrote four books of poems in elegiac couplets, the *Epistulae ex Ponto,* letters to his friends and relations back in Rome.

Ovid's final work was a poem called the *Ibis,* a six-hundred–line attack on a former acquaintance who had tried to profit from Ovid's banishment. Several other short works from this period are now lost; at the time of his death the poet had begun a major poem, the *Halieutica,* about fishing; we have some 130 lines of this poem. Ovid died in Tomis at the age of sixty.

TOPICAL BIBLIOGRAPHY FOR OVID

General: Amores

Boyd, Barbara Weiden. *Ovid's Literary Loves. Influence and Innovation in the "Amores "* (Ann Arbor: University of Michigan Press, 1997).

Buchan, M. *Ovidius Imperamator:* Beginnings and Endings of Love Poems and Empire in the *Amores." Arethusa* 28:53–85.

Cahoon, L. "The Bed as Battlefield: Erotic Conquest and Military Metaphor in Ovid's *Amores." Transactions and Proceedings of the American Philological Association* 118 (1988) 293–307.

Davis, John. T. *Fictus Adulter Poet as Actor in the "Amores"* (Amsterdam: J. C. Gieben, 1989).

Davis, P. J. "Ovid's Amores: A Political Reading." *Classical Philology* 94.4 (1999) 431–499.

Greene, Ellen. *The Erotics of Domination: Male Desire and the Mistress in Latin Love Poetry* (Baltimore: The Johns Hopkins University Press, 1998).

James, Sharon L. "Slave-Rape and Female Silence in Ovid's Love Poetry." *Helios* 24.1 (1995) 60–76.

———. *Learned Girls and Male Persuasion: Gender and Reading in Roman Love Elegy* (Berkeley: University of California Press, 2003).

Keith, A. M. "*Corpus Eroticum:* Elegiac Poetics and Elegiac *Puellae* in Ovid's *Amores." Classical World* 88 (1994) 27–40.

Luck, George. *The Latin Love Elegy* (New York: Barnes and Noble, 1960).

Martin, Christopher. *Policy in Love: Lyric and Public in Ovid, Petrarch, and Shakespeare* (Pittsburgh: Duquesne University Press, 1994).

O'Gorman, Ellen. "Love and the Family: Augustus and Ovidian Elegy." *Arethusa* 30 (1997) 103–24.

Paxson, J., and Cynthia Gravlee, eds. *Desiring Discourse: the Literature of Love, Ovid through Chaucer* (Selinsgrove: Susquehanna University Press, 1998).

Stapleton, M. L. *Harmful Eloquence: Ovid's "Amores" from Antiquity to Shakespeare* (Ann Arbor: University of Michigan Press, 1996).

Tracy, V. A. "Dramatic elements in Ovid's *Amores." Latomus* 36 (1977) 496–500.

Veyne, P. *Roman Erotic Elegy: Love, Poetry and the West*. David. Pellauer, trans. (Chicago: University of Chicago Press, 1988).

Commentaries: Amores

Barsby, John A. *Ovid's "Amores" Book 1* (Oxford: Clarendon Press, 1973).

Booth, Joan. *The Second Book of Amores* (Warminster: Aris & Phillips, 1991).

McKeown, J. C. *Ovid, Amores: text, prolegomena, and commentary* (Liverpool, England: F. Cairns, 1987).

Translations: Amores

Green, P., trans. *Ovid. The Erotic Poems. With Introduction* (New York: Penguin, 1982).

Humphries, Rolfe. *The Loves, The Art of Beauty, The Remedies for Love, and The Art of Love* (Bloomington: Indiana University Press, 1957).

Lee, Guy. *Ovid's Amores* (New York: Viking Press, 1968).

Melville, A. D. *Ovid. The Love Poems* (Oxford: Oxford University Press, 1990).

Showerman, Grant. *Ovid I: Heroides and Amores* (Cambridge: Harvard University Press, Loeb Edition, 1986).

Amores I. 1

Keith, Alison M. "*Amores 1.1*: Propertius and the Ovidian Programme." In *Studies in Latin Literature and Roman History*, ed. C. Deroux (Bruxelles: *Latomus*, 1992) 6.327–344.

Amores I. 3

Barsby, J. A. "*Desultor amoris* in *Amores* 1.3." *Classical Philology* 70 (1975) 44–5.

Olstein, K. "*Amores* 1.3 and Duplicity as a Way of Love." *Transactions and Proceedings of the American Philological Association* 105 (1975) 241–57.

Amores I. 9

McKeown, J. C. "*Militat omnis amans*." *Classical Journal* 90 (1995) 295–304.

Murgatroyd, P. "*Militia amoris* and the Roman Elegists." *Latomus* 34 (1974) 57–59.

———. "The Argumentation in Ovid Amores 1.9" *Mnemosyne* 52.5 (1999) 569–571.

Olstein, K. "*Amores* 1.9 and the Structure of Book I." In *Studies in Latin Literature and Roman History*, ed. C. Deroux. *Latomus* 164 (1979) 286–300.

Amores I. 11

McKie, D. S. " Love in the margin: Ovid, *Amores* 1.11.22." *Proceedings of the Cambridge Studies in Classical Philology* 30 (1984) 79–83.

Amores I. 12

Baker, R. "*Duplices Tabellae:* Propertius 3.23 and Ovid *Amores* 1.12." *Classical Philology* 68 (1973) 109–13.

General: Metamorphoses

Ahl, Frederick. *Metaformations: Soundplay and Word Play in Ovid and other Classical Poets* (Ithaca: Cornell University Press, 1985).

Anderson, William S. "Multiple Changes in the *Metamorphoses*." *Transactions and Proceedings of the American Philological Association* 94 (1963) 1–27.

———. "Aspects of Love in Ovid's *Metamorphoses*. "*Classical Journal* 90 (1995) 265–269.

Barchiesi, Alessandro. *The Poet and the Prince: Ovid and Augustan Discourse* (Berkeley: University of California Press, 1997).

Cahoon, Leslie. "Let the Muse Sing On: Poetry, Criticism, Feminism and the Case of Ovid." *Helios* 17 (1990) 197–211.

Culham, Phyllis. "Decentering the Text: the Case of Ovid." *Helios* 17 (1990) 161–170.

Curran, L. C. "Rape and Rape Victims in the *Metamorphoses*." *Arethusa* 11 (1978) 213–241.

Due, Otto Steen. *Changing Forms: Studies in the Metamorphoses of Ovid* (Copenhagen: Gyldendal, 1974).

Fränkel, Hermann. *Ovid: A Poet Between Two Worlds* (Berkeley: University of California Press, 1945).

Galinsky, G. Carl. *Ovid's Metamorphoses: An Introduction to the Basic Aspects* (Berkeley: University of California Press, 1975).

Glen, Edgar M. *The Metamorphoses: Ovid's Roman Games* (Lanham, MD: University Press of America, Inc., 1986).

Hallett, Judith. "Contextualizing the Text: The Journey to Ovid." *Helios* 17 (1990) 187–95.

Hinds, Stephen. "Generalizing about Ovid." *Ramus* 16 (1987) 4–31.

Kenney, E. J. "The Style of the *Metamorphoses*." In *Ovid*, ed. J. W. Bins (Boston: Routledge and Kegan Paul, 1973) 116–153.

Knox, Peter. *Ovid's Metamorphoses and the Traditions of Augustan Poetry* (Cambridge: Cambridge Philological Society, 1986).

Mack, Sara. *Ovid* (New Haven: Yale University Press, 1988).

Myers, K. Sara. *Ovid's Causes: Cosmology and Aetiology in the Metamorphoses* (Ann Arbor: University of Michigan Press, 1994).

Nagle, Betty Rose. "*Amor, Ira,* and Sexual Identity in Ovid's *Metamorphoses*." *Classical Antiquity* 3 (1984) 236–255.

———. "Ovid: A Poet between Two Novelists." *Helios* 12:1 (1985) 65–73.

Otis, Brooks. *Ovid as an Epic Poet* (Cambridge: Cambridge University Press, 1966).

Richlin, Amy. "Reading Ovid's Rapes." In *Pornography and Representation in Greece and Rome* (Oxford: Oxford University Press, 1994) 158–89.

Segal, Charles. *Landscape in Ovid's Metamorphoses: A Study in the Transformation of a Literary Symbol* (Wiesbaden: Franz Steiner, 1969).

———. "Ovid. *Metamorphoses*, Hero, Poet." *Helios* 12 (1985) 49–63.

Solodow, Joseph. *The World of Ovid's Metamorphoses* (Chapel Hill: University of North Carolina Press, 1988).

Tissol, Garth. *The Faces of Nature: Wit, Narrative, and Cosmic Origins in Ovid's Metamorphoses* (Princeton: Princeton University Press, 1997).

———. "Ovid's Little *Aeneid* and the Thematic Integrity of the *Metamorphoses*," *Helios* 20.1 (1993) 69–79.

Wheeler, Stephen Michael. *A Discourse of Wonders: Audience and Performance in Ovid's Metamorphoses* (Philadelphia: University of Pennsylvania Press, 1999).

Commentaries: Metamorphoses

Anderson, William S. *Ovid's Metamorphoses, Books 1–5* (Norman: University of Oklahoma Press, 1997).

———. *Ovid's Metamorphoses, Books 6–10* (Norman: University of Oklahoma Press, 1972).

Lee, A. G. *Ovid: Metamorphoses Book I* (Wauconda, IL: Bolchazy-Carducci Publishers, 1988).

Translations: Metamorphoses

Hughes, Ted. *Tales from Ovid* (New York: Farrar, Straus and Giroux, 1995).

Mandelbaum, A. *The Metamorphoses of Ovid* (New York: Harcourt Brace, 1993).

Melville, A. D. *Metamorphoses* (Oxford: Oxford University Press, 1986).

Miller, Frank J. *Metamorphoses* (Cambridge, MA: Harvard University Press, 1976).

Raeburn, D. A. *Ovid. Metamorphoses. A new Verse Translation with an Introduction by D. Feeney* (London: Penguin Books, 2004).

Simpson, Michael. *The Metamorphoses of Ovid* (Amherst: University of Massachusetts Press, 2001).

Slavitt, David R. *The Metamorphoses of Ovid* (Baltimore: Johns Hopkins University Press, 1994).

Apollo and Daphne

Barnard, Mary E. *The Myth of Apollo and Daphne from Ovid to Quevedo: Love, Agon and the Grotesque* (Durham: Duke University Press, 1987).

Francese, C. "Daphne, Honor, and Aetiological Action in Ovid's Metamorphoses." *Classical World* 97.2 (2004) 153–157.

Gross, N. P. "Rhetorical Wit and Amatory Persuasion in Ovid." *Classical Journal* 74 (1979) 305–318 [*Met.* I, 504–24, et al.].

Hollis, A. S. "Ovid, *Metamorphoses* 1.455ff.: Apollo, Daphne, and the Pythian Crown." *Zeitschrift für Papyrologie und Epigraphik* 112 (1996) 69–73.

Knox, Peter E. "In Pursuit of Daphne." *Transactions and Proceedings of the American Philological Association* 120 (1990) 183–202.

Nethercut, W. R. "Daphne and Apollo. A Dynamic Encounter."
    Classical Journal 74 (1974) 333–347.

Nicoll, W. S. M. "Cupid, Apollo, and Daphne (Ovid, *Met.* 452ff.)."
    Classical Quarterly (1980) 174–82.

Pyramus and Thisbe

Crockett, Bryan. "The 'Wittiest Partition': Pyramus and Thisbe in
    Ovid and Shakespeare." *Classical and Modern Literature* 12
    (1991) 49–58.

Duke, T. T. "Ovid's Pyramus and Thisbe." *Classical Journal* 66
    (1971) 320–27.

Glendinning, Robert. "Pyramus and Thisbe in the Medieval
    Classroom." *Speculum,* 61 (1986) 103–15.

Jacobson, Howard. "Etymological Wordplay in Ovid's 'Pyramus
    and Thisbe' (MET. 4.55–166)" *Classical Quarterly* 2001 51:
    309–314.

Knox, Peter. "Pyramus and Thisbe in Cyprus." *Harvard Studies in
    Classical Philology* 88 (1989) 315–28.

Newlands, Carole. "The Simile of the Fracture Pipe in Ovid's
    Metamorphoses 4." *Ramus* 15 (1986) 145–53.

Rhorer, Catharine. "Red and White in Ovid's *Metamorphoses:* The
    Mulberry Tree in the Tale of Pyramus and Thisbe." *Ramus* 9
    (1980) 79–88.

Rudd, Niall. "Pyramus and Thisbe in Shakespeare and Ovid: *A
    Midsummer Night's Dream* and *Metamorphoses* 4:1–166." In
    Creative Imitation and Latin Literature, ed. David West and
    Tony Woodman (Cambridge: Cambridge University Press,
    1979) 173–193.

Segal, Charles. "Narrative Art in the *Metamorphoses.*" *Classical
    Journal* 66 (1971) 331–337.

Shorrock, Robert. "Ovidian Plumbing in Metamorphoses 4."
    Classical Quarterly 53.2 (2003) 624–627.

Daedalus and Icarus

Davisson, Mary H. T. "The Observers of Daedalus and Icarus in
    Ovid." *Classical World* 90 (1997) 263–278.

Hoefmans, Marjorie. "Myth into Reality: The Metamorphosis of
    Daedalus and Icarus (Ovid, *Metamorphoses,* VIII, 183–234)."
    L'Antiquité Classique 63 (1994) 137–160.

Pavlock, Barbara. "Daedalus in the Labyrinth of Ovid's *Metamorphoses*," *CW* 92.2 (1998) 141–157.

Rudd, Niall. "Daedalus and Icarus (i) From Rome to the End of the Middle Ages; (ii) From the Resnaissance to the Present Day." In Martindale 1988, 21–53 (see full reference in section **Ovid's Influence on Art and Literature**).

Wise, V. M. "Flight Myths in Ovid's *Metamorphoses*." *Ramus* 6 (1977) 44–59.

Philemon and Baucis

Gamel, M. K. "Baucis and Philemon. Paradigm or Paradox?" *Helios* 11 (1984) 117–131.

Green, Steven J. "Collapsing Authority and 'Arachnean' Gods in Ovid's Baucis and Philemon (Met. 8.611–724)." *Ramus* 32.1 (2003) 39–56.

Griffin, Alan H. F. "Philemon and Baucis in Ovid's Metamorphoses." *Greece and Rome* 38 (1991) 62–74.

Jones, C. P. "A Geographical Setting for the Baucis and Philemon Legend (Ovid, *Metamorphoses* 8.611–724)." *Harvard Studies in Classical Philology* 96 (1997) 200–203.

Pygmalion

Arkins, Brian. "Sexy Statues: Pygmalionism in Irish Literature." *Classical and Modern Literature* 18.3 (1998) 247–250.

Davis, Sally. "Bringing Ovid into the Latin Classroom: Pygmalion." *Classical Journal* 90 (1995) 273–278.

Griffin, A. H. F. "Ovid's *Metamorphoses*." *Greece and Rome* 24 (1977) 57–70. [On the Narcissus and Pygmalion episodes].

James, Paula "She's All That: Ovid's Ivory Statue and the Legacy of Pygmalion on Film." *Classical Bulletin* 79.1 (2003) 63–91.

Knowles, Ronald. "A Kind of Alaska: Pinter and Pygmalion." *Classical and Modern Literature* 16.3 (1996) 231–240.

Miller, J. H. *Versions of Pygmalion*. (Cambridge, MA: Harvard University Press, 1990).

Ovid's Influence on Art and Literature

Aghion, Irene, Claire Barbillon, and Francois Lissarague, eds. *Gods and Heroes of Classical Antiquity* (Flammarion: Paris, 1996). [Source for works of art on myth].

Barkan, Leonard. *The Gods Made Flesh: Metamorphosis and the Pursuit of Paganism*. (New Haven: Yale University Press, 1986).

Boardman, John, et al., eds. *Lexicon Iconographicum Mythologiae Classicae [LIMC]* (Zurich: Artmeis Verlag, 1981–1997). [Eight volumes published (A–Z). Articles in German, English, French, or Italian. Each volume consists of: pt. 1: text ; pt. 2: plates. Includes bibliographies. Focuses on ancient art to the 1200 A.D.].

Hoffman, Michael, and James Lasdun. *After Ovid: New Metamorphoses* (New York: Farrar, Straus and Giroux, 1995). [Poems by contemporary poets modeled on the *Metamorphoses*].

Martindale, Charles, ed. *Ovid Renewed: Ovidian Influences on Literature and Art from the Middle Ages to the Twentieth Century* (Cambridge: Cambridge University Press, 1988).

Reid, Jane D. *The Oxford Guide to Classical Mythology in the Arts 1300–1990s*, 2 vols (Oxford: Oxford University Press, 1993).

Wilkinson, L. P. *Ovid Recalled* (Cambridge: Cambridge University Press, 1955). [General influence].

Web sites with Information on Ovid

http://www.tlg.uci.edu/~tlg/index/resources.html [Electronic Resources for Classicists: links to a number of resources, including bibliographies, projects, course materials, Classics Departments].

http://www.uvm.edu/~hag/ovid/index.html
[Paintings illustrating Ovid's *Metamorphoses* at University of Vermont].

http://www.perseus.tufts.edu/neh.ann.html
[Roman Perseus: Latin texts. Only includes Metamorphoses, to date].

http://www.vroma.org/vromalinks.html
http://www.stoa.org/avclassics/
http://lilt.ilstu.edu/drjclassics/links.htm

The
Amores

© LINDA LARSON 1998

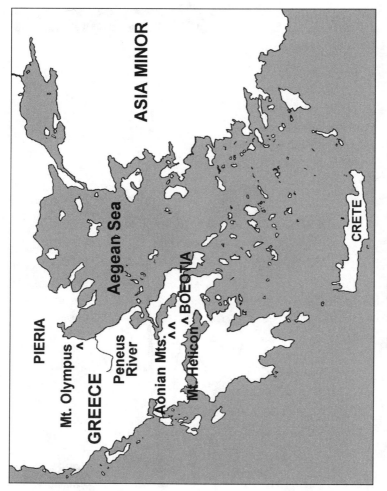

Map of Places in Amores I.1

THE AMORES

Ovid's *Amores* is a collection in three books. In Ovid's epigram to the collection, the poems themselves declare that they were edited from five to three books in order to provide less work for their readers. This explanation sets the humorous tone employed by the poet throughout the *Amores*.

Ovid began his love elegies at the age of 18 in 26 B.C., wrote the bulk of the poems after 20 B.C., and published the second edition around 7 B.C. At the same time, the poet was also composing his other major works (see Ovid's Life and Works), most of which were completed before his exile in 8 A.D.

In choosing to write love elegy, Ovid placed himself squarely among Roman poets who developed a uniquely Roman genre. The topic of the trials and tribulations of the lover was already popular in fourth-century B.C. Greek New Comedy and in the Greek novels of the Hellenistic periods. The metrical form of the elegiac couplet (see Appendix) was used by some of the Greek poets; it was the Romans, however, who developed love elegy as a genre and who first composed collections of love poems addressed to one or more women.

By the time Ovid began his collection, Catullus (c. 88–55 B.C.) had already died, leaving behind his Lesbia poems, a group of poems that describe his tumultuous love affair with Clodia, a married woman from a very distinguished family. Some of Catullus's Lesbia poems were written in the elegiac meter. The popular works, now lost, of the poet Gallus (69–26 B.C.) seem to have been the first to take on the form and characteristic themes we associate with the genre of love elegy. Also important to Ovid were the works of his older contemporaries, Propertius and Tibullus. Their poems similarly described the vicissitudes of a love affair with a married woman and often explored serious issues of life, love, and art. Ovid's challenge in writing his poems was to continue this Roman tradition, but at the same time to achieve something new. He accomplished this by using the traditional themes of love elegy, but at the same time by redefining the characters of the lover and his mistress. His are not the poems of a lover who is deeply and emotionally involved with his beloved. Rather, he presents a *persona*, or character of a lover, who is witty, urbane, but emotionally detached. Ovid appears to be more concerned with demonstrating his poetic skill and versatility than he is with documenting a personal love affair. The degree to which these poems are or are not biographical is far less important than the clever artistry with which the poet develops his themes.

That Ovid wanted to reinvent the genre of love elegy is clear from the very first. Ovid's collection does not begin with a dedicatory poem to his mistress, but with a poem about Cupid's tricking him into writing love elegy (I. 1). The collection ends with a farewell to the poetic form itself (III. 15), not to his mistress, as one might expect. Nevertheless, the poet achieves unity by using the story of the love affair as a loosely chronological narrative that spans the three books. His first book documents the joyous beginnings of a love affair with the mysterious Corinna, a married woman whose true identity and even existence is in question. The second and third books continue with disillusionment and parting—both the girl and the love elegy itself are renounced. But throughout the work, the poet exploits the traditional topics of love poetry, continually overturning established patterns.

AMORES I. 1

This short poem introduces the entire *Amores*. Ovid begins by saying that, although he had attempted an epic poem, he soon discovered he could not write about wars and heroes in dactylic hexameter (the meter traditionally used for epic verses), because Cupid had stolen one metrical foot from the second line. This mischief turned his epic into elegy. (See the Appendix for examples of epic and elegiac meter.) The poet rebukes Cupid for meddling in a realm that does not belong to him. To give weight to his argument against such interference, the poet points out how inappropriate it would be for Venus and Minerva, or Ceres and Diana, to exchange roles, as Cupid has done with the poet. Ovid then adds that, as he has no lover, he has no subject for love elegy. This defiance of the god leads to a surprising consequence: Cupid fires an arrow into the poet that suddenly and dramatically transforms him into both a lover and a love poet. Ovid ends by bidding farewell to epic poetry.

This poem is a humorous and ironic justification of Ovid's decision to write elegy rather than epic. Ovid cleverly pretends that he has been forced into this choice and imagines the scene as a real event with a real conversation between apparent equals.

AMORES I. 1

Arma gravī numero violentaque bella parabam
    edere, materia conveniente modis.
par erat inferior versus; risisse Cupido
    dicitur atque unum surripuisse pedem.
"quis tibi, saeve puer, dedit hoc in carmina iuris?   5
    Pieridum vates, non tua, turba sumus.

✦   ✦   ✦

1   **arma...numero:** recalls the opening line of the *Aeneid: Arma
        virumque cano.*
    gravi numero: refers to the dactylic hexameter traditionally used
        for epic poetry, most particularly by Vergil in the *Aeneid.*
2   **ēdō, -ere, -idī, -itum:** *to give out, put forth, produce.*
    materia: refers back to *arma* and *bella,* the material most suitable for
        epic tales.
    modis: a direct reference to the dactylic hexameter meter required
        for epic verse.
3   **inferior:** in dactylic hexameter all lines are of equal length, six
        metrical feet.
    risisse: from *rīdeō, rīdēre, rīsī, rīsum.*
    Cupido, -inis (m.): the eternally youthful son of Venus whose
        arrows could inflict either love or revulsion upon their victims.
5   **saeve puer:** Ovid here addresses Cupid directly. The scene is
        parallel to the Apollo/Daphne story in *Met.* I. 453 where Ovid
        describes Cupid's wrath as *saeva ira* and to 456 where Apollo
        refers to Cupid as a *lascive puer.* In that scene Apollo expresses
        his annoyance with the boy-god for using a weapon (the bow)
        that Apollo felt was more rightfully suitable to his own epic-
        scale deeds than to the amatory deeds of Cupid. Here, Ovid
        scolds the mischievous god for interfering with the writer's
        desire to compose epic verse.
    iuris: partitive genitive used after the neuter demonstrative
        pronoun *hoc.*
6   **Pīerides, -um (f. pl.):** the Muses from Pieria on the northern slope
        of Mt. Olympus.
    vātēs, -is (m.): *poet, prophet.* Ovid ironically chooses the ancient
        term for a poet, *vates,* which once carried the meaning of
        "prophet."
    turba, -ae (f.): *a crowd of followers, attendants, troop.*

quid si praeripiat flavae Venus arma Minervae,
　　ventilet accensas flava Minerva faces?
quis probet in silvis Cererem regnare iugosis,
　　lege pharetratae virginis arva coli?　　　　　10
crinibus insignem quis acuta cuspide Phoebum

✦　✦　✦

7　**praeripiō, -ere, -ripuī, -reptum:** *to take away, snatch, tear away.* A
　　present subjunctive in the protasis of a future-less-vivid
　　construction with the apodosis understood.
　　flāvus, -a, -um: *yellow, having yellow hair.* The phrase
　　flavae...Minervae is a kind of embracing word order.
　　Venus, -eris (f.): goddess sacred to love and lovers.
　　Minerva, -ae (f.): Ovid here chooses to contrast Love and War
　　(arma).
8　**ventilō, -āre, -āvī, -ātum:** *to brandish in the air, fan.* A second
　　protasis in the future-less-vivid construction.
　　accensas...faces: CHIASMUS. The *faces* refers to the torch symboliz-
　　ing love and always present at marriages, where Venus would
　　be expected to reign.
9　**probō, -āre, -āvī, -ātum:** *to authorize, sanction.* Translated like a
　　potential subjunctive but used to convey doubt.
　　Cerēs, -eris (f.): the goddess of open fields and agriculture.
　　iugōsus, -a, -um: *mountainous.*
10　**pharetrātus, -a, -um:** *furnished with or wearing a quiver, quivered.*
　　pharetratae virginis refers to the goddess of the hunt and of the
　　woodlands, Diana. Just as Ovid has contrasted Love and War in
　　lines 7–8, here there is a contrast between Ceres whose appro-
　　priate territory is the open fields and Diana who frequents
　　wooded areas.
　　arvum, -ī (n.): *ploughed or cultivated land, a field.*
11　**crīnis, crīnis (m.):** *hair, tresses.*
　　insignis, -e: *distinguished, outstanding, memorable.*
　　acūtus, -a, -um: *sharp, pointed.*
　　cuspis, -idis (f.): *spear, javelin, lance.*
　　Phoebus, -ī (m.): an epithet for Apollo as the god of light.

instruat, Aoniam Marte movente lyram?
sunt tibi magna, puer, nimiumque potentia regna:
   cur opus affectas ambitiose novum?
an, quod ubique, tuum est? tua sunt Heliconia tempe?   15
   vix etiam Phoebo iam lyra tuta sua est?
cum bene surrexit versu nova pagina primo,
   attenuat nervos proximus ille meos.

✦ ✦ ✦

12   **instruō, -ere, -xī, -ctum:** *to instruct, equip, furnish.* Translate like a
        potential subjunctive, here used to express doubt, as does
        probet, I. 9.
     Aoniam: refers to Boeotia, a region in Greece, which includes the
        Aonian mountains and Mt. Helicon. Often an epithet for the
        Muses.
     lyra, -ae (f.): *lute, lyre.* The four-word phrase *Aoniam Marte movente*
        lyram is in CHIASTIC word order. The lyre is the standard
        emblem for Apollo and so suggests poetry. Ovid sets up a third
        contrast here between Poetry (Apollo) and War (Mars).
13   **tibi:** dative of possession with *sunt.*
     nimium (adv.): *extremely, very much, too much.*
     potens, -tis: *powerful, mighty, influential.*
14   **affectō, -āre, -āvī, -ātum:** *to strive after a thing, to pursue.*
     ambitiōsus, -a, -um: *ambitious, vain, vainglorious, conceited.*
15   **quod ubique:** supply a missing *est* to complete the clause. It is a
        common occurrence in Ovid for the verb *sum* to be omitted
        from phrases.
     Helicōnius, -a, -um: *of or pertaining to Mt. Helicon, the mountain*
        sacred to the Muses.
     tempe (n. pl.): (indecl.) *valley;* in particular the beautiful valley at
        the foot of Mt. Olympus through which ran the Peneus river.
16   **Phoebo:** dative of reference with *tuta.*
17   **pāgina, -ae (f.):** *page.*
18   **attenuō, -āre, -āvī, -ātum:** *to weaken, enfeeble, lessen, diminish.*
     nervus, -ī (m.): *string of a musical instrument or bow.*

nec mihi materia est numeris levioribus apta,
    aut puer aut longas compta puella comas."   20
questus eram, pharetra cum protinus ille soluta
    legit in exitium spicula facta meum
lunavitque genu sinuosum fortiter arcum
    "quod" que "canas, vates, accipe" dixit "opus."
me miserum! certas habuit puer ille sagittas.   25
    uror, et in vacuo pectore regnat Amor.

✦   ✦   ✦

19   **mihi:** dative of possession with *est*.
        materia...apta: the material most suitable to the light meter (i.e.
            elegiac couplets) is Love. But as the next line reveals, Ovid is
            not in love.
        aptus, -a, -um: (+ dat.) *fitted, suitable, appropriate.*
20   **longas...comas:** CHIASTIC word order. The *longas comas* surround
            the *compta puella* just as her hair would fall about her body. The
            accusative here is a Greek accusative used of the part of the
            body affected.
        comptus, -a, -um: *adorned.*
        coma, -ae (f.): *hair.*
21   **pharetra, -ae (f.):** *quiver.*
22   **exitium, -ī (n.):** *destruction, ruin, hurt.* The expression
            exitium...meum is in CHIASTIC word order.
        spīculum, -ī (n.): *arrow.* Although technically this word refers to a
            pointed end, here it stands for the whole weapon, the arrow or
            dart itself. The figure of speech that uses the part for the whole
            is called SYNECDOCHE.
23   **lūnō, -āre, -āvī, -ātum:** *to bend like a half-moon or crescent.*
        genu, -ūs (n.): *the knee.*
        sinuōsus, -a, -um: *bent, winding, sinuous, pliant.*
        arcus, -ūs (m.): *a bow.*
24   **canas:** subjunctive in a relative clause of characteristic.
25   **me miserum:** accusative used in an exclamation. This is a standard
            phrase by which elegiac poets describe themselves as lovers.
26   **ūrō, -ere, ussī, ustum:** *to burn, inflame, consume with passion.* The use
            of this word here is parallel to the language and situation of
            *Met.*I. 495–96 when Apollo is struck by Cupid's golden-tipped
            arrow.

sex mihi surgat opus numeris, in quinque residat;
   ferrea cum vestris bella valete modis.
cingere litorea flaventia tempora myrto,
   Musa per undenos emodulanda pedes.   30

✦ ✦ ✦

27 **surgat:** a jussive subjunctive.
    residō, -ere, -sēdī, -sessum: *to sink or settle down, subside, grow calm.*
       Here, a jussive subjunctive.
28 **ferreus, -a, -um:** *hard, unfeeling, made of iron.*
    modis: this is the last reference to dactylic hexameter, the meter of
       epic poetry and war. It echoes lines 1 and 2 of the poem.
29 **lītoreus, -a, -um:** *of the seashore.*
    litorea…myrto: CHIASTIC word order.
    flāvens, -entis: *golden-yellow.*
    tempus, -oris (n.): *the temple of the head.*
    myrtus, -ī (f.): *a myrtle tree.*
30 **undēnī, -ae, -a:** *eleven each, eleven at a time.*
    ēmodulor, -ārī, -ātum: *to sing, celebrate in rhythm.* Ovid ends with a
       reference to the meter of Love, the defined theme of all three
       books of the *Amores.*

AMORES I. 3

In this poem the poet swears eternal love for a girl *(puella)* who is as yet unnamed. He prays that the girl will love him in return and that there will be eternal fidelity between them. Neither rich nor of an aristocratic lineage, he admits that his credentials may not impress her, but argues that three gods, Apollo, Bacchus, and Cupid, can support him and that his best personal attributes are his fidelity and his integrity. He maintains that he is not fickle, and that his beloved, by loving him, will provide the subject matter for his finest poetry. But all this promise of immortality must be considered in the light of the mythological examples that Ovid offers in the poet's defense. They consist of women who have been loved by Jupiter, the most notorious adulterer in the Olympian pantheon.

The poet here explores and exploits the traditional subject matter of love poetry, especially the concept of *fides,* or fidelity.

AMORES I. 3

Iusta precor: quae me nuper praedata puella est,
   aut amet aut faciat, cur ego semper amem.
a, nimium volui: tantum patiatur amari,
   audierit nostras tot Cytherea preces.
accipe, per longos tibi qui deserviat annos;   5
   accipe, qui pura norit amare fide.
si me non veterum commendant magna parentum

✦ ✦ ✦

1   **precor, -ārī, -atus:** *to pray for, beg, implore.*
    praedor, -ārī, -ātus: *to take as prey, catch.*
    puella: the first reference to the girl Ovid will love. We now know
       that the subject of his poetry will be heterosexual love. *Puella* is
       the traditional word used by Latin love elegists for the young
       woman who is the object of their desire.
2   **amet:** a jussive subjunctive, as is *faciat.*
    amem: a deliberative subjunctive in a question implying doubt or
       indignation.
3   **a:** exclamation expressing anguish.
    nimius, -a, -um: *too much, too great.*
    patiatur: a jussive subjunctive.
4   **audierit:** a syncopated form of the future perfect indicative.
    nostras: Ovid here employs a poetic convention in using a first
       person plural adjective with singular intent.
    Cytherēa, -ae (f.): refers to Venus; an epithet taken from the name
       of the island in the Aegean Sea known for its worship of the
       goddess.
    prex, -cis (f.): *prayer.*
5   **dēserviō, -īre:** *to devote oneself, serve zealously.* Here, a present
       subjunctive used in a relative clause of characeristic. Ovid refers
       to a standard idea of Latin love elegy that the lover is enslaved
       by his lover or by his emotion.
6   **accipe:** this ANAPHORA draws attention to the poet's offering
       himself as a devoted, skilled lover.
    noscō, -ere, nōvī, nōtum: *to learn.* Here it is a syncopated form of
       the perfect subjunctive *noverit.* Like *deserviat* (5), it too occurs in
       a relative clause of characteristic.
7   **si:** *etsi.*
    commendō, -āre, -āvī, -ātum: *to recommend, make agreeable or
       attractive.* This is the first protasis in a series of four simple
       conditions all using the present indicative.

nomina, si nostri sanguinis auctor eques,
nec meus innumeris renovatur campus aratris,
    temperat et sumptus parcus uterque parens,   10
at Phoebus comitesque novem vitisque repertor
    hac faciunt et me qui tibi donat Amor
et nulli cessura fides, sine crimine mores,
    nudaque simplicitas purpureusque pudor.
non mihi mille placent, non sum desultor amoris: 15

✦   ✦   ✦

8   **si...eques:** another phrase in which an *est* is needed to complete its meaning.

    nostri: another poetic use of the plural with singular intent.

9   **aratrum, -ī (n.):** *a plow.*

10   **temperō, -āre, -āvī, -ātum:** *to moderate, regulate.*

    sumptus, -ūs (m.): *expenditure.*

    parcus, -a, -um: *frugal, thrifty.*

11   **comitesque novem:** refers to the nine Muses. Here begins the apodosis to balance the four conditions set forth in the protasis. It first names four deities (Apollo, the Muses, Bacchus, Love) and continues with four honorable human qualities (fidelity, character, simplicity, modesty).

    vītis, -is (f.): *the grapevine.*

    repertor, -ōris (m.): *originator, discoverer.* Here it refers to Bacchus.

12   **hac faciunt:** an unusual idiomatic construction meaning either "act on my behalf" or "are on my side."

    faciunt: there are a total of eight subjects for this verb: *Phoebus* (11), *comitesque* (11), *repertor* (11), *Amor* (12), *fides* (13), *mores* (13), *simplicitas* (14), *pudor* (14).

14   **purpureus, -a, -um:** *radiant, glowing, blushing.*

    pudor, -ōris (m.): *modesty.* Note the ASSONANCE and ALLITERATION drawing attention to this culminating qualification. In light of what Ovid has already said and will go on to say in this poem, this phrase is a good example of Ovid's playful self-mockery.

15   **dēsultor, -ōris (m.):** *a circus rider who leaps from horse to horse.* Ovid uses the word here to suggest an inconstant or fickle lover. It provides a very graphic image of a lover leaping from partner to partner.

tu mihi, si qua fides, cura perennis eris;
  tecum, quos dederint annos mihi fila sororum,
    vivere contingat teque dolente mori;
  te mihi materiem felicem in carmina praebe:
    provenient causa carmina digna sua.   20
  carmine nomen habent exterrita cornibus Io
    et quam fluminea lusit adulter ave

✦ ✦ ✦

16   **qua:** *aliqua.*
      si…fides: another ELLIPSIS of *sum*, probably *sit.*
17   **fīlum, -ī (n.):** *thread, yarn.*
      sororum: refers to the Fates, the three sisters: Clotho, who spun;
        Lachesis, who measured; and Atropos, who severed the thread
        of life at one's birth.
18   **contingat:** a jussive subjunctive, here used impersonally.
      mori: present infinitive of *morior;* a second complementary
        infinitive with *contingat.*
19   **mātēriēs, -ēi (f.):** *material, subject matter.*
20   **prōveniō, -īre, -vēnī, -ventum:** *to come into being, arise.*
      causa…sua: CHIASTIC word order.
      dignus, -a, -um: *worthy.*
21   **habent:** this verb has three subjects—*Io* (21); the clause *quam…ave*
        (22) with an understood antecedent *ea;* and the clause
        quaeque…tenuit (23–24), also with an understood antecedent *ea.*
      exterreō, -ēre, -uī, -itum: *to frighten, terrify.*
      Io: Io was a maiden beloved by Jupiter who, in order to hide her
        from Juno, transformed Io into a heifer. Juno, suspecting
        Jupiter's infidelity, asked for the heifer and set Argus with his
        hundred eyes to watch over her. Jupiter sent Hermes to kill
        Argus and later released Io from her disguised shape.
22   **quam:** a reference to Leda, also beloved by Jupiter, who wooed her
        in the guise of a swan.
      flūmineus, -a, -um: *of or pertaining to a river.*
      lusit: from *ludō, lūdere, lūsī, lūsum.*
      adulter, -erī (m.): *an adulterer.*

quaeque super pontum simulato vecta iuvenco
   virginea tenuit cornua vara manu.
nos quoque per totum pariter cantabimur orbem   25
   iunctaque semper erunt nomina nostra tuis.

✦ ✦ ✦

23   **quaeque:** refers to the maiden Europa whom Jupiter deceived in the guise of a bull.

        pontus, -ī (m.): *the sea.*

        vecta: from *vehō, vehere, vexī, vectum*—to carry.

        iuvencus, -ī (m.): *a young bull.*

24   **virginea...manu:** because this line is not symmetrical, it is a variation of a GOLDEN LINE—a single verb accompanied by two adjective/noun pairs. When Ovid chooses to include here three mythologial characters loved by Jupiter, he may in fact reveal a truth about the poet as lover. Io is described with the word *exterrita*, the phrase depicting Leda uses the verb *lusit*, and Jupiter is described as an *adulter* in conjunction with Leda and as *simulato* in the Europa couplet. These stories do not illustrate eternal fidelity.

        vārus, -a, -um: *bent outwards.*

25   **nos:** refers both to Ovid and his yet-to-be-revealed lover.

26   **nomina nostra:** here probably with singular intent referring specifically to the poet.

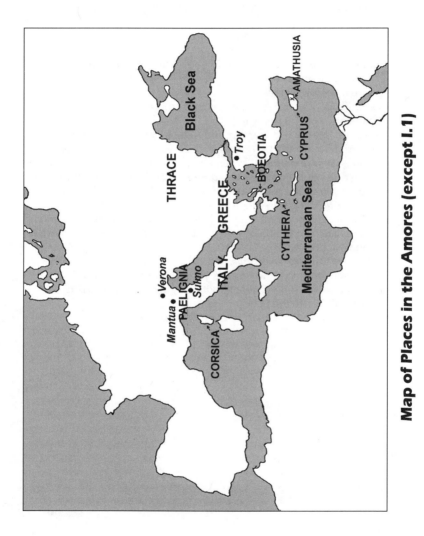

Map of Places in the Amores (except I.1)

AMORES I. 9

Ovid addresses this poem to a man called Atticus, with the pretense that Atticus has accused the poet of devoting himself to making love and thus of leading a lazy and non-productive life. Ovid argues that the lover is a soldier and that the rigors of warfare are identical to those of love. He gives several examples of how these parallels work, and, typically, provides three mythological examples of famous warriors, Achilles, Hector, and Mars himself, who were also lovers.

Again, the poet inverts an established theme of elegiac poetry, because the conventional poetic treatment of Love and War contrasted rather than equated the two. While the traditional lover preferred *otium* to *negotium*, Ovid playfully suggests that the earnest lover is as busy as the soldier and has no time for leisure.

AMORES I. 9

Militat omnis amans, et habet sua castra Cupido;
    Attice, crede mihi, militat omnis amans.
quae bello est habilis, Veneri quoque convenit aetas:
    turpe senex miles, turpe senilis amor.
quos petiere duces animos in milite forti,   5
    hos petit in socio bella puella viro:
pervigilant ambo, terra requiescit uterque;
    ille fores dominae servat, at ille ducis.

✦   ✦   ✦

1   **mīlitō, -āre, -āvī, -ātum:** *to be a soldier, serve as a soldier.* Ovid
        employs a METAPHOR here, the lover as soldier / warrior. Roman
        poets often felt that the lover fought a kind of war either with
        his mistress, a rival, or his own overpowering emotion.
        amans, -ntis (m., f.): *a lover.*
        Cupido: Cupid is not so much seen by Ovid as an enemy but rather
        the general under whom the soldier / lover serves.
2   **Attice:** it is unusual for Ovid to have an addressee in his love
        elegies. It is not known, with any certainty, who Atticus was.
3   **habilis, -e:** *suitable, fit.*
        conveniō, -īre, -vēnī, -ventum: *to be suitable or adapted for.*
        aetas: the age that suits the best soldiering and lovemaking is
        youth, according to Ovid.
4   **turpis, -e:** *loathsome, repulsive, shameful.*
        turpe senex miles: supply a missing *est.* The neuter predicate
        adjective works like a noun.
        senīlis, -e: *old, aged.*
5   **petiere:** the alternate spelling for the 3rd person plural perfect active
        indicative, a common usage in Ovid.
6   **bella:** a wordplay of both sound and sense. The striking ASSONANCE
        with *puella* and the hint of *bellum* draw attention to the replace-
        ment of the general Cupid by the girl.
7   **ambō, -ae, -ō:** *both.*
        terra: poetic use of the ablative of place where without a preposi-
        tion.
8   **ille, ille:** the first refers to the lover (*amans*) and the second to the
        soldier (*miles*).
        foris, foris (f.): *door, double door.*

militis officium longa est via: mitte puellam,
    strenuus exempto fine sequetur amans;   10
ibit in adversos montes duplicataque nimbo
    flumina, congestas exteret ille nives,
nec freta pressurus tumidos causabitur Euros
    aptave verrendis sidera quaeret aquis.
quis nisi vel miles vel amans et frigora noctis   15
    et denso mixtas perferet imbre nives?
mittitur infestos alter speculator in hostes,
    in rivale oculos alter, ut hoste, tenet.
ille graves urbes, hic durae limen amicae
    obsidet; hic portas frangit, at ille fores.   20

✦   ✦   ✦

9   **mitte:** here in the sense of dispatching, sending away or ahead.
10   **eximō, -ere, -ēmī, -emptum:** *to take away.*
11   **duplicō, -āre, -āvī, -ātum:** *to double in size or amount.*
     nimbus, -ī (m.): *cloudburst, rainstorm.*
12   **congestus, -a, -um:** *piled up.*
     exterō, -ere, -trīvī, -trītum: *to wear down, trample on.*
     nix, nivis (f.): *snow.*
13   **fretum, -ī (n.):** *strait, sea.*
     premō, -ere, pressī, -ssum: *to press on, push.*
     causor, -ārī, -ātus: *to plead as an excuse or reason.*
     tumidos: used in an active sense of causing the sea to swell.
     Eurus, -ī (m.): *the east wind.*
14   **aptave...sidera:** constellations, which would suggest favorable
        conditions for sailing.
     aptus, -a, -um: (+ dat.) *appropriate, fitting, suited.*
     -ve (conj.): *or.*
     verrō, -ere, versum: *to pass over, skim, sweep, row.*
     sīdus, -eris (n.): *constellation.*
15   **frīgus, -oris (n.):** *cold, chill.*
16   **et...nives:** a variation on a GOLDEN LINE in INTERLOCKED WORD
        ORDER.
     perferō, -ferre, -tulī, -lātum: *to suffer, endure, undergo.*
17   **speculātor, -ōris (m.):** *a scout, spy.*
18   **rīvalis, -is (m.):** *a rival.*
20   **obsideō, -ēre, -sēdī, -sessus:** *to beseige.*
     at ille fores: there is an ELLIPSIS in this phrase. Supply another
       frangit.

saepe soporatos invadere profuit hostes
caedere et armata vulgus inerme manu.
sic fera Threicii ceciderunt agmina Rhesi,
et dominum capti deseruistis equi.
nempe maritorum somnis utuntur amantes   25
et sua sopitis hostibus arma movent.
custodum transire manus vigilumque catervas
militis et miseri semper amantis opus.
Mars dubius, nec certa Venus: victique resurgunt,
quosque neges umquam posse iacere, cadunt.   30
ergo desidiam quicumque vocabat amorem,
desinat: ingenii est experientis Amor.

✦ ✦ ✦

21 **sopōrō, -āre, -āvī, -ātum:** *to put asleep.*
   invādō, -ere, -vāsī, -vāsum: *to attack, set on.*
   prōsum, -desse, -fuī, -futūrus: *to be advantageous, helpful, useful.*
22 **armata...manu:** CHIASMUS.
23 **ferus, -a, -um:** *fierce, savage, wild.*
   Thrēicius, -a, -um: *from Thrace,* a region northeast of Greece.
   Rhēsus, -ī (m.): *a Thracian who fought on the side of the Trojans.*
      Odysseus and Diomedes sneaked into his camp at night,
      slaughtered his men, and stole his famous white chariot horses.
   sic...Rhesi: a variant of a GOLDEN LINE in INTERLOCKED WORD ORDER.
24 **deserō, -ere, -uī, -tum:** *to abandon, leave.* Here, an APOSTROPHE.
25 **nempe** (conj.): *to be sure, yet, certainly.*
   somnis: perhaps a sleepiness induced by too much strong wine at
      dinner.
26 **sōpītus, -a, -um:** *sleepy.* Recalls the *soporatos hostes* of 21.
27 **transeō, -īre, -īvī, -ītum:** *to cross, go across.* The subject of a missing
      est to be supplied in line 28.
   vigil, -ilis (m.): *guard, sentry.*
29 **dubius, -a, -um:** *uncertain, wavering.*
   resurgō, -ere, -surrexī, -surrectum: *to rise up again.*
30 **neges:** a subjunctive in a relative clause of characteristic.
31 **dēsīdia, -ae (f.):** *idleness, inactivity, leisure.*
   quicumque: presumably *Atticus* of 2.
32 **desinat:** a jussive subjunctive.
   ingenii...experientis: genitive of quality or description.

ardet in abducta Briseide magnus Achilles
    (dum licet, Argeas frangite, Troes, opes);
Hector ab Andromaches complexibus ibat ad arma,   35
    et galeam capiti quae daret, uxor erat;
summa ducum, Atrides visa Priameide fertur
    Maenadis effusis obstipuisse comis.
Mars quoque deprensus fabrilia vincula sensit:
    notior in caelo fabula nulla fuit.   40

✦   ✦   ✦

33   **abdūcō, -ere, -dūxī, -ductum:** *to carry off.*
      Brīsēis, -idis (f.): *Achilles's slave and lover* whom Agamemnon stole
        but later returned. Ablative of cause with *in.*
      Achillēs, -is (m.): *Greek hero of the Trojan War, son of Peleus and*
        Thetis. When Agamemnon stole Briseis, Achilles sulked in his
        tent, refusing to fight and later even refused to take her back.
        He was eventually killed in battle by the Trojan, Paris.
34   **Argēus, -a, -um:** *Greek.*
      frangite: APOSTROPHE.
      Trōs, -ōis (m.): *Trojan.*
35   **Hector, -oris (m.):** *prince of Troy, eldest son of Priam.* He fought
        valiantly to save Troy but was defeated and killed by Achilles.
      Andromachē, -ēs (f.): *wife of Hector.*
36   **galea, -ae (f.):** *helmet.*
      daret: subjunctive in a relative clause of characteristic.
37   **summa:** a nominative neuter plural standing in apposition to the
        masculine singular *Atrides.*
      Atrīdēs, -ae (m.): *a descendant of Atreus,* usually used of Agamemnon.
      Priamēis, -idos (f.): *Cassandra,* daughter of Priam, king of Troy. She
        was carried off as a prize of war by Agamemnon; however,
        both the hero and his lover were murdered by Clytemnestra,
        his wife, when they reached Greece.
38   **Maenas, -adis (f.):** *a female worshipper of Bacchus, a Bacchante,*
        Maenad. The association here is due most likely to the loose,
        flowing hair common to both the Maenads and Cassandra, a
        sign of madness in both.
      obstipescō, -ere, -stipuī: *to be amazed, astonished.*
      coma, -ae (f.): *hair.*
39   **Mars…sensit:** refers to the story of Mars and Venus who were
        caught in an adulterous affair by means of a fine mesh net
        forged by Venus's husband, Vulcan.
      dēprendō, -dere, -dī, -sum: *to catch, discover.*
      fabrīlis, -e: *of or pertaining to a metal worker, skilled, fabricated.*
      vinculum -ī (n.): *chain, bond.*

ipse ego segnis eram discinctaque in otia natus;
    mollierant animos lectus et umbra meos;
impulit ignavum formosae cura puellae,
    iussit et in castris aera merere suis.
inde vides agilem nocturnaque bella gerentem: 45
    qui nolet fieri desidiosus, amet.

✦ ✦ ✦

41   **segnis, -e:** *inactive, sluggish.*
        discinctus, -a, -um: *undisciplined, easygoing.*
        ōtium, -ī (n.): *leisure.*
        natus: perfect participle of *nascor,* used as an adjective.
42   **molliō, -īre, -īvī, -ītum:** *to soften, weaken, enfeeble.*
        lectus et umbra: HENDIADYS. The two nouns carry the meaning of a
            single, modified noun, a shady couch.
43   **impellō, -ere, -pulī, -pulsum:** *to push, urge on.*
        ignavum: modifies an assumed *me.*
        formōsus, -a, -um: *beautiful.*
44   **in castris...suis:** reminiscent of *sua castra* (1). This wording returns
            the reader to the original intent of the poem.
        aes, aeris (n.): *money, pay.*
45   **vides:** perhaps addressing *Atticus.*
        agilis, -e: *active, busy.*
46   **amet:** a jussive subjunctive.

AMORES I. 11

In poem I. 5 Ovid finally tells us that his mistress's name is Corinna. *Amores* I. 11 is addressed to Corinna's maid Nape. In it, the poet flatters Nape, calling her *docta, cognita utilis,* and *ingeniosa,* in order to obtain her aid in carrying to Corinna a message in which the poet requests a night with her. Ovid suggests that Nape's own experiences with love oblige her to support his suit. Having gained Nape as his ally, the poet provides detailed instructions on how and when his message can best be delivered. His repeated requests that the maid use all haste are emphasized when he directs her to elicit from Corinna a simple, single word reply: "come." In a final humorous appeal for divine aid in his mission, the poet promises to dedicate his message tablets to Venus, should he be successful.

Throughout this poem, the poet argues that he desperately needs Corinna; surprisingly, he presents this argument to her maid, for he provides no clue to what is actually written on the tablets. He again exploits the traditional subject matter of elegiac love poetry: here, the theme of "carpe diem" is used to convince the girl to enjoy love while there is still time.

AMORES I. 11

Colligere incertos et in ordine ponere crines
    docta neque ancillas inter habenda Nape
inque ministeriis furtivae cognita noctis
    utilis et dandis ingeniosa notis,
saepe venire ad me dubitantem hortata Corinnam,   5
    saepe laboranti fida reperta mihi,

✦ ✦ ✦

1   **colligō, -ere, -lēgī, -lectum:** *to gather.*
      incertus, -a, -um: *disarranged, not fixed.*
2   **docta:** Ovid begins with a compliment to Corinna's maid in an
        attempt to win her favor and support.
      ancillas: placed before the preposition.
      neque...habenda: note that this participle is negative, i.e., Nape is
        no common handmaid like others. It is another flattery on
        Ovid's part.
      Napē, -ēs (f.): one of Corinna's personal maids who acts as a go-
        between for Ovid and his mistress. His flattery continues as he
        addresses her as more than a simple hairdresser—a conspirator.
3   **ministerium, -ī (n.):** *office, duty.*
      furtīvus, -a, -um: *clandestine, secret.* Although this genitive modifies
        noctis, its placement attracts its meaning also to *ministeriis.*
4   **ingeniōsus, -a, -um:** *clever.*
      nota, -ae (f.): *a note.*
5   **Corinnam:** the first time we have seen Ovid's mistress's name.
6   **saepe:** ANAPHORA serving to emphasize Ovid's meaning here as
        well as to unite the couplet.
      laboranti: perhaps meant to recall the activities of both soldiers
        and lovers as expressed in *Amores* I. 9.
      fīdus, -a, -um: *faithful, loyal.*
      reperiō, -īre, repperī, repertum: *to find, discover.*

accipe et ad dominam peraratas mane tabellas
  perfer et obstantes sedula pelle moras.
nec silicum venae nec durum in pectore ferrum
  nec tibi simplicitas ordine maior adest;   10
credibile est et te sensisse Cupidinis arcus:

✦ ✦ ✦

7   **dominam:** refers to Nape's mistress who is Ovid's as well.
    perārō, -āre, -āvī, -ātum: *to plow through, inscribe.*
    tabella, -ae (f.): these are the pair of wooden tablets, each half
        covered on one side with wax, in which Ovid's message was
        engraved with a writing stylus. The tablets were then tied
        together with the message concealed in the middle. The
        METAPHOR from plowing suits since a metal plow furrows
        through the earth just as the stylus scratches its way through
        the surface of the wax leaving behind its message. It is also a
        fine example of Ovid's applying a rather ordinary word to a
        novel situation.
8   **obstō, -āre, -itī, -ātum:** *to stand in the way, block the path.*
    sēdulus, -a, -um: *attentive, persistent.*
    pelle: the third imperative in two lines and the second in this line
        emphasizes the haste Ovid feels to communicate with his
        mistress. The imperatives combined with *obstantes…moras* give
        a graphic image of the poet's urgency.
9   **silex, -icis (m.):** *hard rock or stone, flint.*
    vēna, -ae (f.): *blood vessel, vein;* the first element in a TRICOLON
        CRESCENDO.
    ferrum, -ī (n.): *iron, steel.*
10 **tibi:** dative of possession with a compound of *sum.*
    adest: singular verb with multiple subjects: *venae* (9), *ferrum* (9),
        and *simplicitas* (10).
11 **arcus, -ūs (m.):** *a bow.*
    Cupidinis arcus: reminiscent of *Amores* I. 9 when Ovid sees himself
        as a soldier in Cupid's army, as well as of I. 1 when Ovid first
        feels the sting of Cupid's arrows. In employing the METAPHOR
        here Ovid includes Nape as a fellow soldier/lover, creating an
        even closer link with her and garnering yet more favor.

in me militiae signa tuere tuae.
si quaeret quid agam, spe noctis vivere dices;
    cetera fert blanda cera notata manu.
dum loquor, hora fugit: vacuae bene redde tabellas,   15
    verum continuo fac tamen illa legat.
aspicias oculos mando frontemque legentis:
    et tacito vultu scire futura licet.

✦ ✦ ✦

12   **mīlitia, -ae (f.):** *military service.*
      tueor, -ērī, tuitus: *to observe, watch over, guard.* Here, the imperative
        singular.
13   **quid agam:** present subjunctive in an indirect question. An
      idiomatic expression here meaning "how I am doing."
      spēs, -eī (f.): *hope.*
      spe noctis: this love affair, like most carried on with married
        women, occurs under the cover of darkness.
      vivere: Ovid here suggests that his very existence is dependent on
        this love affair.
14   **cetera:** scan the line carefully to determine the quantity of all the
      final -*as* in this line heavy with ASSONANCE.
      blandus, -a, -um: *charming, seductive.*
      cēra, -ae (f.): *wax, beeswax;* but here meaning the letter inscribed in
        the wax.
15   **dum...fugit:** a variation on the *carpe diem* theme used by the lover
      to persuade his mistress to yield to him.
      vacuae: dative with *redde* referring to his mistress.
      bene: note the correspondence between the meaning of the line and
      the fast pace created by repeated dactyls.
16   **verum (conj.):** *but.*
      continuō (adv.): *immediately, forthwith, without delay.*
      legat: present subjunctive in an indirect command after the
      imperative *fac* without *ut.*
17   **aspicias:** present subjunctive after *mando* without the *ut,* as often in
      poetry.
      mandō, -āre, -āvī, -ātum: *to order, bid.*

nec mora, perlectis rescribat multa iubeto:

    odi, cum late splendida cera vacat.   20

comprimat ordinibus versus, oculosque moretur

    margine in extremo littera †rasa† meos.

quid digitos opus est graphio lassare tenendo?

✦ ✦ ✦

19   **rescribat:** present subjunctive in an indirect command with the *ut*
       omitted.

       iubeto: a future imperative. Ovid's fourth command in the last
       three couplets.

20   **ōdī, odisse, ōsum:** *to hate, dislike.*

       splendidus, -a, -um: *bright, shining.*

       vacō, -āre, -āvī, -ātum: *to be empty, vacant, unfilled.* Note the slow
       rhythm in the first half of the line created by repeated spondees
       reflecting the poet's displeasure.

21   **comprimō, -ere, -pressī, -pressum:** *to pack closely or densely.* Here, a
       jussive subjunctive.

       versus: these are not necessarily verses of poetry but simply lines
       of writing. The image contrasts with *splendida cera vacat* (20).

       moretur: subject is *littera* (22); another jussive subjunctive. The
       abrupt change of subject here suggests the eagerness with
       which the lover addresses Nape.

22   **margō, -inis (m.):** *margin.*

       extrēmus, -a, -um: *farthest.*

       rādō, -ere, rāsī, -sum: *to rub out or erase; to scratch* but here assumed
       to mean "inscribed" by the context, although an erasure may
       suggest a carefully thought-out composition. In either case the
       poet is suggesting that he wants an extensive reply from his
       lover. The daggers show that modern editors are uncertain
       whether *rasa* is the correct reading.

       meos: The exaggerated separation of the adjective from its noun
       lends even more intensity to the lover's eagerness for a re-
       sponse.

23   **graphium, -ī (n.):** *stylus*—a sharp, pointed instrument used for
       incising letters onto waxed writing tablets.

       lassō, -āre, -āvī, -ātum: *to tire, exhaust.*

hoc habeat scriptum tota tabella "veni."
non ego victrices lauro redimire tabellas   25
    nec Veneris media ponere in aede morer.
subscribam VENERI FIDAS SIBI NASO MINISTRAS
    DEDICAT. AT NUPER VILE FUISTIS ACER.

✦   ✦   ✦

24   **habeat:** a jussive subjunctive.
      veni: from first fearing that the wax tablets will return to him
          empty in line 20, to requesting that Corinna fill them as full as
          possible with writing (21–22), Ovid at last decides that he
          would prefer the tablets to return with but one word written on
          them.
25   **victrix, -īcis:** *victorious.*
      lauro: this was the plant used to crown victorious generals and it
          also crowned their dispatches reporting their victories to the
          Roman Senate.
      redimiō, -īre, -iī, -ītum: *to wreathe, encircle.*
26   **Veneris…morer:** Ovid here mimics the custom of triumphant
          generals who dedicated their laurels to Jupiter in his temple on
          the Capitoline Hill.
      morer: potential subjunctive.
27   **Naso:** Publius Ovidius Naso, nominative.
28   **vīlis, -e:** *worthless, common, ordinary.*
      fuistis: PERSONIFICATION.
      acer, -eris (n.): maple wood.

AMORES I. 12

In poem I. 11, the poet asks Nape to deliver a message to his mistress; in I. 12 we learn that Corinna has replied that she is unable to entertain her lover today. Ovid initially scolds the hapless Nape for tripping as she carried the tablets, thus bringing bad luck to his message, and even implies that she was drunk when she set out. He then devotes the major portion of this poem to a long and detailed curse directed against the wax and wood on which the poet's message was incised. Both wax and wood are described as ominous and death-bearing, and the poet castigates himself for having chosen to send a love message on such deadly materials.

When Ovid curses the writing tablets that provoked his lover's rebuke, he employs another conventional topic of lyric and elegiac poetry. Both Propertius (III. 23) and Horace (*Carm.* II. 13) had made similar protests. In this poem, Ovid's humorous and exaggerated anger is not that of a miserably disappointed lover; rather his "anger" is constructed to showcase the poet's skill and versatility and reflects his pleasure in his own clever virtuosity.

AMORES I. 12

Flete meos casus: tristes rediere tabellae;
    infelix hodie littera posse negat.
omina sunt aliquid: modo cum discedere vellet,
    ad limen digitos restitit icta Nape.
missa foras iterum limen transire memento   5
    cautius atque alte sobria ferre pedem.

✦ ✦ ✦

1   **flete:** the appeal for sympathy in an otherwise lighthearted
        treatment establishes exaggerated emotional outburst as the
        poet's main device in this poem.
     rediere: the 3rd person plural perfect active alternate form.
     tabella, -ae (f.): *writing tablet.*
2   **infēlix, -icis:** *unhappy, ill-fated.*
     littera: the singular is used here to denote the whole of the writing.
     posse negat: an indirect statement with the subject understood.
3   **modo** (adv.): *just now, recently.*
     vellet: imperfect subjunctive used in a *cum*-circumstantial clause.
        Here it means "starting to."
4   **ad...Nape:** the unusual initial spondee and the repetitions of *i* and *t*
        mimic and intensify Nape's stumbling.
     digitos: a Greek accusative (used of the part of the body affected,
        i.e., the toes) with the perfect participle *icta*.
     restō, -āre, -itī: *to linger, remain; to stop.*
     iciō, -ere, īcī, ictum: *to strike.*
5   **memento:** a future active imperative which, with this verb, will
        translate as the present tense.
6   **altē** (adv.): *at a great height.*
     sōbrius, -a, -um: *sober, not intoxicated.* Perhaps the first time Nape
        set out on her mission she was not completely sober. If so, her
        tripping on the threshold would more likely suggest human
        frailty rather than divine intervention. Ovid here paints a quite
        different picture of this same maid from that of I. 11.

ite hinc, difficiles, funebria ligna, tabellae,
   tuque, negaturis cera referta notis,
quam, puto, de longae collectam flore cicutae
   melle sub infami Corsica misit apis.   10
at tamquam minio penitus medicata rubebas:

✦ ✦ ✦

7   **hinc:** *from here, from this place.*
      difficiles...tabellae: two vocative plural pairs in CHIASTIC word
         order personifying the tablets.
      lignum, -ī (n.): *wood.*
8   **tuque:** vocative singular personifying the *cera referta.*
      negaturis...notis: Ovid continues the vocative reprimand in
         CHIASTIC word order intensifying his displeasure by the use of
         ASSONANCE.
      cēra, -ae (f.): *wax.*
      nota, -ae (f.): *note, mark.*
      cera referta: vocative singular.
9   **puto:** suggests that Ovid may not be completely serious in what he
         says about the wax. Note the SYSTOLE in this metrical foot which
         scans as a dactyl.
      colligō, -ere, -lēgī, -lectum: *to gather together, collect.*
      cicūta, -ae (f.): *poisonous hemlock (conium maculatum).* Hemlock was
         given to criminals as poison. The most well-known individual
         to die from hemlock poisoning was Socrates. The plant was also
         considered to be an antaphrodisiac and thus might have
         contributed to the cause of Corinna's refusal.
10   **mel, mellis (n.):** *honey.*
      infāmis, -e: *infamous, disgraced.* Corsican honey was infamous for
         being bitter, due, according to ancient sources, to the large
         number of box trees, yew trees, and thyme on the island
         (McKeown, 328).
      Corsicus, -a, -um: *of or belonging to the island of Corsica* off the
         western coast of Italy, north of Sardinia.
      apis, -is (f.): *a bee.*
11   **minium -ī (n.):** *cinnabar, a bright red dye.*
      medicō, -āre, -āvī, -ātum: *to dye.*
      rubeō, -ēre: *to turn bright red.* Directed to the wax which, unlike
         ordinary wax that was dyed black, was red.

ille color vere sanguinulentus erat.
proiectae triviis iaceatis, inutile lignum,
    vosque rotae frangat praetereuntis onus.
illum etiam, qui vos ex arbore vertit in usum,   15
    convincam puras non habuisse manus.
praebuit illa arbor misero suspendia collo,
    carnifici diras praebuit illa cruces;
illa dedit turpes raucis bubonibus umbras,

✦ ✦ ✦

12   **color, -ōris (m.):** *color, pigment.*
       vērē (adv.): *truly, indeed.*
       sanguinulentus, -a, -um: *blood-red, crimson.* This adjective is
          suggestive of the deadly power of these tablets already men-
          tioned, *funebria ligna* (7).
13   **prōiciō, -ere, -iēci, -iectum:** *to fling to the ground.* There is no
          expressed noun in this couplet for this adjective to modify.
          Supply a missing *tabellae.*
       trivium, -ī (n.): *the meeting place of three roads; a crossroads.*
       iaceatis: addresses the supplied *tabellae* in a jussive subjunctive. A
          continuation of the PERSONIFICATION.
       inūtilis, -e: *useless.*
14   **frangat:** another jussive subjunctive.
16   **convincō, -ere, -vīcī, -victum:** *to prove, demonstrate.*
17   **suspendium, -ī (n.):** *hanging* (as a means of execution or suicide.)
       collum, -ī (n.): *the neck.*
18   **carnifex, -ficis (m.):** *an executioner.*
       dīrus, -a, -um: *awful, dreadful, frightful.*
       crux, -ucis (f.): *a wooden frame or cross on which criminals were hanged*
          or impaled.
19   **turpis, -e:** *loathsome, repulsive, shameful.*
       turpes...umbras: CHIASTIC word order.
       raucus, -a, -um: *harsh-sounding, raucous.*
       būbō, -ōnis (m.): *the horned owl;* its call sounded funereal and was
          considered a bad omen.

vulturis in ramis et strigis ova tulit.   20
his ego commisi nostros insanus amores
    molliaque ad dominam verba ferenda dedi?
aptius hae capiant vadimonia garrula cerae,
    quas aliquis duro cognitor ore legat;
inter ephemeridas melius tabulasque iacerent,   25
    in quibus absumptas fleret avarus opes.
ergo ego vos rebus duplices pro nomine sensi:

✦ ✦ ✦

20   **vultur, -uris (m.):** *a vulture.* These are birds of prey and hence were
        believed to be evil.
        rāmus, -ī (m.): *a branch.*
        strix, -igis (f.): *an owl, screech-owl.* The Romans believed these birds
        attacked infants in their cradles (Barsby, 137).
21   **his:** note the first position prominence in this clause.
        nostros…amores: poetic use of the plural.
        insānus, -a, -um: *frenzied, mad.*
23   **aptus, -a, -um:** (+ dat.) *fit, suitable, appropriate.*
        capiant: a potential subjunctive.
        vadimōnium, -ī (n.): *a legal term referring to an agreement of both
        parties in a legal suit to appear in court on an appointed day.*
        garrulus, -a, -um: *loquacious.* This word contrasts with the one-
        word reply Ovid had hoped for in I. 11.
24   **aliquis…ore:** INTERLOCKED WORD ORDER (SYNCHESIS).
        cognitor, -ōris (m.): *a legal representative, attorney.*
        legat: subjunctive by attraction, dependent on the subjunctive in
        line 23.
25   **ephēmeris, -idos (f.):** *a record book, day book.*
        iacerent: a potential subjunctive expressing past time.
26   **absumō, -ere, -sumpsī, -sumptum:** *to use up, spend, squander.*
        fleret: imperfect subjunctive again by attraction, dependent on
        iacerent (25).
        avārus, -a, -um: *greedy, avaricious, miserly.*
27   **duplex, -icis:** *two-faced, deceitful.* The adjective is used here in both
        its figurative sense in that the tablets have not delivered the
        message the poet had hoped for and in its literal sense since
        there are two halves to the tablets.

auspicii numerus non erat ipse boni.
quid precer iratus, nisi vos cariosa senectus
rodat, et immundo cera sit alba situ?   30

✦   ✦   ✦

28   **auspicium, -ī (n.):** *portent, fortune, luck*—with *boni,* a genitive of
quality (descriptive genitive).
29   **precor, -ārī, -ātus:** *to pray for, implore, beg.* Here, a deliberative
subjunctive.
cariōsus, -a, -um: *decayed.*
senectūs, -ūtis (f.): *old age.*
30   **rōdō, -ere, rōsī, -sum:** *to eat away, erode.* Here, an optative subjunctive, as is *sit.*
immundus, -a, -um: *unclean, foul.*

AMORES III. 15

In this last poem of the three books, Ovid addresses Venus and tells her that she must find a new love poet. He declares that his poetry has made him as distinguished to Sulmo as Vergil is to Mantua or Catullus to Verona, ranking himself among the greatest of the Roman poets. The poet says farewell to Cupid and to Venus. He proclaims that Bacchus now calls him to a greater work, most likely a tragedy, since Bacchus was the patron god of the theater. The poet in fact did write a single tragedy, the *Medea*, now lost. *Amores* III. 15 concludes with the traditional wish that his elegies survive him.

This poem looks back to I. 1 where the poet described his "accidental" birth as a love elegist. But, it is also a reply to III. 1. In that poem, the poet constructed a mock dialogue between elegy and tragedy in which tragedy argues that Ovid is now ready to write more serious poetry, whereas elegy claims him for herself. In reply, the poet asks tragedy for a little more time for his love poetry, although he recognizes that he will soon have to assume a greater task. This last poem of the elegies is also reminiscent of Horace, *Odes* III. 30, in which Horace announces that his odes will be more lasting than any material monument.

AMORES III. 15

Quaere novum vatem, tenerorum mater Amorum:
   raditur haec elegis ultima meta meis;
quos ego composui, Paeligni ruris alumnus,
   (nec me deliciae dedecuere meae)
si quid id est, usque a proavis vetus ordinis heres,   5
   non modo militiae turbine factus eques.
Mantua Vergilio gaudet, Verona Catullo;

✦ ✦ ✦

1   **vātēs, -is (m.):** *prophet, poet.* The oldest word for poet but one that
      had fallen out of favor. It was restored to prominence by the
      Augustan poets.
      tener, -era, -erum: *tender, sensitive.*
      mater Amorum: refers to Venus.
2   **rādō, -ere, rāsī, -sum:** *to scrape, graze.*
      elegī, -ōrum (m.): *elegiac verses.*
      meta: used of the turning posts at either end of a circus. Chariots
      competing in races would try to make the turn at the end of the
      circus as closely as possible, often grazing the post with the
      chariot.
3   **Paelignus, -a, -um:** *of or pertaining to the mountainous region in
      central Italy, east of Rome;* Ovid's province by birth.
      alumnus, -ī (m.): *a "son" or "foster son"; a product of a particular
      region or environment.*
4   **deliciae:** refers to the elegies, but also used by Catullus of his
      beloved in poems 2 and 3.
      dēdecet, -ēre, -uit: *to disgrace, dishonor.*
5   **proavus, -ī (m.):** *a forefather, ancestor.*
      vetus ordinis heres: this phrase gives us some important bio-
      graphical information about Ovid and his family: that Ovid is
      an *eques* by birth, not by a recent reward for military service; as
      well as a glimpse of the poet's fascination with genealogy,
      which is more obvious in his stories of the *Metamorphoses.*
6   **modo (adv.):** *just now, recently.*
      mīlitia, -ae (f.): *military service.*
      turbō, -inis (m.): *a whirlwind.*
7   **Mantua, -ae (f.):** *birthplace of the poet Vergil in the north of Italy.*
      Vērōna, -ae (f.): like Vergil's, Catullus's birthplace also lay in the
      far north of the Italian penninsula.

Paelignae dicar gloria gentis ego,
quam sua libertas ad honesta coegerat arma,
   cum timuit socias anxia Roma manus.   10
atque aliquis spectans hospes Sulmonis aquosi
   moenia, quae campi iugera pauca tenent,
"quae tantum" dicet "potuistis ferre poetam,
   quantulacumque estis, vos ego magna voco."
culte puer puerique parens Amathusia culti,   15
   aurea de campo vellite signa meo:
corniger increpuit thyrso graviore Lyaeus;

✦   ✦   ✦

9   **honestus, -a, -um:** *honorable.* Ovid speaks here from the point of
        view of a Paelignian, proud of his region's uprising in its
        struggle to maintain equality when threatened by Rome.

10   **anxius, -a, -um:** *anxious, distressed, worried.*

11   **Sulmō, -ōnis (m.):** *the town in Paelignia where Ovid was born.*
        aquōsus, -a, -um: *watery, wet.* Because Paelignia was a mountain-
        ous region it was filled with running streams.

12   **iūgerum, -ī (n.):** *a measurement of land equal approximately to two-
        thirds of an acre and measuring 240 feet by 120 feet.*

14   **quantuluscumque, -acumque, -umcumque:** *however small.*

15   **cultus, -a, -um:** *refined, sophisticated, elegant.* The final *-e* is short
        making this the vocative singular modifying *puer.*
        puer: Cupid; prompts a memory of I. 1, where, described with the
        adjective *saeve*, he was declared to be the reason for these
        poems having been written.
        Amathusius, -a, -um: *of or pertaining to a town in the southern part of
        Cyprus,* sacred to Venus, hence an epithet for Venus.

16   **aurea:** modifies *signa* but its first position in the line places it close
        to *Amathusia* who was often thought of as golden-haired.
        vellō, -ere, vulsī, vulsum: *to pull up.* When used with *signa* forms a
        military term meaning to break camp; reminiscent of I. 9.

17   **corniger, -era, -erum:** *having horns.* Bacchus is often referred to as
        "bull-horned."
        increpō, -āre, -uī, -itum: *to rattle, clang.*
        thyrsus, -ī (m.): *a wand,* usually covered with vine leaves and
        carried by worshippers of Bacchus.
        Lyaeus, -ī (m.): another name for *Bacchus* highlighting his role as
        the patron god of the theater who provides relaxation and
        release from care. Here Ovid invokes him for his own release
        from elegy.

pulsanda est magnis area maior equis.
imbelles elegi, genialis Musa, valete,
    post mea mansurum fata superstes opus.   20

✦ ✦ ✦

18   **magnis…equis:** CHIASTIC word order.
       area maior: a reference to the poet's future work, most probably
          the *Medea* but possibly a hint at the epic-scale *Metamorphoses*.
19   **imbellis, -e:** *not suited for war, unwarlike.* Here, a PERSONIFICATION
          with *elegi.*
       genialis, -e: *creative.*
20   **superstes, -itis:** *surviving after death.*

The
Metamorphoses

THE METAMORPHOSES

Ovid's *Metamorphoses*, a poem of fifteen books, is written in dactylic hexameters, the meter of the three great epic poems of antiquity, the *Iliad*, the *Odyssey*, and the *Aeneid*. While its meter suggests that the *Metamorphoses* is an epic, the subject matter, as well as its structure, places the poem in a category of its own. The focus on love seems more appropriate for elegy than for epic; the length and scope of the poem are more epic than elegiac. The poem consists of several hundred metamorphoses, or transformations, described in over 250 tales that begin with the creation of the world and of man, and end in the time of Augustus, first of the Roman emperors. The range of narratives includes the lives and loves of the gods, divine wrath, stories from the *Iliad*, the *Odyssey*, and the *Aeneid*, and accounts of important mythological and human families.

Ovid sets forth the plan for his massive undertaking in the first four lines of the poem:

> In nova fert animus mutatas dicere formas
> corpora; di, coeptis (nam vos mutastis et illas)
> adspirate meis primaque ab origine mundi
> ad mea perpetuum deducite tempora carmen!
>
> I plan to tell of forms changed into new bodies; you gods
> (for you yourselves have made these changes)
> look favorably on what I am beginning and spin out my
>   song to be continuous
> from the first origin of the world to my own times.
>   *Met.* I. 1–4

Most of the tales explain the origin *(aition)* of a natural phenomenon, such as a particular flower, tree, or bird, the name of a river or sea, the reason for a particular custom or tradition such as the color of the fruit of the mulberry tree or the wearing of the laurel wreath. The final transformation of the poem is that of Julius Caesar into a god and a star, and Ovid ends the poem, as he promises in his prelude, in his own time, the age of Augustus, first of the Roman emperors.

The idea of metamorphosis was extremely popular in Greek poetry, especially the poetry of the Hellenistic period. The poet Callimachus, writing in Alexandria in the third century B.C., wrote a narrative elegy of some four thousand lines in four books, which he called *Aitia*, or causes. (Ovid also used this meter for his love poetry: see the Appendix on meter.) Callimachus described the loves of the gods and the origin of many local religious practices. Other Alexandrian poets also wrote about metamorphoses, and, although these works are largely lost to us, Ovid had access to them and consulted these poets for information and inspiration. In Ovid, a metamorphosis most often transforms a human into a plant, animal, or stone; in the case of Pygmalion's statue, a stone into a woman. But in each instance the transformation affects only the physical body; the basic character of the individual survives the metamorphosis and usually determines it; Daphne, for example, who is changed into a laurel tree to escape the pursuing god Apollo, as a tree still shrinks from Apollo's advances; Baucis and Philemon, devoted to the gods and completely faithful to one another, are transformed into a pair of intertwined trees.

The poem may be divided into three major sections (Anderson [1996], 13): Books 1–6 are chiefly concerned with stories about gods and men; Books 7–11 primarily with stories that focus on human beings and their destructive passions; and Books 12–15 with stories that tell of Troy, Rome, and the deification of the great Roman heroes. In this textbook, the stories of Apollo and Daphne and Pyramus and Thisbe come from the first section; the tales of Daedalus and Icarus, of Philemon and Baucis, and of Pygmalion are from the second. Yet often the stories defy classification or categorization and the tremendous appeal of Ovid's great work throughout the ages is due, in large measure, to the complex and varied narrative.

Although the overarching theme that unifies the poem is metamorphosis, Ovid does seem to use two devices to create a kind of unity within the three sections of this complex tapestry of stories. Sometimes one story, like a frame, encompasses a series of tales, such as the cycle of stories told by the daughters of

Minyas to pass the time while they stay at home, having re-
fused to join in the worship of Bacchus; the story of Pyramus
and Thisbe is told by one of the Minyeides. In addition, Ovid
repeats patterns of thematically related stories; so, for example,
stories like the Apollo and Daphne episode also consider the
disastrous passions of the gods for mortal females.

To find a central theme for such a complex poem is difficult.
The poem is about endless change and the helplessness of
human beings in a world where the gods are generally cruel
or indifferent. Like his Alexandrian predecessors, Ovid is fascinated more by the narrative potential inherent in myth than
in its possible truths; he loves to tell stories for their own sake.
Some of his stories are serious and moving, or full of pathos
such as the poignant tale praising the simple piety of Philemon
and Baucis. Other stories, however, have a far less serious
tone, even when the subject matter itself is tragic; the poet
recounts the loss of Daedalus' son in a dramatic story which
appears to be about parental grief but the pathos is under-
mined by the larger context of the story (see the introduction
to Daedalus and Icarus below). The story of the doomed love
of Pyramus and Thisbe is not as serious as it first seems; neither is the story of the "pious" Pygmalion simply the tale of a
righteous and religious man. No single label fits this remarkable collection of stories.

With the loss of a number of collections of mythological tales
that Ovid had available to him, the *Metamorphoses* remains
the only source now for many classical myths. For centuries,
it has provided and continues to provide inspiration for poets, novelists, musicians, playwrights, and artists. Perhaps no
other single work of literature except the Bible has had a similar impact.[1]

---

[1] For a listing of literary, musical, and artistic works based on myth, especially the
Metamorphoses, see Jane Reid, *The Oxford Guide to Classical Mythology in the Arts 1300–
1900s*, 2 vols., Oxford and New York, 1993.

Apollo and Daphne

LARSON 1998

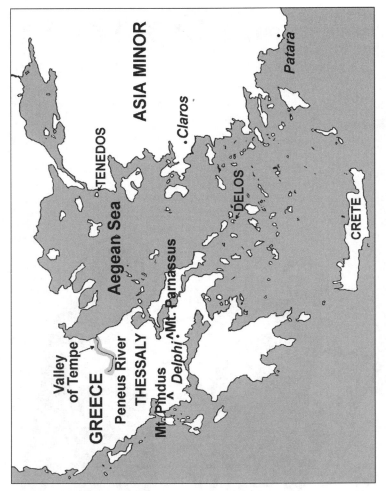

Map of Places in Apollo and Daphne

APOLLO AND DAPHNE
Met. I. 452–567

This is the first love story of the *Metamorphoses*. It follows the opening narratives of the poem, which describe the Creation, the Ages of Man, and the Flood. From the aftermath of the flood comes a snake-like creature called Python, which Apollo killed with his bow and arrow. Apollo's victory over Python was commemorated by the Pythian Games, although the wreath-crowns given the victors as prizes were made of oak leaves, not laurel, since the laurel tree was not yet known. The story of Apollo and Daphne is, in part, about the origin of the laurel, and the ending of the story connects the Rome of Ovid to the past by explaining the practice of awarding Roman victors a laurel wreath. This association with the past, so revered by Romans, was especially important to the emperor Augustus. By linking himself with the founder of Rome, Aeneas, and to the heroic deeds and practices of the past, he justified and glorified his own new role as princeps.

This myth of transformation includes many internal transformations of its own. When Apollo, full of boastful pride because of his victory over Python, claims to be a better archer than Cupid, the god of love immediately strikes him with an arrow so that he is consumed with love for the woodland nymph Daphne, daughter of the river god Peneus. At the same time, Cupid strikes Daphne with an arrow that has the opposite effect, so that she is immediately revolted and terrified by the god's advances. Ovid describes Daphne as if she were the love object of an elegiac lover; at the same time, as she flees the god, he compares her to a hare running for its life from a hound, in language reminiscent of epic. The god's pursuit of his unwilling victim is both tragic and comic; this blending of perspectives is typical of Ovid throughout the poem. Daphne, terrified by the fear of rape, is pitiful; the god, reduced to the status of a desperate mortal lover who pleads that his love be acknowledged and accepted, is comic. Both god and nymph have been transformed from their normal states, and as the nymph's capture becomes imminent, she prays to her father for help, and is willingly changed into a laurel tree rather than suffer the god's violent embrace.

The Apollo and Daphne episode is followed by the story of Zeus and Io, another in the series of narratives concerned with acts of rape, either attempted or performed, by the gods.

Perhaps no tale by Ovid has been so enormously popular for artists and writers. The subject of wall paintings and mosaics in antiquity, it has been reinterpreted by artists as diverse as Botticelli, Bernini, Dürer, Rubens, and Sargent, by musicians such as Handel and Scarlatti, and by poets including Spenser, Dryden, and Milton.

APOLLO AND DAPHNE

Met. I. 452–567

Primus amor Phoebi Daphne Peneia, quem non
fors ignara dedit, sed saeva Cupidinis ira,
Delius hunc nuper, victa serpente superbus,
viderat adducto flectentem cornua nervo   455

✦ ✦ ✦

452 **Phoebus, -ī (m.):** one of many appellations for Apollo. This one
refers to him as the god of light. There is an ELLIPSIS in this line:
supply a form of *esse* to join the two nominative phrases: *Primus
amor* and *Daphne Peneia.*

Daphnē, -ēs (f.): nominative singular in apposition to *amor.*

Pēnēius, -a, -um: a patronymic referring to Daphne as the daughter of the river deity *Peneus.* Peneus is the name of a principal
river in Thessaly, which rises in Mt. Pindus and flows through
the Vale of Tempe, noted for its beauty. *Daphne Peneia* make up
nearly half the syllables of the line and establish Daphne's
importance in this story.

quem non: antecedent is *amor.* This is an uncommon occurrence of
two monosyllables at a line end. Following the uncommon fifth
foot bucolic diaeresis, they represent a break with the introduc-
tory information and signal the beginning of the story.

453 **fors, -tis (f.):** *chance, luck.*

saeva Cupidinis ira: Ovid, like Vergil (*Aeneid* I. 4–12) begins a
section of his epic with reference to the wrath of the gods, but
Cupid's wrath is far less disastrous than Juno's. The adjective
saeva is one Ovid uses to describe Cupid at *Amores* I. 1.5.

454 **Dēlius, -iī (m.):** a standard epithet for Apollo derived from Delos,
the island of his birth.

serpens, -ntis (f., m.): *snake, serpent.* Here, feminine.

superbus: introduces Apollo in this episode as arrogant and
haughty, qualities that incite Cupid's wrath.

455 **cornua:** a SYNECDOCHE referring to the bow by naming its basic
parts. Bows were generally made from naturally bent horns
held together with a central piece of metal.

nervus, -ī (m.): *string of a musical instrument or bow.* The drawn-out
bowstring stretches from one end of the bow to the other just as
the words describing that string, *adducto...nervo,* lie at either
end of the phrase expressing the bow.

"quid" que "tibi, lascive puer, cum fortibus armis?"
dixerat: "ista decent umeros gestamina nostros,
qui dare certa ferae, dare vulnera possumus hosti,
qui modo pestifero tot iugera ventre prementem
stravimus innumeris tumidum Pythona sagittis.   460

✦ ✦ ✦

456 **que:** a simple connective interrupting the flow of the quotation and
    helping the line to move with a light and energetic rhythm.
    lascīvus, -a, -um: *naughty, unrestrained, mischievous.*
    tibi: take with *quid* and translate loosely as "what do you want
    with."
    armis: weapons common both to Apollo and Cupid—arrows.
457 **umerus, -ī (m.):** *the shoulder.*
    gestāmen, -inis (n.): *load, burden.*
    nostros: Ovid's use of the plural with singular intent.
458 **dare…dare:** ANAPHORA used to swell Apollo's arrogance.
    fera, -ae (f.): *wild animal.*
    possumus: another use of "we" for "I."
459 **qui:** taken with the *qui* of 458 creates an ANAPHORA emphasizing
    the prowess of Apollo as a hunter. Because the first *qui* intro-
    duces two clauses, his boast here forms a variation of a
    TRICOLON CRESCENDO.
    pestifer, -era, -erum: *deadly, pernicious, pestilential.*
    iūgerum, -ī (n.): *a measurement of land equal approximately to two-*
    thirds of an acre and measuring 240 feet by 120 feet.
    venter, -tris (m.): *the belly or underside.*
    premō, -ere, pressī, -ssum: *to press on, push, cover.*
460 **sternō, -ere, strāvī, strātum:** *to strew, lay low, spread over an area,*
    throw down.
    tumidus, -a, -um: *swollen.*
    Pythōn, -ōnis (m.): the Python, a serpent that Apollo killed near
    Delphi. The Pythian games were inaugurated in honor of this
    achievement. Ovid recounts that story just prior to the Apollo/
    Daphne episode. Here, a Greek masculine accusative singular
    form ending in *-a.*
    sagitta, -ae (f.): *arrow.*
    innumeris tumidum Pythona sagittis: HYPERBOLE in CHIASTIC word
    order.

tu face nescio quos esto contentus amores
inritare tua, nec laudes adsere nostras!"
filius huic Veneris "figat tuus omnia, Phoebe,
te meus arcus" ait; "quantoque animalia cedunt
cuncta deo, tanto minor est tua gloria nostra."   465
dixit et eliso percussis aere pennis
inpiger umbrosa Parnasi constitit arce

✦ ✦ ✦

461 **fax, facis (f.):** *torch, firebrand.* .
  nescio quos: with *amores.* A dismissive, haughty remark. The *-o* of
    nescio is short by SYSTOLE.
  esto: future singular imperative.
  contentus, -a, -um: *content, satisfied.*
462 **inrītō, -āre, -āvī, -ātum:** *to provoke, rouse.*
  tua: ablative singular modifying *face,* 461. The HYPERBATON creates
    suspense and sustains interest throughout the clause.
  laus, laudis (f.): *praise.*
  adserō, -ere, -uī, -tum: *to lay claim to.*
463 **Venus, -eris (f.):** Venus, the goddess most associated with love and
    sexual attraction.
  fīgō, -ere, -xī, -xum: a concessive subjunctive; translate as "al-
    though," or "even though."
464 **te meus arcus:** supply a missing *figet* to balance *figat* from line 463.
    It is a practice common to Ovid to omit duplicate words in
    parallel constructions. Although the first clause is subjunctive,
    this second will be future indicative.
  arcus, -ūs (m.): *a bow.*
  quanto...tanto: these correlatives used as ablatives of degree of
    difference introduce a comparison of the sort "*by as much as
    ...by just so much....*"
466 **ēlīdō, -ere, -sī, -sum:** *to expel, force out, drive forth.*
  eliso percussis aere pennis: SYNCHESIS and multiple spondees
    graphically exaggerate Cupid's flying motions.
  āēr, -āeris (m.): *air.* Here, a three syllable word (both *e*'s are short).
  penna, -ae (f.): *wing, feather.*
467 **inpiger, -era, -erum:** *tireless, energetic, quick.*
  umbrosus, -a, -um: *shady.*
  Parnāsus, -ī (m.): a mountain in Greece at the base of which is
    Delphi; sacred to both Apollo and the Muses.
  constō, -āre, -itī: *to take up a position.*

eque sagittifera prompsit duo tela pharetra
diversorum operum: fugat hoc, facit illud amorem;
quod facit, auratum est et cuspide fulget acuta,   470
quod fugat, obtusum est et habet sub harundine plumbum.
hóc déus in nympha Pēnēide fixit, at illō
laésit Apollineas traiecta per ossa medullas;

✦ ✦ ✦

468 **eque:** *ex que = et ex.*
   sagittifer, -era, -erum: *loaded with arrows.*
   prōmō, -ere, -psī, -ptum: *to bring forth, draw forth, produce.*
   pharetra, -ae (f.): *quiver.* Note that the words describing the quiver,
   sagittifera…pharetra, surround the weapons within.
469 **dīversus, -a, -um:** *differing, distinct.*
   fugō, -āre, -āvī, -ātum: *to cause to flee, drive away, repel.*
   hoc…illud: the first of several ANTITHESES Ovid sets up in the next
   few lines to demonstrate the very different effects Cupid's
   arrows have on Apollo and Daphne.
470 **quod facit:** with *quod fugat,* 471, forms an ANAPHORA used to draw
   attention to the ANTITHESIS. Although parallel in form these two
   lines reflect the opposite effects of the two arrows.
   aurātus, -a, -um: *golden.*
   cuspis, -idis (f.): *spear, lance; sharp point, tip.*
   fulgeō, -ēre, fulsī: *to glisten, gleam.*
   acūtus, -a, -um: *sharp, pointed.*
471 **obtūsus, -a, -um:** *dull, blunt.*
   harundō, -inis (f.): *the shaft of an arrow.*
472 **nympha, -ae (f.):** *nymph, a demi-goddess.* Although this word most
   often refers to a woodland spirit, here it may also carry its
   original Greek meaning of unmarried girl.
   Pēnēis, -idos: *daughter of the river god Peneus.* Here, a Greek
   feminine ablative adjective modifying *nympha.*
   illo: completes another ANTITHESIS begun with *hoc.*
473 **Apollineus, -a, -um:** *of or pertaining to Apollo.*
   trāiciō, -ere, -iēcī, -iectum: *to pierce, transfix.*
   medulla, -ae (f.): *marrow;* often representing the inmost soul. This
   wound will have a dramatic effect on Apollo, changing him
   from an epic-scale hero into a frustrated elegiac lover, just as
   Cupid's arrow does to Ovid himself in *Amores* I. 1.

protinus alter amat, fugit altera nomen amantis
silvarum latebris captivarumque ferarum   475
exuviis gaudens innuptaeque aemula Phoebes:
vitta coercebat positos sine lege capillos.
multi illam petiere, illa aversata petentes
inpatiens expersque viri nemora avia lustrat

✦ ✦ ✦

474   **alter...altera:** graphic CHIASMUS succinctly pointing out the ANTITH-
       ESIS.
       amans, -tis (m.): *a lover.* This line, full of ASSONANCE, completes the
       fourth ANTITHESIS within five lines. The same words (*alter, amo*),
       in varying forms, are employed to describe two different effects
       on two different characters. The phrase *nomen amantis* consti-
       tutes a PLEONASM for Apollo.
475   **latebra, -ae (f.):** *hiding place.*
476   **exuviae, -ārum (f.):** *skin torn from a hunted animal, spoils.*
       innuptus, -a, -um: *unmarried.*
       aemula, -ae (f.): *a female imitator.*
       Phoebē, -ēs (f.): *Diana,* twin sister to Apollo; the virgin goddess
       most associated with forests and the hunt. Here, a Greek
       genitive singular ending.
477   **vitta:** a headband was worn by both married and unmarried
       women; but married women wore their hair tied up while
       unmarried women let it hang loose (*sine lege*) as Daphne does
       here.
       coerceō, -ēre, -uī, -itum: *to restrain, restrict, control.*
478   **petiere:** the third person plural perfect active alternate form. Here
       meaning *to seek the hand of in marriage, to court.*
       āversor, -ārī, -ātus: *to turn away from in disgust, to reject.*
       petentes: an accusative plural present participle used here as a
       substantive to represent Daphne's suitors.
479   **inpatiens, -ntis:** *impatient.*
       expers, -ertis: *lacking experience or knowledge.*
       nemus, -oris (n.): *wood, sacred grove.*
       āvius, -a, -um: *uncharted, remote, distant.*
       lustrō, -āre, -āvī, -ātum: *to move through or around, traverse, roam.*

nec, quid Hymen, quid Amor, quid sint conubia curat. 480
saepe pater dixit: "generum mihi, filia, debes,"
saepe pater dixit: "debes mihi, nata, nepotes";
illa velut crimen taedas exosa iugales
pulchra verecundo suffuderat ora rubore
inque patris blandis haerens cervice lacertis   485
"da mihi perpetua, genitor carissime," dixit
"virginitate frui! dedit hoc pater ante Dianae."

✦ ✦ ✦

480   **quid...quid...quid:** sets up a TRICOLON emphasizing strongly that in which Daphne has no interest.
    Hymēn: *the god of marriage* and, by extension, marriage.
    cōnūbium, -ī (n.): *the rite or ceremony of marriage.*

481   **gener, -erī (m.):** *a son-in-law.*

482   **saepe pater dixit:** ANAPHORA drawing attention to Peneus's words which embody the purpose of Roman marriage, to produce children.
    generum...debes, debes...nepotes: graphic CHIASMUS.
    nāta, -ae (f.): *daughter.*

483   **velut:** *just as, in the same way that;* often introduces a SIMILE. Here, with *crimen.*
    taedas: these were the pine torches carried in marriage processions that escorted a bride to her husband's house the night of the wedding. Here, a METONYMY referring to the marriage state.
    exōsus, -a, -um: *hating, despising.*
    iugālis, -e: *matrimonial, nuptial.*

484   **pulchra...rubore:** a GOLDEN LINE—a five-word line made up of a central verb flanked by an adjective/noun pair in INTERLOCKED WORD ORDER on each side.
    ora: an accusative plural direct object.
    verēcundus, -a, -um: *modest.*
    suffundō, -ere, -fūdī, -fūsum: *to pour into, overspread; to color, redden, blush.*
    rubor, -ōris (m.): *redness.*

485   **blandus, -a, -um:** *charming, seductive, caressing.*
    cervix, -īcis (f.): *the neck.*
    lacertus, -ī (m.): *the upper arm from elbow to shoulder.* The word order here may portray Daphne with her arms entwined about her father's neck.

486   **genitor, -ōris (m.):** *father.*

487   **virginitās, -tātis (f.):** *maidenhood.*
    Dianae: at the age of three, Diana is said to have asked for and been granted the gift of Virginity from her father, Jupiter (see Calimachus *Hymn to Artemis, I*).

ille quidem obsequitur, sed te decor iste quod optas
esse vetat, votoque tuo tua forma repugnat:
Phoebus amat visaeque cupit conubia Daphnes,   490
quodque cupit, sperat, suaque illum oracula fallunt,
utque leves stipulae demptis adolentur aristis,
ut facibus saepes ardent, quas forte viator
vel nimis admovit vel iam sub luce reliquit,
sic deus in flammas abiit, sic pectore toto   495

✦ ✦ ✦

488 **obsequor, -sequī, -secūtus:** *to comply, humor, gratify.*

te: APOSTROPHE—heightens sympathy for Daphne and her impossible situation: beauty that attracts unwanted male advances.

decor, -ōris (m.): *beauty, good looks.*

489 **vōtum, -ī (n.):** *vow, oath.* Here, a dative after a compound verb. The preponderance of harsh *t* sounds and the juxtapositions of *vetat, voto* and *tuo, tua* all reinforce Daphne's hopeless situation.

repugnō, -āre, -āvī, -ātum: *to resist, fight against.*

490 **Daphnes:** here an objective genitive dependent on *conubia*. This noun has a Greek declension: *Daphnē, Daphnēs, Daphnae, Daphnēn, Daphnē.*

491 **suaque...fallunt:** Apollo, the god most associated with prophecy, is unable to see the futility of his own desire. He is self-deceived.

ōrāculum, -ī (n.): *oracle, divine utterance.*

492 **utque:** introduces a SIMILE.

stipula, -ae (f.): *stubble, the stalks left in the field after a harvest.*

dēmō, -ere, dempsī, demptum: *to remove, take away.*

adoleō, -ēre, -uī, adultum: *to burn.*

arista, -ae (f.): *harvest.*

493 **ut:** ANAPHORA and ASYNDETON introducing a second SIMILE about burning.

saepēs, -is (f.): *hedge.*

494 **vel...vel:** the correlatives balance the line creating a parallel structure just as *sic, sic* will do in the next line.

sub luce: translate idiomatically as *at dawn.*

495 **sic...sic:** these resolve the earlier two SIMILES introduced by *utque* (492) and *ut* (493).

abeō, -īre, -iī, -itum: *to change, be transformed into.*

uritur et sterilem sperando nutrit amorem.
spectat inornatos collo pendere capillos
et "quid, si comantur?" ait. videt igne micantes
sideribus similes oculos, videt oscula, quae non
est vidisse satis; laudat digitosque manusque   500
bracchiaque et nudos media plus parte lacertos;
si qua latent, meliora putat. fugit ocior aura

✦   ✦   ✦

496   **urō, -ere, ussī, ustum:** *to burn, inflame with passion;* parallel to
     Amores I. 1.26 when Ovid, the lover, is struck with one of
     Cupid's arrows.

     sterilis, -e: *futile;* an appropriate adjective as Apollo's love for
     Daphne is all in vain. Unlike the *stipulae* in 492, which make the
     fields more fertile, Apollo burns with a love that will never be
     fruitful; it will never be rewarded or fulfilled.

     sperando: here a simple ablative gerund.

     nūtriō, -īre, -īvī, -ītum: *to encourage, foster.*

497   **collum, -ī (n.):** *the neck.*

     pendeō, -ēre, pependī: *to hang.*

498   **comō, -ere, -psī, -ptum:** *to adorn, arrange.* Here, a subjunctive in a
     future-less-vivid condition with the apodosis understood.

499   **sīdus, -eris (n.):** *star, constellation.* Here, dative with *similes.*

     osculum -ī (n.): *mouth, lips.*

500   **...que...que:** with the third *-que* immediately in 501 create
     POLYSYNDETON isolating and highlighting each part as Apollo
     runs his eyes over her body.

501   **brācchium, -ī (n.):** *arm.*

     nudos...lacertos: a CHIASTIC arrangement of words drawing
     attention to her partially exposed arms that excite the young
     god. *media* and *parte* are ablatives of comparison with the
     adverbial *plus,* which modifies *nudos.* Translate roughly *her arms*
     more than half naked.

502   **qua:** variant form of *aliquae* after *si.* Ovid leaves out the details but
     provides ample room for imagination.

     ōcior, ōcius: *swifter, faster.*

     aura, -ae (f.): *a breeze.*

illa levi neque ad haec revocantis verba resistit:
"nympha, precor, Penei, mane! non insequor hostis;
nympha, mane! sic agna lupum, sic cerva leonem,   505
sic aquilam penna fugiunt trepidante columbae,
hostes quaeque suos: amor est mihi causa sequendi!
me miserum! ne prona cadas indignave laedi
crura notent sentes et sim tibi causa doloris!

✦   ✦   ✦

503   **illa levi:** completes the INTERLOCKED phrase begun with *ocior aura*,
502. The ENJAMBMENT between 502–503 helps to reflect the
speed and intention with which Daphne flees her pursuer.

504   **precor, -ārī, -ātus:** *to pray for, implore, beg.* It is of note that Apollo, a
god, is here reduced to praying to a maiden.

Pēnēi: here, a Greek vocative ending in short *-i.* The multiple
CAESURAE, in this line as well as in the next several lines
describing Apollo's pursuit of the maiden, suggest intermittent
utterances during the chase. We can almost hear him gasping
for air as he pursues her.

insequor, -sequī, -secūtus: *to pursue.*

505   **sic:** the first of three phrases that, introduced with this same
adverb, create a TRICOLON CRESCENDO full of IRONY because,
although he claims not to be, Apollo behaves exactly like the
wolf, the lion, and the eagle, all predatory hunters.

agna, -ae (f.): *a ewe lamb.*

cerva, -ae (f.): *a deer.*

506   **aquila, -ae (f.):** *an eagle.*

penna, -ae (f.): *a wing; feather.*

columba, -ae (f.): *a dove,* a bird especially associated with Venus.

508   **me miserum:** an accusative of exclamation typical of the elegiac
lover (see *Amores* I. 1.25).

cadas: an optative subjunctive, as are *notent* and *sim* (509), introduced by *ne.*

indignus, -a, -um: *not deserving.*

laedō, -ere, laesī, laesum: *to harm, injure.*

509   **crūs, crūris (n.):** *the lower leg, shin.*

notō, -āre, -āvī, -ātum: *to mark.*

sentis, -is (m.): *a briar or bramble.*

sim...doloris: nearly the same structure as *amor...sequendi* (507).
Because of its separation from the negative particle *ne,* the clause
sounds positive and foreshadows the true ending of the chase.

aspera, qua properas, loca sunt: moderatius, oro,　　　510
curre fugamque inhibe, moderatius insequar ipse.
cui placeas, inquire tamen: non incola montis,
non ego sum pastor, non hic armenta gregesque
horridus observo. nescis, temeraria, nescis,
quem fugias, ideoque fugis: mihi Delphica tellus　　　515
et Claros et Tenedos Patareaque regia servit;
Iuppiter est genitor; per me, quod eritque fuitque

✦　✦　✦

510　**qua:** adverb formed from the relative pronoun—*in which direction,*
　　　where.
　　　moderatius: the comparative of the adverb.
511　**inhibeō, -ēre, -uī, -itum:** *to restrain, check.*
512　**cui:** dative with *placeas.*
　　　inquīrō, -ere, -quīsīvī, -sītum: *to inquire, ask.*
　　　non: introduces a TRICOLON CRESCENDO with ASYNDETON. His
　　　　TRICOLON here reflects the one at 505–506.
　　　incola: the verb for this phrase is found in the next line—*sum.*
513　**pastor, -ōris (m.):** *a shepherd.*
　　　hīc: *here, in this place.*
　　　armentum, -ī (n.): *a herd.*
　　　grex, gregis (m.): *a flock.*
514　**horridus, -a, -um:** *rough in manner, rude, uncouth; hairy.*
　　　nescis...nescis: repetition for emphasis.
　　　temerārius, -a, -um: *thoughtless, reckless, hasty.*
515　**fugias:** subjunctive in an indirect question.
　　　tellūs, -ūris (f.): *land, country.*
516　**et...et...-que:** POLYSYNDETON emphasizes just how many places on
　　　　earth recognize the greatness of this deity.
　　　Claros, -ī (f.): a small town, sacred to Apollo, on the central coast of
　　　　Asia Minor.
　　　Tenedos, -ī (f.): an island in the Aegean, sacred to Apollo.
　　　Patarēus, -a, -um: *of or related to Patara,* a coastal city in southern
　　　　Asia Minor with an oracle of Apollo.
　　　rēgia, -ae (f.): *royal palace, court.*
517　**Iuppiter est genitor:** Apollo comically tries to place himself back
　　　　into the realm of deities even while he is possessed by very
　　　　human emotions and in hot pursuit of Daphne.
　　　per me: ANAPHORA and ENJAMBMENT drawing yet more attention to
　　　　the boast.

estque, patet; per me concordant carmina nervis.
certa quidem nostra est, nostra tamen una sagitta
certior, in vacuo quae vulnera pectore fecit!   520
inventum medicina meum est, opiferque per orbem
dicor, et herbarum subiecta potentia nobis.
ei mihi, quod nullis amor est sanabilis herbis
nec prosunt domino, quae prosunt omnibus, artes!"
     Plura locuturum timido Peneia cursu   525
fugit cumque ipso verba inperfecta reliquit,

✦ ✦ ✦

518   **...-que:** the third in a series creating POLYSYNDETON that isolates and
        emphasizes each of the three verbs and adds weight to Apollo's
        boast about his prophetic powers. Nonetheless he is unable to
        foresee his own failure in this chase.
        concordō, -āre, -āvī, -ātum: *to agree, harmonize.*
        nervus, -ī (m.): *a string of a musical instrument.* Here, an ablative,
        probably of place where without the preposition.
519   **nostra:** nominative but difficult to see because of ELISION; modifies
        sagitta.
        nostra: ablative of comparison with *certior,* 520.
        sagitta, -ae (f.): *arrow.* Take with both clauses in the line.
        una: Cupid's.
521   **inventum, -ī (n.):** *discovery, invention.*
        medicina: Apollo is known as the god of healing. It is IRONIC that
        just as his power of foresight has earlier failed him, so too do
        his powers fail to heal the wound caused by Cupid's arrow.
        opifer, -era, -erum: *aid-bringing, helper.*
522   **herba, -ae (f.):** *plant, herb.*
        sūbiciō -ere, -iēcī, -iectum: *to subject to, put under the control of.*
        Supply *est.*
        potentia, -ae (f.): *power, influence.*
523   **ei:** interjection used to express anguish, *oh!*
        mihi: dative of reference.
        quod: take with the interjection and translate *alas, that.*
        sānābilis, -e: *curable.* For the elegiac lover, love is a disease, often
        incurable.
525   **plura:** neuter accusative plural object of *locuturum.*
        locuturum: future active participial direct object of *fugit.* Modifies
        him (Apollo).
526   **inperfectus, -a, -um:** *unfinished.*

tum quoque visa decens; nudabant corpora venti,
obviaque adversas vibrabant flamina vestes,
et levis inpulsos retro dabat aura capillos,
auctaque forma fuga est. sed enim non sustinet ultra   530
perdere blanditias iuvenis deus, utque monebat
ipse Amor, admisso sequitur vestigia passu.
ut canis in vacuo leporem cum Gallicus arvo
vidit, et hic praedam pedibus petit, ille salutem;

✦   ✦   ✦

527   **tum...decens:** supply *est* to complete the perfect passive with *visa*.
       corpora: often used in poetry in the plural to stand for the whole
            person.
       venti: the first of three words (with *flamina,* 528 and *aura,* 529) used
            in three lines referring to the movement of air and its effects on
            Daphne's body and clothing. Note the parallel structure of the
            lines, particularly 528–29.
528   **obvius, -a, -um:** *opposing, confronting.*
       vibrō, -āre, -āvī, -ātum: *to wave, flutter.*
       flāmen, -inis (n.): *wind, breeze.*
529   **inpellō, -ere, -pulī, -pulsum:** *to push, drive, set in motion.*
530   **auctaque ...est:** the ASSONANCE of *a* sounds smoothes the line and
            with the ELISION quickens the pace of her flight, which only
            serves to make her more desirable and attractive to the god.
            The mid-line break in sense allows but a brief pause in the
            narrative for both reader and pursuer.
       ultra: *further, beyond that point.*
531   **blanditia, -ae (f.):** *charm, flattery.*
532   **Amor:** because of the *ipse,* this must be translated as *Cupid.*
       admisso: *having been given full rein, at full speed.*
533   **ut canis:** a SIMILE of epic proportions. Apollo gains strength in the
            SIMILE and resumes his former stature of the skilled, proven
            hunter. The god seems here to become the actual enemy of real
            prey; this he had earlier (504) claimed not to be.
       cum: conjunction.
       Gallicus, -a, -um: *of Gaul.*
       arvum, -ī (n.): *field, ploughed land.*
534   **hic...ille:** *hic* refers to the nearer of the two possible antecedents,
            the *Gallicus (canis),* and *ille* to the hare, the farther of the two.
            They form a parallel ANTITHESIS.
       praeda, -ae (f.): *prey.*

alter inhaesuro similis iam iamque tenere   535
sperat et extento stringit vestigia rostro,
alter in ambiguo est, an sit conprensus, et ipsis
morsibus eripitur tangentiaque ora relinquit:
sic deus et virgo est hic spe celer, illa timore.
qui tamen insequitur pennis adiutus Amoris,   540
ocior est requiemque negat tergoque fugacis
inminet et crinem sparsum cervicibus adflat.

✦ ✦ ✦

535   **alter:** the beginning of another ANTITHESIS.
     inhaereō, -rēre, -sī, -sum: *to stick, cling, attach.* Here, the masculine
      dative future active participle with *similis.*
     iam iamque: adds speed to the meter and vividness to the SIMILE.
536   **vestigia:** recalls the *vestigia* of 532 that referred directly to Daphne.
      Here, refers not just to the impression left by the foot but to the
      foot itself.
     rostrum, -ī (n.): *muzzle, snout.*
537   **alter:** completes the ANTITHESIS begun in 535.
     ambiguum, -ī (n.): *uncertainty, doubt.*
     an sit conprensus: an indirect question introduced by *an.*
     conprendō, -ere, -dī, -sum: *to seize, catch hold of.*
538   **morsus, -ūs (m.):** *a bite.*
     eripitur: this passive form carries a reflexive meaning—*snatches*
      itself away. This is a line filled with harsh sounds that reflect the
      frightening situation.
539   **hic...illa:** another ANTITHESIS with parallel structure. In this
      instance, because of the clear genders, *hic* and *illa* are not *the*
      former and *the latter*, but rather *he* and *she.*
     spēs, -eī (f.): *hope, expectation.*
540   **adiuvō, -āre, -iūvī, -iūtum:** *to help, assist.*
541   **ōcior, -ius:** *swifter.* The subject is the *qui*-clause in 540.
     requiēs, -ētis (f.): (*requiem,* acc.) *rest, relaxation.*
     tergo: dative after *inminet* (542).
     fugax, -ācis: *fleeing, running away—the one who is fleeing,* i.e.,
      Daphne. The rapid succession of increasingly longer clauses
      helps to give the effect of speed and of the ever-gaining Apollo.
542   **inmineō, -ēre:** *to press closely on, to be almost on.*
     spargō, -ere, sparsī, sparsum: *to scatter, strew.*
     cervix, -īcis (f.): *neck.*
     adflō, -āre, -āvī, -ātum: *to breathe onto, blow onto.*

viribus absumptis expalluit illa citaeque
victa labore fugae spectans Peneidas undas
"fer, pater," inquit "opem! si flumina numen habetis,   545
qua nimium placui, mutando perde figuram!"   547
vix prece finita torpor gravis occupat artus,
mollia cinguntur tenui praecordia libro,
in frondem crines, in ramos bracchia crescunt,   550
pes modo tam velox pigris radicibus haeret,

✦ ✦ ✦

543 **absumō, -ere, -sumpsī, -sumptum:** *to use up, squander, spend.*
     expallescō, -ere, -paluī: *to turn pale.*
     citus, -a, -um: *rapid, speedy.*
544 **victa:** modifies the subject, Daphne.
     Peneidas undas: direct object of *spectans.* Refers to her father, the
       river.
545 **fer:** imperative singular.
     flumina: nominative plural subject of *habetis.* Since her father was
       the divinity of the river, she refers to him as the water itself.
547 **qua:** refers to *figuram*; ablative of means or instrument. The lack of
       a line 546 is due to uncertainties and inaccuracies in the ancient
       texts.
     nimium: *excessively, extremely, very much.*
548 **torpor, -ōris (m.):** *numbness, heaviness.*
     artus, -ūs (m.): *limb of a tree or body.*
549 **tenuis, -e:** *fine, thin.*
     praecordia, -ōrum (n.): *chest, heart, breast.*
     liber, -brī (m.): *the inner bark of a tree.*
550 **frons, -dis (f.):** *foliage, leafy boughs.*
     crescunt: with both clauses of the line.
551 **vēlox, -ōcis:** *swift, speedy.* The strong, principal CAESURA of this line
       falls between two ANTONYMS, *velox* | | *pigris,* which graphically
       reflect the change brought about by Daphne's ongoing meta-
       morphosis.
     piger, -gra, -grum: *sluggish, inactive.*
     rādix, -īcis (f.): *a root*; here, ablative with *haeret.*
     haereō, -ēre, haesī, haesum: *to cling.* The many SPONDEES and
       multiple consonant clusters slow down the pace of the line
       perhaps mimicing Daphne's feet, which become slow and stuck
       to the ground.

ora cacumen habet: remanet nitor unus in illa.
    Hanc quoque Phoebus amat positaque in stipite dextra
sentit adhuc trepidare novo sub cortice pectus
conplexusque suis ramos ut membra lacertis   555
oscula dat ligno; refugit tamen oscula lignum.
cui deus "at, quoniam coniunx mea non potes esse,
arbor eris certe" dixit "mea! semper habebunt
te coma, te citharae, te nostrae, laure, pharetrae;

✦ ✦ ✦

552   **cacūmen, -cūminis (n.):** *top or tip of a tree.*
       nitor, -ōris (m.): *brilliance, brightness, splendor, elegance.* Though this
          word is modified with the adjective *unus*, it may nonetheless
          have a dual reference: to the sheen of the new leaves and to her
          former glowing beauty. Note the metrical contrast to line 551
          where the line is heavily SPONDAIC; here the line is all DACTYLIC.
553   **stīpes, -itis (m.):** *tree trunk; woody branch.*
554   **cortex, -icis (m.):** *outer bark of a tree.*
555   **membrum, -ī (n.):** *part of the body; limb of a tree or body.*
       lacertus, -ī (m.): *upper arm.* With *suis*, the CHIASTIC word order
          places Apollo's arms around the branches/limbs.
556   **lignum, -ī (n.):** *wood, firewood.* Note double use of the word in
          different cases in this line.
       refugit: her transformation has been purely physical. Even in her
          new guise, Daphne remains true to her former character,
          shrinking still from Apollo's attention.
559   **te...te...te...:** the pronouns are given great prominence in this line.
          Ovid employs ANAPHORA to introduce a TRICOLON CRESCENDO,
          each element of which contains a well-known Apollonian
          attribute.
       coma, -ae (f.): *hair.*
       cithara, -ae (f.): *lyre.*
       laurus, -ī (f.): *foliage of the laurel (bay) tree; the bay tree.*
       pharetra, -ae (f.): *quiver.*

tu ducibus Latiis aderis, cum laeta Triumphum   560
vox canet et visent longas Capitolia pompas;
postibus Augustis eadem fidissima custos
ante fores stabis mediamque tuebere quercum,
utque meum intonsis caput est iuvenale capillis,
tu quoque perpetuos semper gere frondis honores!"   565

✢   ✢   ✢

560   **ducibus:** dative with *adsum*. A general celebrating a triumph
          would wear a garland made of bay and carry a branch of it—
          the bay being a sign of victory.
          Latius, -a, -um: a poetic adjective for Rome, taken from the name of
          the ancient territory in which Rome was founded. Ovid here
          links a contemporary Augustan practice to a divine past.
          Triumphum: the sacred and glorious procession by which a
          Roman general was welcomed back to the city of Rome and
          honored for victories on the battlefield.
561   **longas:** the procession included officials of the government, spoils
          captured from the defeated people, sacrificial white bulls,
          prisoners of war, musicians, and the general and his troops.
          Capitolia: used poetically in the plural. The Capitoline was one of
          the seven hills of Rome, on which sat the great temple to Jupiter
          Optimus Maximus and the sacred citadel. The procession,
          which began in the Campus Martius, ended at the Temple of
          Jupiter on the Capitoline where the general performed a ritual
          sacrifice and dedicated his laurel/bay wreath.
562   **postibus Augustis:** ablative with *stabis* (563) without a preposition.
          fīdus, -a, -um: *faithful, loyal.*
563   **foris, -is (f.):** *door;* most frequently in the plural because doors on
          Roman houses were double doors made of two halves.
          tueor, -ēri, tuitus: *to observe, watch over, guard.* Here, the second
          person singular, future deponent alternate *-re* ending instead of
          the more common *-ris.*
          quercum: over the door to Augustus's house on the Palatine Hill
          hung a garland of oak leaves called the civic crown.
564   **intonsus, -a, -um:** *unshorn, uncut.*
          iuvenālis, -e: *youthful.*
565   **semper:** the *laurus nobilis* or Mediterranean bay tree is an evergreen
          tree; it never loses its leaves.
          gere: second person singular imperative.

finierat Paean: factis modo laurea ramis
adnuit utque caput visa est agitasse cacumen.

✦ ✦ ✦

566 **finierat:** pluperfect indicative formed with the syncopated perfect stem.

Paeān, -nis (m.): yet one more appellation for Apollo; this one suggests his capacity to heal, although he has healed no one in this story. This word is also used of a hymn of praise to Apollo.

laurea, -ae (f.): *the laurel/bay tree.*

567 **adnuō, -ere, -uī, -ūtum:** *to nod, to nod in approval.*

visa est: offers an element of doubt—either she *was seen* or *seemed* to use her treetop as a head to nod her consent to Apollo's words.

agitō, -āre, -āvī, -ātum: *to shake, brandish.*

cacūmen: it is significant that the line ends not with *caput* but with *cacumen*. Daphne's metamorphosis is complete. She has lost all semblance of human form and henceforth will be a tree.

Pyramus
and Thisbe

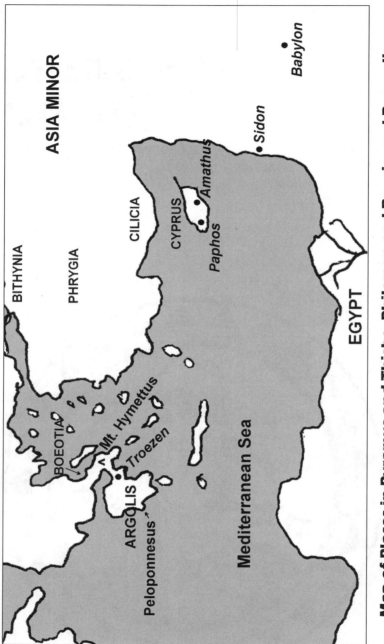

Map of Places in Pyramus and Thisbe, Philemon and Baucis, and Pygmalion

PYRAMUS AND THISBE
Met. IV. 55–166

The episode of Pyramus and Thisbe is a story within a story. It is the first of four told by the three daughters of Minyas, who have chosen to ignore the festival of Bacchus and the priest's call to all women to honor the divinity of the god in wild revels. These daughters have denied the divinity of Bacchus and pursue, while remaining at home, their never-ending tasks of spinning and weaving. By the time the Minyeides have finished their stories, each an account of a metamorphosis, the god whom they have denied and whose holy day they have profaned takes his revenge by changing them into bats.

Ovid sets the scene for Pyramus and Thisbe in the environs of Babylon and gives the two lovers exotic Oriental names. In this tale of forbidden love, the parents will not allow them to marry. The wall that separates their two houses becomes a symbol of this prohibition. But through a chink in the wall they communicate and make plans to meet near a tomb outside the city. Thisbe arrives first and is frightened away by a lioness, who, having just killed a prey, bloodies the cloak that Thisbe has left behind. Pyramus, finding the cloak, concludes that Thisbe is dead and, remorseful and grief-stricken, kills himself. When Thisbe returns she finds him dead and the white berries on the tree next to his body changed to red. She kills herself with his sword so that she may join him in death; in her final words she prays to their parents that they be buried together.

The Pyramus and Thisbe story provided inspiration for the English poet Chaucer and the Italian poet Petrarch. This pair of young, star-crossed lovers also becomes the model for Shakespeare's *Romeo and Juliet*, Schmidt and Jones' *Fantastiks*, and Leonard Bernstein's *West Side Story*, among others. Ovid imbued his tragic tale with a tone that is light and sentimental, and even on occasion mocking and irreverent (see lines 122–124, for example, or consider Thisbe's long speech, lines

141–165). Shakespeare, who knew Latin and had certainly read this story, created a comic version of it in his *Midsummer's Night's Dream* that reflects Ovid's juxtaposition of a serious subject with a light and even humorous tone. Many painters have illustrated the story, including Rembrandt and Poussin.

PYRAMUS AND THISBE
Met. IV. 55–166

"Pyramus et Thisbe, iuvenum pulcherrimus alter,
altera, quas Oriens habuit, praelata puellis,   56
contiguas tenuere domos, ubi dicitur altam
coctilibus muris cinxisse Semiramis urbem.
notitiam primosque gradus vicinia fecit,
tempore crevit amor; taedae quoque iure coissent,   60
sed vetuere patres; quod non potuere vetare,
ex aequo captis ardebant mentibus ambo.

✦ ✦ ✦

55 **Pyramus, -ī (m.):** this name comes from a river in the Roman
province of Cilicia (modern Turkey near the Syrian border).
Thisbē, -ēs (f.): *Thisbe*. As with the Apollo/Daphne passage, this
story also begins with the two names of the main characters.

56 **Oriens, -entis (m.):** the setting for this story, as the two main
characters' names suggest, is the East, described by Roman
writers as an exotic locale.
praeferō, -ferre, -tulī, -lātum: (+ dat.) *to prefer, esteem more.*

57 **contiguus, -a, -um:** *adjacent, neighboring.*
tenuere: third person plural alternate perfect form—subject is
Pyramus et Thisbe (55).
altam: HYPERBATON. The noun that this adjective modifies, *urbem*, is
held until the end of the next line. Such exaggerated separation
creates suspense, holds the reader's attention, and mimics the
walls that embrace the city.

58 **coctilis, -e:** *of baked bricks.*
Semīramis, -idis (f.): the legendary queen of Assyria and builder of
Babylon.

59 **nōtitia, -ae (f.):** *acquaintance.*

60 **taedae:** a METONYMY for marriage.
coeō, coīre, coiī, coitum: *to come together, unite.* Here, a pluperfect
subjunctive in a mixed contrary-to-fact clause.

61 **vetuere...vetare:** an ANTITHESIS involving wordplay.

62 **ex aequo:** *equally.*
ardebant: the imperfect tense reflects the progress of their love.
Note the ASSONANCE of *a* sounds in this line and the long,
drawn-out rhythm caused by the succession of spondees.

conscius omnis abest, nutu signisque loquuntur,
quoque magis tegitur, tectus magis aestuat ignis.
fissus erat tenui rima, quam duxerat olim,   65
cum fieret, paries domui communis utrique.
id vitium nulli per saecula longa notatum—
quid non sentit amor?—primi vidistis amantes
et vocis fecistis iter, tutaeque per illud
murmure blanditiae minimo transire solebant.   70
saepe, ubi constiterant hinc Thisbe, Pyramus illinc,
inque vices fuerat captatus anhelitus oris,

✦ ✦ ✦

63 **conscius, -ī (m.):** *accomplice.*
    abest: the shift to the present indicative in the next few lines creates
      a more vivid scene as is customary with the historic present.
      Translate as past tense.
    nūtus, -ūs (m.): *nod.*
64 **quoque:** because of the long first syllable this is not the familiar
      adverb *quoque* but rather the adverb *quo* plus *-que.*
    magis tegitur, tectus magis: CHIASTIC arrangement around the
      central caesura that divides the line in imitation of the lovers
      separated by the wall.
    aestuō, -āre, -āvī, -ātum: *to blaze, seethe.*
65 **findō, -ere, fidī, fissum:** *to split.*
    rīma, -ae (f.): *crack.*
66 **fieret:** functions as a passive of *faciō.* Its subject is *paries.*
    domui: here the fourth declension dative with *communis.*
67 **vitium, -ī (n.):** *defect, fault.*
    nulli: dative of agent with *notatum.*
68 **vidistis:** APOSTROPHE bringing the lovers vividly into the narrative
      and placing them immediately before us.
70 **murmure...minimo:** alliterative ONOMATOPOEIA; the strong sound
      of *m*s graphically describes the murmurs passing through the
      walls.
    blanditia, -ae (f.): *flattery, charm.*
71 **hinc...illinc:** a CHIASMUS arranging the lovers on opposite sides of
      the wall with a strong diaeresis in the middle of the phrase.
72 **fuerat:** read *erat.*
    in vices: an idiomatic usage meaning *by turns, alternately.*
    anhēlitus, -ūs (m.): *gasp, panting.*

'invide' dicebant 'paries, quid amantibus obstas?
quantum erat, ut sineres toto nos corpore iungi,
aut, hoc si nimium est, vel ad oscula danda pateres?   75
nec sumus ingrati: tibi nos debere fatemur,
quod datus est verbis ad amicas transitus auris.'
talia diversa nequiquam sede locuti
sub noctem dixere 'vale' partique dedere
oscula quisque suae non pervenientia contra.   80
postera nocturnos Aurora removerat ignes,
solque pruinosas radiis siccaverat herbas:
ad solitum coiere locum. tum murmure parvo
multa prius questi statuunt, ut nocte silenti

✦   ✦   ✦

73   **invidus, -a, -um** : *envious, malevolent.* Here, the vocative.
     paries: APOSTROPHE personifying the wall.
74   **erat:** an imperfect indicative in place of an imperfect subjunctive
           meaning "would be."
     sineres: imperfect subjunctive in a consecutive clause.
75   **ad:** introduces a gerundive of purpose.
     pateres: a continuation of the condition introduced by *ut* (74).
76   **ingrātus, -a, -um:** *ungrateful, thankless.*
77   **quod:** the conjunction here meaning *that, the fact that.*
     auris, -is (f.): *ear.* Here the accusative plural *-is* ending for *i*-stem
           nouns.
78   **sēdēs, -is (f.):** *house, dwelling.* A nicely balanced line with the
           adjective/noun pair, which describes the house separated by
           the adverb *nequiquam* just as the wall separates the two houses.
79   **dixere:** third person plural perfect active alternate form, as are
           dedere and *coiere* (83).
80   **quisque:** nominative singular, in apposition to the subject of *dixere*
           and *dedere.*
81   **Aurōra, -ae (f.):** *Aurora, goddess of the dawn.*
82   **pruīnōsus, -a, -um:** *frosty.*
     radius, -ī (m.): *ray of light.*

fallere custodes foribusque excedere temptent,   85
cumque domo exierint, urbis quoque tecta relinquant,
neve sit errandum lato spatiantibus arvo,
conveniant ad busta Nini lateantque sub umbra
arboris: arbor ibi niveis uberrima pomis,

✦   ✦   ✦

85   **custodes:** like *patres* (61), *custodes* are also traditional obstacles to
the fulfillment of love in elegy.
foris, foris (f.): *door, double-door.*
temptent: present subjunctive after *statuunt ut* (84), expressing
intent.

86   **relinquant:** present subjunctive in a continuation of the *statuunt ut*
construction begun in 84. As the lovers, driven by the power of
their passions, leave behind the protection of their parents,
their doorkeepers, and the city, they expose themselves to the
wilderness that will destroy them in the end.
tecta: a SYNECDOCHE.

87   **neve:** introduces a negative purpose clause, hence the continued
use of the subjunctive.
sit errandum: the passive periphrastic expressing necessity or
obligation.
spatior, -ārī, -ātus: *to walk about.* Here, a present participle referring
to the two lovers. This word supplies the dative of agent for the
passive periphrastic.

88   **bustum, -ī (n.):** *a tomb*—here a poetic plural with singular intent.
Ninus, -ī (m.): king of Assyria and second husband to Semiramis;
the romance between Ninus and Semiramis was legendary.
umbra: together with *arbor* (89), *pomis* (89), *gelido* (90), and *fonti* (90),
constitute the major characteristics of a *locus amoenus* (a
pleasant place). Generally speaking, a *locus amoenus* represents
relaxation, protection, comfort, or simple pleasures; it is the
ideal setting for romance.

89   **niveus, -a, -um:** *snow-white, snowy.*
ūber, -eris: *plentiful, abundant.*
pōmum, -ī (n.): *a fruit.*

ardua morus, erat, gelido contermina fonti. 90
pacta placent; et lux, tarde discedere visa,
praecipitatur aquis, et aquis nox exit ab isdem.
"Callida per tenebras versato cardine Thisbe
egreditur fallitque suos adopertaque vultum
pervenit ad tumulum dictaque sub arbore sedit. 95

✦   ✦   ✦

90   **arduus, -a, -um:** *tall, lofty*. The emphatic wording in this elaborate description of the mulberry tree reminds us that it provides the essential *aition* (origin) for the tale.
  mōrus, -ī (f.): *the mulberry tree*.
  gelidus, -a, -um: *icy cold*. Here a dative after the adjective *contermina*.
  conterminus, -a, -um: *nearby, adjacent*.

91   **pactum, -ī (n.):** *agreement*. From the perfect passive participle of *pacisco*, this verb often connotes a person who is betrothed, much as the characters in this story wish to be.
  tarde: three of the six feet in this line are spondees slowing down the rhythm in step with the slow-setting sun.

92   **praecipitatur:** in contrast, this line is filled with DACTYLS, which quicken the pace of the line and mimic the action of the sun here.
  isdem: an alternate ablative plural form of *idem*. This does not mean the same spot in which the sun set but rather the same region, i.e., the sea.

93   **callidus, -a, -um:** *clever, resourceful*. This quality is normally considered essential to the elegiac lover in his schemes, but here Thisbe's cleverness will lead to the tragic deaths of the two lovers.
  versō, -āre, āvī, -ātum: *to turn*.
  cardō, -inis (m.): *hinge*.

94   **suos:** modifies a missing *patres* or more likely her *custodes* of line 85, which is used there with the same verb, *fallo*, as here.
  adoperiō, -perīre, -peruī, -pertum: *to cover over*. Her covering allows her not to be recognized and successfully to deceive the doorkeepers.
  vultum: an accusative of specification, or Greek accusative, found in poetry to denote the part of the body affected.

95   **tumulum, -ī:** *a grave, tomb*.

audacem faciebat amor. venit ecce recenti
caede leaena boum spumantis oblita rictus,
depositura sitim vicini fontis in unda;
quam procul ad lunae radios Babylonia Thisbe
vidit et obscurum timido pede fugit in antrum,   100
dumque fugit, tergo velamina lapsa reliquit.
ut lea saeva sitim multa conpescuit unda,
dum redit in silvas, inventos forte sine ipsa

✦   ✦   ✦

96   **faciebat:** the shift to the imperfect tense after a series of perfect verbs
        stresses the continuous effect love is having on her. Love is
        transforming her into something she had not been before.
      venit: the first syllable is short, making this the historic present
        tense, shifting the reader's perspective back to the maiden's
        immediate situation.
      ecce: this adverbial demonstrative makes the reader an eyewitness.
97   **boum:** genitive plural of *bōs, bovis* with *caede recenti.*
      spumō, -āre, -avī, -ātum: *to foam, froth.* Here, the final syllable is
        long, making this the accusative plural of the present participle
        with *i*-stem endings. It modifies *rictus.*
      oblinō, -ere, -lēvī, -litum: *to besmear, make dirty.* Modifies *leaena.*
      rictus, -ūs, (m.): *the opening of the jaws*—another Greek accusative of
        the part of the body affected.
98   **depositura:** future active participle agreeing with *leaena* (97) and
        expressing intention.
      sitis, -is (f.): *thirst.*
99   **ad:** *by the light of.*
      Babylonia Thisbe: a reference to the city of her birth.
100   **obscūrus, -a, -um:** *dim, dark.*
      timido: her recent boldness disappears quickly with the threat
        from the lioness.
      antrum, -ī (n.): *a cave.*
101   **lapsa:** from *labor, labī, lapsus.*
102   **conpescō, -ere, -pescuī:** *to quench.*
103   **forte:** may be taken with either *inventos* or *sine ipsa,* or both. It
        reminds us of the purely accidental cause of this tragedy.
      ipsa: refers to Thisbe.

ore cruentato tenues laniavit amictus.
serius egressus vestigia vidit in alto   105
pulvere certa ferae totoque expalluit ore
Pyramus; ut vero vestem quoque sanguine tinctam
repperit, 'una duos' inquit 'nox perdet amantes,
e quibus illa fuit longa dignissima vita;
nostra nocens anima est. ego te, miseranda, peremi,   110
in loca plena metus qui iussi nocte venires
nec prior huc veni. nostrum divellite corpus
et scelerata fero consumite viscera morsu,

✦   ✦   ✦

104   **cruentō, -āre, -āvī, -ātum:** *to stain with blood.*
       tenuis, -e: *thin, slender.*
       laniō, -āre, -āvī, -ātum: *to tear, mangle.*
       amictus, -ūs (m.): *cloak;* modified by *inventos* (103). This adjective/
          noun pair encloses the clause as the cloak earlier enclosed
          Thisbe.

105   **sērus, -a, -um:** *late, after the expected time.* Here, the neuter compara-
       tive adverb.

107   **tingō, -ere, -nxī, -nctum:** *to wet, soak.*

108   **reperiō, -īre, repperī, repertum:** *to find, discover.*
       una duos: the ANTITHESIS created by the juxtaposition of these two
          words adds emphasis. Note the INTERLOCKED WORD ORDER in the
          remainder of the line: *una duos...nox...amantes.*

110   **nostra:** the meaning is singular, as it also is in 112.
       ego...peremi: the words referring to Pyramus embrace *te,*
          miseranda, referring to Thisbe. For the second time in this
          lament, for dramatic effect, Ovid's narrator draws attention to
          Pyramus's words by APOSTROPHE.
       peremō, -ere, -ī, -ptum: *to kill.*

111   **venires:** *iubeo* is used with the imperfect subjunctive minus the
       expected *ut* to introduce an indirect command.

112   **divellō, -ere, -vulsī, -vulsum:** *to tear apart, tear open, tear in two.*

113   **scelerātus, -a, -um:** *wicked, accursed, impious.*
       morsus, -ūs (m.): *a bite.*
       et...morsu: is a variation of a GOLDEN LINE.

o quicumque sub hac habitatis rupe leones!
sed timidi est optare necem.' velamina Thisbes   115
tollit et ad pactae secum fert arboris umbram,
utque dedit notae lacrimas, dedit oscula vesti,
'accipe nunc' inquit 'nostri quoque sanguinis haustus!'
quoque erat accinctus, demisit in ilia ferrum,
nec mora, ferventi moriens e vulnere traxit.   120
ut iacuit resupinus humo, cruor emicat alte,
non aliter quam cum vitiato fistula plumbo
scinditur et tenui stridente foramine longas

✦ ✦ ✦

114 **quicumque:** modifies *leones*.
rūpēs, -is (f.): *rocky cliff.*
leones: vocative case.
115 **timidi:** a genitive of quality or characteristic with a *hominis* understood.
nex, necis (f.): *death.*
Thisbes: a Greek genitive ending.
116 **paciscor, -ī, pactus:** *to agree upon.*
117 **notae...vesti:** HYPERBATON.
118 **haustus, -ūs (m.):** *a drawn quantity of liquid, a drink.*
119 **accingō, -ere, -xī, -ctum:** *to gird, equip.*
ilia, -ium (n. pl.): *gut, groin.*
120 **nec mora:** *there was no delay.*
fervens, -ntis: *hot, fresh.*
traxit: from *traho, trahere, traxī, tractum.*
121 **resupīnus, -a, -um:** *lying on one's back.*
humus, -ī (f.): *ground, earth.*
cruor, -ōris (m.): *blood, gore.*
ēmicō, -āre, -āvī, -ātum: *to spurt, shoot forth.*
122 **non aliter quam:** an example of LITOTES, expressing the affirmative by denying the opposite. It introduces a SIMILE.
vitiō, -āre, -āvī, -ātum: *to impair, cause defects in.*
fistula, -ae (f.): *pipe, tube.*
plumbum, -ī (n.): *lead.*
123 **stridō, -ere, -ī:** *to make a high-pitched sound; to whistle, shriek, hiss.*
forāmen, -inis (n.): *a hole, aperture.*

eiaculatur aquas atque ictibus aera rumpit.
arborei fetus adspergine caedis in atram   125
vertuntur faciem, madefactaque sanguine radix
purpureo tinguit pendentia mora colore.
    "Ecce metu nondum posito, ne fallat amantem,
illa redit iuvenemque oculis animoque requirit,
quantaque vitarit narrare pericula gestit;   130
utque locum et visa cognoscit in arbore formam,
sic facit incertam pomi color: haeret, an haec sit.
dum dubitat, tremebunda videt pulsare cruentum

✦   ✦   ✦

124 **eiaculor, -ārī, -ātus:** *to shoot forth.*
     ictus, -ūs (m.): *a blow, stroke, thrust.*
     āēr, āeris (n.): *the air.* This is a three-syllable word with a Greek
         accusative ending.
125 **fētus, -ūs (m.):** *fruit or product of a plant.*
     adspergō, -ginis (f.): *a sprinkling, scattering, splashing.*
     āter, ātra, ātrum: *black, dark-colored, stained.*
126 **faciēs, -ieī (f.):** *appearance, looks.*
     madefaciō, -ere, -fēcī, factum: *to soak, drench.*
127 **purpureus, -a, -um:** *purple, crimson.*
     pendeō, -ēre, pependī: *to hang.*
     mōrum, -ī (n.): *the fruit of the mulberry tree.*
128 **ecce:** signals a shift in scene and character. Thisbe returns to the
         scene.
130 **vitō, -āre, -āvī, -ātum:** *to avoid;* here the syncopated form of the
         perfect subjunctive used in an indirect question.
     gestiō, -īre, -īvī: *to desire eagerly, want, be anxious to.*
131 **utque:** a correlative with *sic* (132) meaning *although...still.*
132 **haereō, -ēre, haesī, haesum:** *to be brought to a standstill, be perplexed,
         hesitate.*
     sit: present subjunctive in an indirect question. The diaeresis and
         the three monosyllabic words that end the line underscore
         Thisbe's reluctance to proceed toward the tree.
133 **tremebundus, -a, -um:** *trembling, quivering.*

membra solum, retroque pedem tulit, oraque buxo
pallidiora gerens exhorruit aequoris instar,   135
quod tremit, exigua cum summum stringitur aura.
sed postquam remorata suos cognovit amores,
percutit indignos claro plangore lacertos
et laniata comas amplexaque corpus amatum
vulnera supplevit lacrimis fletumque cruori   140
miscuit et gelidis in vultibus oscula figens
'Pyrame,' clamavit, 'quis te mihi casus ademit?
Pyrame, responde! tua te carissima Thisbe

✦   ✦   ✦

134   **membrum, -ī (n.):** *limb.*
   solum, -ī (n.): *earth, soil.* These two nouns follow their adjectives in a separate line. The slowed resolution of adjective with noun mimics Thisbe's own gradual realization of what has happened.
   buxus, -ī (f.): *boxwood.* The wood of the boxwood is well known for its light color.
135   **exhorreō, -ēre:** *to shudder.*
   instar (n.): *like, just like*—usually takes the genitive case. Sets up a SIMILE comparing Thisbe's shaking to trembling water.
136   **tremit:** phonetically connects Thisbe to Pyramus's *tremebunda.*
   exiguus, -a, -um: *small, slight.*
   aura, -ae (f.): *breeze.*
137   **remoror, -ārī, -ātus:** *to linger, delay.*
   amores: the plural is a standard variant in poetry, generally taken to mean *beloved.*
138   **percutiō, -ere, -cussī, -cussum:** *to beat, strike.*
   clārus, -a, -um: *loud, shrill.*
   plangor, -oris (n.): *beating, lamentation.*
   lacertus, -ī (m.): *upper arm.* Thisbe's actions here and in line 139 are the typical ritual gestures of the woman as mourner in the ancient world.
139   **coma, -ae (f.):** *hair.* Here a Greek accusative of respect.
   amplector, -ī, -plexus: *to embrace.*
140   **suppleō, -ēre, -ēvī, -ētum:** *to fill up.* HYPERBOLE stretching all imagination.
141   **vultibus:** a poetic plural.
142   **mihi:** dative of separation.
   adimō, -ere, -ēmī, -emptum: *to take away, remove.*
143   **Pyrame:** ANAPHORA adding pathos to her lament.
   responde: the first of three imperatives setting up a TRICOLON.
   tua te: ALLITERATION linking the two lovers with the same sound.

nominat; exaudi vultusque attolle iacentes!'
ad nomen Thisbes oculos a morte gravatos   145
Pyramus erexit visaque recondidit illa.
  "Quae postquam vestemque suam cognovit et ense
vidit ebur vacuum, 'tua te manus' inquit 'amorque
perdidit, infelix! est et mihi fortis in unum
hoc manus, est et amor: dabit hic in vulnera vires.   150
persequar extinctum letique miserrima dicar
causa comesque tui: quique a me morte revelli
heu sola poteras, poteris nec morte revelli.

✦   ✦   ✦

144   **nōminō, -āre, -āvī, -ātum:** *to call by name.*
      attollō, -ere: *to lift up, raise.*
145   **Thisbes:** it is the mention of her name, not his, that stirs him.
      gravō, -āre, -āvī, -ātum: *to make heavy, weigh down.* The many
          SPONDEES weigh down the line just like Pyramus's eyes, which
          are weighed down by Death.
146   **ērigō, -ere, -exī, -ectum:** *to raise.*
      recondō, -ere, -idī, -itum: *to close again.*
147   **quae:** feminine nominative singular referring to Thisbe. Along with
          -que, connects this sentence to the previous one—*and when she.*
      ensis, -is (m.): *a sword.*
148   **ebur, -oris (n.):** *ivory*—through SYNECDOCHE means *a scabbard.*
      tua te: modifying *manus* and referring to Pyramus, this phrase
          mimics 143.
149   **perdidit:** an example of ZEUGMA.
      et: the first of two correlatives *et...et* meaning *both...and.*
      mihi: dative of possession with *est.*
      unum: with *hoc* of 150 means *for this one thing.*
150   **amor:** here *amor* will give her strength; in 96 *amor* made her bold.
      hic: antecedent is *amor,* giving precedence to the power of her love.
151   **persequor, -sequī, -secūtus:** *to follow all the way, accompany.*
      lētum, -ī (n.): *death.*
152   **revellō, -ere, -vellī, -vulsum:** *to remove, tear away.* The two occur-
          rences of this verb, here and in 153, form a paradox: death,
          which has taken him away from her will, in fact, not take him
          away from her because of her own suicide.
153   **nec:** *not even.*

hoc tamen amborum verbis estote rogati,
o multum miseri meus illiusque parentes,   155
ut, quos certus amor, quos hora novissima iunxit,
conponi tumulo non invideatis eodem;
at tu, quae ramis arbor miserabile corpus
nunc tegis unius, mox es tectura duorum,
signa tene caedis pullosque et luctibus aptos   160

✦ ✦ ✦

154   **hoc...rogati:** a heavily spondaic line. The slow, plodding meter
lends weight and importance to the request she is about to
make. The passive *rogati* takes the accusative *hoc.*
estote: this is the future plural imperative emphatically expressing
a command to be carried out in the future. Thisbe directly
addresses the absent fathers in an APOSTROPHE.

155   **o:** sets up a direct address.
multum: adverbial modifying the adjective *miseri.*
miseri: vocative case modifying *parentes* at line end. Thisbe earlier
used this adjective to describe herself in 151.
meus: the use of the singular adjective refers to Thisbe's father as
the genitive *illius* does to Pyramus's.

156   **ut:** introduces an indirect command after *rogati* (154).
quos...quos: ANAPHORA. These relative pronouns are each direct
objects in their own clauses. The implied antecedents, *eos* or *nos,*
of these pronouns function as subjects of the passive infinitive
conponi (157).
novissimus, -a, -um: *last, final.*

157   **conponi:** a present passive infinitive used in an indirect statement
with *invideatis.*
invideō, -ēre, -vīdī, -vīsum: *to refuse, be unwilling.*

158   **tu...arbor:** PERSONIFICATION.

159   **es tectura:** an active periphrastic expressing what is about to be.

160   **tene:** imperative singular, continuation of the direct address to the
tree, as is *habe* (161). The metamorphosis and *aition* are established.
pullus, -a, -um: *dingy, sombre, drab-colored.*
luctus, -ūs (m.): *grief, mourning.*
aptus, -a, -um: (+ dat.) *appropriate, fitting, suited.*

semper habe fetus, gemini monimenta cruoris.'
dixit et aptato pectus mucrone sub imum
incubuit ferro, quod adhuc a caede tepebat.
vota tamen tetigere deos, tetigere parentes:
nam color in pomo est, ubi permaturuit, ater,   165
quodque rogis superest, una requiescit in urna."

✦   ✦   ✦

161   **fetus:** once again a noun is held until the end of its clause to create
        suspense and to bring an emphatic end to the declaration.
      geminus, -a, -um: *double.*
      monimentum, -ī (n.): *memorial.*
      cruor, -ōris (m.): *bloodshed, gore.*
162   **mucrō, -ōnis (m.):** *tip, point of a sword.*
163   **incubō, -āre, -uī, -itum:** *to throw oneself upon.*
      tepeō, -ēre: *to be warm, tepid.* The line begins and ends with
        gruesome verbs marking her suicide.
165   **permātūrescō, -ere, -tūruī:** *to become fully ripe.*
166   **rogus, -ī (m.):** *funeral pyre.* In the plural because there were two
        funeral pyres.
      supersum, -esse, -fuī: *to remain, be left over.*
      una...urna: Ovid ends this tale of two lovers, separated at the
        beginning but joined into one in death with a strong image
        symbolizing their union—a single urn for their combined ashes.

Daedalus
and Icarus

© LINDA LARSON 1998

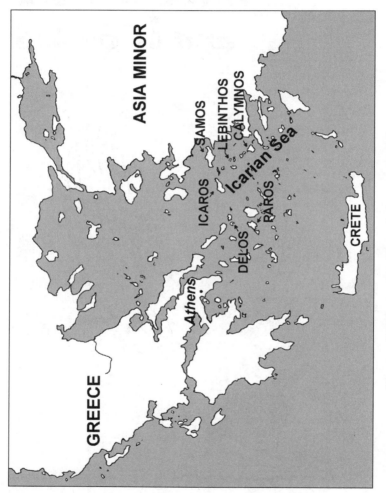

Map of Places in Daedalus and Icarus

DAEDALUS AND ICARUS
Met. VIII. 183–235

The story of Daedalus and Icarus is part of a continuous narrative begun in Book 7 about King Minos of Crete. Daedalus, introduced as an *ingenio fabrae celeberrimus artis* (a man most famous for his skill in the arts, VIII. 159), is the constructor of the labyrinth for Minos. The maze, so complex that the artist himself could scarcely find his way out of it, was built to contain the Minotaur, a monster, half man, half bull, the offspring of an unnatural union between the king's wife, Pasiphae, and a bull. Although little is said of Daedalus's sojourn in Crete, the poet describes him as discontented with his lengthy exile there. To escape, he fashions from bird feathers and beeswax wings for himself and his son Icarus, with which they seek flight.

It is not until this moment that the poet provides Daedalus's full history. After Icarus has fallen from the sky and drowned, and Daedalus has buried him, a *garrula perdix* (a chattering partridge), clapping her wings and singing with joy, confronts Daedalus as a reproach to him. The partridge was once his own twelve-year-old nephew Perdix, whom Daedalus had attempted to murder by throwing him off the Acropolis out of jealousy for the boy's artistic talent, which rivaled his own. As Perdix fell, he was saved by Athena, who transformed him into the partridge that emerges from the mud. Now the bird clearly rejoices in the justice of Daedalus's loss of his own son. This closing scene stands in stark contrast to the whole of the Daedalus and Icarus passage. The tale ostensibly describes a loving father who longs for his own land and plans to escape in flight with his son, whom he advises appropriately on the dangers of flying too high or too low. Yet the poet intends us to see the attempted murder as the reason for the long exile.

The story also illustrates an essential precept of Aristotelian philosophy, that man be moderate in all things. Both Daedalus and Icarus violate this law. Icarus flies too close to the sun, and Daedalus, by constructing wings for himself and his son, has attempted to change nature itself. This violation of the natural order of the world is doomed to fail.

Because this story epitomizes so beautifully the nature of artistic creativity, it has been a favorite topic for artists from antiquity until today. As the epigram to his novel *The Portrait of an Artist as a Young Man*, James Joyce chose from this story the words *ignotas animum dimittit in artes* (188), and he named the hero of his story Stephen Dedalus. The story has provided inspiration for numerous other writers, including Baudelaire, W. H. Auden, and Mallermé, and has been a favorite subject for artists such as Bruegel, Rubens, Tintoretto, Picasso, and Chagall.

DAEDALUS AND ICARUS

Met. VIII. 183–235

Daedalus interea Creten longumque perosus
exilium tactusque loci natalis amore
clausus erat pelago. "terras licet" inquit "et undas   185
obstruat: et caelum certe patet; ibimus illac:
omnia possideat, non possidet aera Minos."
dixit et ignotas animum dimittit in artes
naturamque novat. nam ponit in ordine pennas
a minima coeptas, longam breviore sequenti,   190
ut clivo crevisse putes: sic rustica quondam

✦ ✦ ✦

183 **Crētē, Crētēs (f.):** *Crete,* an island in the eastern Mediterranean Sea.
Daedalus had fled to Crete after being condemned for
murdering his nephew (*Met.* VIII. 241–259). While on the island
he designed and constructed the labyrinth to hold the
Minotaur. He was not permitted off the island for fear of
revealing the secret of its passages. This is the accusative
singular form of the noun; a direct object of *perosus.*
perōdī, -disse, -sum: *to despise, loathe.* This verb has lost its present
tense forms therefore its perfect forms carry present meaning.
Its perfect participle functions actively, so *perosus* may translate
as *hating, loathing.*
184 **loci natalis:** Daedalus was an Athenian by birth.
185 **licet:** here, used as a conjunction meaning *although,* it introduces a
subjunctive clause with *obstruat,* with Minos as an implied
subject.
et: here means *also.*
186 **illāc:** *by that way.*
187 **possideat:** a concessive subjunctive—*even though he possesses.*
aera: accusative plural of *āēr.*
Mīnōs, -ōis (m.): *Minos,* king of Crete, husband to Pasiphae, father
of Ariadne, and the one who ordered the labyrinth built.
188 **ignōtus, -a, -um:** here suggesting *previously unknown.*
189 **naturamque novat:** this begins the description of the manmade
metamorphosis.
191 **ut:** introduces a result clause without the expected *tam* or *talis.*
clīvus, -ī: *slope, incline.*
sic: introduces a SIMILE.

fistula disparibus paulatim surgit avenis;
tum lino medias et ceris alligat imas
atque ita conpositas parvo curvamine flectit,
ut veras imitetur aves. puer Icarus una   195
stabat et, ignarus sua se tractare pericla,
ore renidenti modo, quas vaga moverat aura,
captabat plumas, flavam modo pollice ceram
mollibat lusuque suo mirabile patris
impediebat opus. postquam manus ultima coepto   200
inposita est, geminas opifex libravit in alas
ipse suum corpus motaque pependit in aura;
instruit et natum "medio" que "ut limite curras,

✦   ✦   ✦

192 · **fistula, -ae (f.):** *pipe, pan-pipe.*
      dispār, -ris: *unequal, dissimilar.*
      avena, -ae (f.): *stem, stalk.*
193   **līnum, -ī (n.):** *thread, string*—probably made from the flax plant.
      alligō, -āre, -āvī, -ātum: *to tie, fasten.*
194   **curvāmen, -minis (n.):** *curvature, arc.*
195   **Īcarus, -ī (m.):** *Icarus,* Daedalus's son.
      ūnā (adv.): *at the same time.*
196   **tractō, -āre, -āvī, -ātum:** *to handle, manage.*
      pericla: a syncopated form of *pericula.*
197   **renīdeō, -ēre:** *to smile with pleasure, beam.*
      modo: these correlatives lend an immediacy and visual element to
          the narrative. The reader is invited to watch as young Icarus
          chases the feathers and meddles with the wax, hindering his
          father's work.
      vagus, -a, -um: *shifting, moving about.*
198   **flavus, -a, um:** *yellow.*
      pollex, -icis (m.): *the thumb.*
199   **molliō, -īre, -īvī, -itum:** *to soften, weaken.*
      lūsus, -ūs (m.): *playing, sporting.*
200   **impediō, -īre, -īvī, -ītum:** *to hinder, impede.*
      manus ultima: i.e., the finishing touch.
201   **opifex, -ficis (m.):** *craftsman, artisan.*
      lībrō, -āre, -āvī, -ātum: *to level, balance.*
202   **pendeō, -ēre, pependī:** *to hang.*
203   **medio:** the essence of Daedalus's speech (203–204) to his son is
          found in this first word of fatherly advice.

Icare," ait "moneo, ne, si demissior ibis,
unda gravet pennas, si celsior, ignis adurat: 205
inter utrumque vola. nec te spectare Booten
aut Helicen iubeo strictumque Orionis ensem:
me duce carpe viam!" pariter praecepta volandi
tradit et ignotas umeris accommodat alas.
inter opus monitusque genae maduere seniles,   210
et patriae tremuere manus; dedit oscula nato
non iterum repetenda suo pennisque levatus
ante volat comitique timet, velut ales, ab alto
quae teneram prolem produxit in aera nido,

✦   ✦   ✦

204 **ne:** introduces two negative purpose clauses (*gravet* and *adurat*)
with ASYNDETON.
dēmissus, -a, -um: *low, close to the ground.*

205 **celsus, -a, -um:** *high, lofty.*
adūrō, -ere, -ussī, -ussum: *to burn, scorch.*

206 **Boōtes, -ae (m.):** a bright constellation in the North known as the
Deer-keeper, next to the Great Bear (Ursa Major) constellation.
Here, the accusative case as direct object of *spectare*.

207 **Helicē, -ēs (f.):** the Greek name for the constellation Ursa Major.
Here, another accusative direct object of *spectare*, 206.
stringō, -ere, -nxī, strictum: *to unsheath.*
Ōrīōn, -onis (m.): the constellation in the South known as the
Hunter. Its rising and setting are often associated with storms.

209 **ignotas:** perhaps meant to recall 188 and the *ignarus* of 196.
Foreshadows the tragedy about to beset Icarus.

210 **gena, -ae (f.):** *the cheek.*
madeō, -ēre, -uī: *to grow wet.*
senīlis, -e: *old, aged.*

212 **suo:** the separation of the adjective from its noun, HYPERBATON,
heightens the pathos of the scene.

213 **comitique:** dative of reference showing for whom he was
concerned.
āles, -itis (m., f.): *a bird.*

214 **tener, -era, -erum:** *tender, sensitive, fragile.*
nīdus, -ī (m.): *a nest.* The exaggerated separation of the noun from
its adjective, HYPERBATON, creates suspense and interest until
the SIMILE is resolved. The placement of *nido* next to *aera*
intensifies the height of the nest.

hortaturque sequi damnosasque erudit artes   215
et movet ipse suas et nati respicit alas.
hos aliquis tremula dum captat harundine pisces,
aut pastor baculo stivave innixus arator
vidit et obstipuit, quique aethera carpere possent,
credidit esse deos. et iam Iunonia laeva   220
parte Samos (fuerant Delosque Parosque relictae)
dextra Lebinthos erat fecundaque melle Calymne,
cum puer audaci coepit gaudere volatu
deseruitque ducem caelique cupidine tractus

✦ ✦ ✦

215 **damnōsus, -a, -um:** *destructive, ruinous.*
     ērudiō, -īre, -īvī, -ītum: *to teach, instruct.*
217 **harundō, -dinis (f.):** *a reed, sharpened reed, arrow.* Here, a rod for
     fishing.
218 **baculum, -ī, (n.):** *walking stick, staff.*
     stīva, -ae (f.): *the shaft of a plough handle.*
     innītor, -ī, -nixus: *to lean on, rest on.*
     arātor, -ōris (m.): *a ploughman.*
219 **obstipescō, -ere, -stipuī:** *to be amazed, astonished.*
     possent: subjunctive in a relative clause of characteristic explaining
     why Daedalus and Icarus are believed to be gods.
220 **Iūnōnius, -a, -um:** *of or pertaining to Juno.*
     laevus, -a, -um: *left, lefthand.*
221 **Samos, -ī (f.):** an island in the eastern Mediterranean off the coast
     of Asia Minor between Ephesus and Miletus. Its temple to Juno,
     built in the sixth century B.C., was the largest in the Greek world
     at the time.
     Dēlos, -ī (f.): a small (two square miles) island in the Aegean
     revered as the birthplace of Apollo and Diana.
     Paros, -ī (f.): another island in the Aegean most known for its fine
     white marble and as the birthplace of the seventh-century
     Greek poet Archilochus.
222 **Lebinthos, -ī (f.):** an island in the Sporadic chain, off the east coast
     of mainland Greece.
     fēcundus, -a, -um: *fertile, fruitful.*
     Calymnē, -ēs (f.): an island off the coast of Asia Minor near Rhodes.
     It is known for its honey. Note Greek ending.
223 **volātus, -ūs (m.):** *flying, flight.*

altius egit iter. rapidi vicinia solis   225
mollit odoratas, pennarum vincula, ceras;
tabuerant cerae: nudos quatit ille lacertos,
remigioque carens non ullas percipit auras,
oraque caerulea patrium clamantia nomen
excipiuntur aqua, quae nomen traxit ab illo.   230
at pater infelix, nec iam pater, "Icare," dixit,
"Icare," dixit "ubi es? qua te regione requiram?"
"Icare," dicebat: pennas adspexit in undis
devovitque suas artes corpusque sepulcro
condidit, et tellus a nomine dicta sepulti.   235

✦ ✦ ✦

225 **egit iter:** refers to his flying.
226 **mollit:** reminiscent of the young boy mischievously softening the
      wax, with the warmth of his own thumb (199). Now the sun
      softens the wax.
227 **tabescō, -ēre, tābuī:** *to melt gradually.*
228 **rēmigium, -ī (n.):** *oars, wings.*
229 **caeruleus, -a, -um:** *blue, greenish blue.* HYPERBATON separates this
      adjective from its noun in the next line. This tightly constructed
      phrase (*oraque...aqua*) consists of a double CHIASMUS entwined
      with a SYNCHESIS, perhaps to reflect the contorted spiraling fall
      of Icarus from the sky.
230 **excipiō, -ere, -cēpī, -ceptum:** *to accept, receive.*
      quae: the antecedent is *aqua*, the body of water known as the
      Icarian Sea.
234 **dēvoveō, -ēre, -ōvī, -ōtum:** *to curse.*
235 **sepeliō, -īre, -īvī, sepultum:** *to bury.* Here, genitive singular with
      nomine, and referring to the boy, Icarus.
      tellus: this is the island Icaria near Samos. Once again Ovid ends
      his tale with a reference to an *aition* (origin).

Philemon
and Baucis

© LINDA LARSON 1998

PHILEMON AND BAUCIS
Met. VIII. 616–724

Ovid places this story of piety and loyalty to the gods immediately after a series of tales that illustrate how the gods reward or punish mortals through metamorphosis. At a dinner party where storytelling provides the evening's entertainment, Pirithous scoffs at the notion that the gods are powerful enough to change the shapes of things. Lelex, a companion of the hero Theseus, in direct response to Pirithous's remarks, tells of the transformations of Philemon and Baucis in order to demonstrate the power and justice of the gods. This story, in turn, is followed by another about Erysichthon's illicit love and consequent metamorphosis, with a long digression on his egregiously impious act of cutting down a tree sacred to the goddess Ceres.

We do not know the precise origin of Ovid's story of Philemon and Baucis. It is, however, one of a number of stories from the ancient world that illustrate the importance of the unwritten law of hospitality: hosts had a moral obligation to provide food, drink, and shelter to guests without questioning their identity. Stories of visits from divinities who test mortals' application of this rule appear in both Judaic and Graeco-Roman culture. In Genesis, for example, the stories of God's visit to Abraham and Sarah, Chapter 18, and the visit to Lot of two angels, Chapter 19, provide important variations of this story. We have no evidence that Ovid read Genesis; he, however, probably knew the *Hecale*, a lost poem by the Greek poet Callimachus that describes how a poor old woman gave hospitality to the hero Theseus. Ovid considered this basic story important enough to include additional variations of it in *Metamorphoses* I. 212ff. and *Fasti* V. 495ff.

Ovid's narrative of the pious Philemon and Baucis is enhanced through the emphasis of their simple home and humble food. He painstakingly lists the steps for preparing the meal and the courses served by the humble hosts to the great gods Jupiter and Mercury, who appear in human guise. This lengthy description highlights the spontaneous, unqualified generosity of the mortal husband and wife. The couple give all they have to their guests, long before they perceive that they are entertaining divinities. Their simple piety receives the highest reward: they are granted their request to die together. Their transformations into trees, she into a linden and he into an oak, assure for them a kind of immortality: the oak and linden will henceforth be reminders of the pious couple's generosity.

This tale portrays a kind of love rarely seen in the *Metamorphoses,* for just as Baucis and Philemon love and honor the gods without reservation, so do they love each other truly, faithfully, and unconditionally. The simple goodness of Philemon and Baucis was re-created by Rembrandt in his famous depiction of the story. Others, including Dryden and Swift, have chosen instead to write parodies of it.

PHILEMON AND BAUCIS
Met. VIII. 616–724

obstipuere omnes nec talia dicta probarunt,
ante omnesque Lelex animo maturus et aevo,
sic ait: "inmensa est finemque potentia caeli
non habet, et quicquid superi voluere, peractum est,
quoque minus dubites, tiliae contermina quercus   620
collibus est Phrygiis modico circumdata muro;

✦ ✦ ✦

616   **obstipescō, -ere, -stipuī:** *to be amazed, astonished.* Here, the third
        person plural perfect active alternate form.
        omnes: this includes Theseus, the hero of Book VII, and his
        comrades who had taken shelter from the rains and swollen
        rivers in the home of the river god Achelous, where they were
        entertained with food and stories.
        talia: accusative plural direct object of *probarunt*. The things
        referred to are the words of doubt (lines 614–615) about the
        powers of the gods that Pirithous utters (see introduction).
        probō, -āre, -āvī, -ātum: *to authorize, sanction, approve.* Here, the
        syncopated third person plural perfect active: *probaverunt*.
617   **Lelex:** a participant in the hunt for the Calydonian boar, also
        recounted in Book VIII. With his companions, he has taken
        refuge from the storm in Achelous's house and it is he who will
        tell the story of Baucis and Philemon in order to prove that the
        gods possess the power of metamorphosis.
        mātūrus, -a, -um: *experienced, mature.*
        aevum, -ī (n.): *lifetime, experience, years of age.*
619   **quicquid:** variant form of *quidquid*.
        peragō, -ere, -ēgī, -actum: *to carry out, perform.*
620   **quoque:** *et quo.*
        tilia, -ae (f.): *a lime (linden) tree.* Here, a dative after *contermina*.
        conterminus, -a, -um: *nearby, adjacent.* Here, modifies *quercus*. This
        is the only mention of the types of trees the couple are changed
        into at the end of the tale.
        quercus, -ūs (f.): *an oak tree.*
621   **Phrygia, -ae (f.):** a region in central Asia Minor.
        modicus, -a, -um: *moderate in size.*
        circumdō, -are, -edī, -atum: (+ abl.) *to surround, encircle.*

ipse locum vidi; nam me Pelopeia Pittheus
misit in arva suo quondam regnata parenti.
haud procul hinc stagnum est, tellus habitabilis olim,
nunc celebres mergis fulicisque palustribus undae;   625
Iuppiter huc specie mortali cumque parente
venit Atlantiades positis caducifer alis.
mille domos adiere locum requiemque petentes,
mille domos clausere serae; tamen una recepit,

✢   ✢   ✢

622 **Pelopēius, -a, -um:** of or pertaining to Pelops, king of Argos, from
whom the Peloponnesian peninsula gets its name.
Pittheus, -eī (m.): king of the ancient city Troezen of Argolis on the
Peloponnesian peninsula. He was grandfather to Theseus and
son of Pelops.

623 **arvum, -ī (n.):** *territory, country.*
parens: refers to Pittheus's father, Pelops. Here, a dative of agent
with the perfect passive participle *regnata.*

624 **stagnum, -ī (n.):** *a pool, standing water.*
tellūs, -ūris (f.): *land, country.*

625 **nunc:** immediately following *olim* (624), this adverb sets up an
ANTITHESIS to emphasize the change brought about by the
metamorphosis.
celeber, -bris, -bre: *crowded, populous.*
mergus, -ī (m.): *a seabird, gull.*
fulica, -ae (f.): *a waterfowl, coot.*
paluster, -tris, -tre: *marshy.*

626 **parente:** refers to Jupiter, Mercury's father.

627 **venit:** this verb has two subjects, *Iuppiter* (626) and *Atlantiades*, but
agrees with only one.
Atlantiadēs, -ae (m.): although this noun may refer to any offspring of Atlas, here it refers specifically to Mercury, whose
mother, Maia, was a daughter of Atlas. He carries the caduceus.
positis...alis: these had to be set aside in order for the god to
assume a human guise.

628 **adiere:** third person plural perfect active alternate form.
locum requiemque: HENDIADYS.

629 **mille domos:** the ANAPHORA emphasizes the rejection of the gods at
all the houses in the neighborhood thereby setting off their
welcome into the humble cottage of Baucis and Philemon.
sera, -ae (f.): *a crossbar for locking a door.*

parva quidem, stipulis et canna tecta palustri, 630
sed pia Baucis anus parilique aetate Philemon
illa sunt annis iuncti iuvenalibus, illa
consenuere casa paupertatemque fatendo
effecere levem nec iniqua mente ferendo;
nec refert, dominos illic famulosne requiras: 635
tota domus duo sunt, idem parentque iubentque.

✦   ✦   ✦

630   **parva, tecta:** modify a missing *domus* or anticipate the *casa* of 633.
         Ovid here stresses the simplicity and humble state of the
         couple's house.
         stipula, -ae (f.): *stubble.*
         canna, -ae (f.): *a small reed.*

631   **Baucis, -idis (f.):** *Baucis,* wife of Philemon.
         anus, -ūs (f.): *old woman.*
         parilis, -e: *similar, like.*
         Philēmōn, -ōnis (m.): *Philemon,* husband of Baucis.

632   **illa:** ablative of place where modifying *casa* (633), as does the final
         illa in this line. Note the slowed rhythm of this heavily
         SPONDAIC line, the ASSONANCE of *i* and *a*, and the balance created
         from the repetition of *illa*. The first occurrence refers to their
         youth spent in this house, the second to their old age.
         iuvenālis, -e: *youthful.*

633   **consenescō, -ere, -senuī:** *to grow old.*
         fateor, -ērī, fassus: *to profess, agree, acknowledge.*

634   **effecere:** third person plural perfect active alternate form.
         nec iniqua: LITOTES.
         inīquus, -a, -um: *discontented, resentful.*
         ferendo: its near repetition of *fatendo* in the same position in the
         line above graphically accentuates their humility.

635   **rēfert, -ferre, -tulit:** *it is of importance.*
         illīc (adv.): *there, in that place.*
         famulus, -ī (m.): *servant, attendant.*
         -ne: *or;* introduces the second alternative only in a double question.
         requiras: a present subjunctive in a substantive clause with *refert*.
         The second person address reminds us of the original setting in
         which this story is being told and of the audience listening.

636   **sunt:** the story now shifts into the historical present, drawing in the
         reader as a part of the audience too.

ergo ubi caelicolae parvos tetigere penates
summissoque humiles intrarunt vertice postes,
membra senex posito iussit relevare sedili;
cui superiniecit textum rude sedula Baucis   640
inque foco tepidum cinerem dimovit et ignes
suscitat hesternos foliisque et cortice sicco
nutrit et ad flammas anima producit anili
multifidasque faces ramaliaque arida tecto
detulit et minuit parvoque admovit aeno,   645

✦ ✦ ✦

637   **caelicola, -ae (m., f.):** *an inhabitant of heaven.*
       tetigere: from *tangō,* in the alternate perfect active form.
       penātēs, -ium (m. pl.): *the household gods.* Here, a METONYMY for the
          small cottage.
638   **summittō, -ere, -mīsī -issum:** *to lower.* This is a GOLDEN LINE with
         the adjective / noun pair in INTERLOCKED WORD ORDER.
       humiles: in both the literal (*submisso vertice*) sense because their
         humble cottage would not have been tall and in the figurative
         since the couple were poor and of humble origin. The line also
         suggests that the gods were tall in stature.
       intrarunt: third person plural syncopated form of *intraverunt.*
       vertex, -icis (m.): *the top of the head.*
639   **relevō, -āre, -āvī, -ātum:** *to relieve, ease.*
       sedīle, -is (n.): *a seat.*
640   **superiniciō, -ere, -iniēcī, -iniectum:** *to throw over the surface.*
       sēdulus, -a, -um: *attentive.*
641   **focus, -ī (m.):** *fireplace, hearth.*
       cinis, -eris (m.): *ashes, embers.*
       dīmoveō, -ēre, -mōvī, -mōtum: *to move about.*
642   **suscitō, -āre, -āvī, -ātum:** *to rouse, restore.*
       hesternus, -a, -um: *yesterday's.*
       folium, -ī (n.): *the leaf of a plant.*
       cortex, -icis (m.): *the outer bark of a tree.*
643   **anima, -ae (f.):** *breath.*
       anīlis, -e: *of or pertaining to an old woman.*
644   **multifidus, -a, -um:** *split, splintered.*
       rāmāle, -is (n.): *branches, twigs.*
645   **parvoque:** a reminder that everything associated with this couple
         is small and simple.
       aēnum, -ī (n.): *a pot or cauldron made of bronze.*

quodque suus coniunx riguo conlegerat horto,
truncat holus foliis; furca levat ille bicorni
sordida terga suis nigro pendentia tigno
servatoque diu resecat de tergore partem
exiguam sectamque domat ferventibus undis.   650
interea medias fallunt sermonibus horas   651
concutiuntque torum de molli fluminis ulva   655
inpositum lecto sponda pedibusque salignis.
vestibus hunc velant, quas non nisi tempore festo

✦ ✦ ✦

646 **riguus, -a, -um:** *irrigated, well-watered.*
647 **truncō, -āre, -āvī, -ātum:** *to strip off foliage.*
     holus, -eris (n.): *vegetable*—probably cabbage or turnip.
     furca, -ae (f.): *a length of wood with a forked end.*
     bicornis, -e: *having two prongs.*
648 **sūs, suis (m., f.):** *pig, sow.*
     tignum, -ī (n.): *timber, rafter.*
649 **resecō, -āre, -secuī, -sectum:** *to cut back, trim.*
     tergus, -oris (n.): *the back of an animal.*
650 **exiguus, -a, -um:** *small, slight.*
     secō, -āre, -cuī, -ctum: *to cut.* Here, the perfect participle used as an
        adjective.
     domō, -āre, -āvī, -ātum: *to boil soft.*
     fervens, -ntis: *boiling, bubbling.*
651 **fallō, -ere, fefellī, falsum:** *to while away, beguile.*
652–655a: four lines are of questionable authenticity and are omitted
        from this text.
655 **concutiō, -ere, -cussī, -cussum:** *to shake.*
     torus, -ī (m.): *a cushion.*
     ulva, -ae (f.): *rush, marsh grass.*
656 **sponda, -ae (f.):** *the frame of a bed or couch.* Here, an ablative of
        description.
     salignus, -a, -um: *willow wood.* A simple wood to contrast with the
        luxurious furnishings of a wealthy Roman household. Modifies
        both *pedibus* and *sponda.*
657 **vēlō, -āre, -āvī, -ātum:** *to cover.*
     festus, -a, -um: *suitable for a holiday, festival.*

sternere consuerant, sed et haec vilisque vetusque
vestis erat, lecto non indignanda saligno.
adcubuere dei. mensam succincta tremensque   660
ponit anus, mensae sed erat pes tertius inpar:
testa parem fecit; quae postquam subdita clivum
sustulit, aequatam mentae tersere virentes.
ponitur hic bicolor sincerae baca Minervae
conditaque in liquida corna autumnalia faece   665
intibaque et radix et lactis massa coacti

✦ ✦ ✦

658   **sternō, -ere, strāvī, strātum:** *to strew, spread over an area, throw down.*
    consuescō, -ere, -suēvī, -suētum: *to be in the habit of, become*
      accustomed to.
    vilis, -e: *worthless, common, ordinary.*
659   **non indignanda:** a LITOTES stressing how noble the simple little
    couch is. A gerundive modifying *vestis.*
660   **adcumbō, -ere, -cubuī, -cubitum:** *to recline at table.*
    succinctus, -a, -um: *to have one's clothing bound up with a girdle or belt*
      to allow for freedom of movement.
662   **testa, -ae (f.):** *a fragment of earthenware.*
    subditus, -a, -um: *situated beneath.*
    clīvus, -ī (m.): *slope, incline.*
663   **aequō, -āre, -āvī, -ātum:** *to make level.*
    menta, -ae (f.): *mint.*
    tergeō, -ēre, tersī, tersum: *to wipe clean.*
664   **sincērus, -a, -um:** *unblemished.*
    bāca, -ae (f.): *olive.*
665   **conditus, -a, -um:** *preserved.*
    liquida…faece: CHIASTIC word order. The preserving liquid
      surrounds the fruits.
    cornum, -ī (n.): *the cornelian cherry.* This comes from the *cornus* tree,
      more commonly known as the dogwood. The fruit of certain
      varieties is red and edible.
    faex, faecis (f.): *the dregs or sediment of any liquid, particularly of wine;*
      brine.
666   **intibum, -ī (n.):** *chicory or endive.*
    rādix, -īcis (f.): *root.* Here, the radish.
    lac, lactis (n.): *milk.*
    massa, -ae (f.): *heap, lump, mass.*
    coactus, -a, -um: *curdled.*

ovaque non acri leviter versata favilla,
omnia fictilibus. post haec caelatus eodem
sistitur argento crater fabricataque fago
pocula, qua cava sunt, flaventibus inlita ceris; 670
parva mora est, epulasque foci misere calentes,
nec longae rursus referuntur vina senectae
dantque locum mensis paulum seducta secundis:
hic nux, hic mixta est rugosis carica palmis

✦ ✦ ✦

667 **non acri:** here meaning *warm*, but not burning.
favilla, -ae (f.): *ashes from a fire.*

668 **fictile, -is (n.):** *earthenware dish or pottery.* Further proof that this
meal consists entirely of items found easily near the cottage.
Presumably the object of a missing *in.*
caelō, -āre, -āvī, -ātum: *to engrave, emboss.*

669 **sistō, -ere, stetī, statum:** *to set, set down.*
argento: with *eodem* (668). Ovid employs comic IRONY—all the
previous dishes were of earthenware, not silver.
crātēr, -ēris (m.): *a bowl used for mixing wine.*
fāgus, -ī (f.): *the beech tree.*

670 **pōculum, -ī (n.):** *a cup for drinking.*
flāvens, -entis: *yellow.*
inlinō, -ere, -lēvī, -litum: *to smear, coat.*

671 **epulae, -ārum (f.):** *feast, banquet.*
caleō, -ēre, -uī: *to be hot or warm.*

672 **referuntur:** the same wine used for the first course is here used
again for the main course, a vulgarity to a wealthy Roman
who varied his wine to suit the course.

673 **mensis...secundis:** the course that followed the main course at a
dinner. It usually consisted of fruits, fresh and dried, and nuts.
sēdūcō, -ere, -dūxī, -ductum: *to draw apart, move away.*

674 **hic...palmis:** the slowed rhythm of SPONDEES helps to elaborate this
course which, unlike the prior course of boiled cabbage and
ham, has a greater variety to it.
nux, nucis (f.): *a nut.*
rūgōsus, -a, -um: *wrinkled.*
cāricus, -a, -um: *carian*, a type of fig.
palma, -ae (f.): *fruit of the date palm, a date.*

prunaque et in patulis redolentia mala canistris   675
et de purpureis conlectae vitibus uvae,
candidus in medio favus est; super omnia vultus
accessere boni nec iners pauperque voluntas.
    "Interea totiens haustum cratera repleri
sponte sua per seque vident succrescere vina: 680
attoniti novitate pavent manibusque supinis
concipiunt Baucisque preces timidusque Philemon
et veniam dapibus nullisque paratibus orant.
unicus anser erat, minimae custodia villae:

✦   ✦   ✦

675   **prūnum, -ī (n.):** *a plum.*
       patulus, -a, -um: *broad, wide.*
       redoleō, -ēre: *to give off a smell, be fragrant.*
       mālum, -ī (n.): *an apple.*
       canistrum, -ī (n.): *a basket.* Ovid varies the rhythm by inserting this
          line filled with DACTYLS.
676   **vītis, vītis (f.):** *the grapevine.*
677   **favus, -ī (m.):** *honeycomb.*
678   **accēdō, -ere, -cessī, -cessum:** *to be added.*
679   **hauriō, -īre, hausī, haustum:** *to swallow up, consume.*
       repleō, -ēre, -ēvī, -ētum: *to refill, replenish.*
680   **spons, spontis (f.):** *will, volition;* here, an idiomatic expression
          meaning *automatically.*
       succrescō, -ere, succrēvī: *to grow up as a replacement, to be supplied*
          anew. Note the heavy ALLITERATION of s sounds.
681   **attonitus, -a, -um:** *dazed, astounded, amazed.*
       novitās, -tātis (f.): *novelty, strange phenomenon.*
       paveō, -ēre: *to be frightened.*
       supīnus, -a, -um: *turned palm upwards.*
682   **concipiō, -ere, -cēpī, -ceptum:** *to produce, form.*
683   **venia, -ae (f.):** *justification, excuse, indulgence.*
       daps, dapis (f.): *feast, meal.*
       nullis: not in the strictly negative sense but rather meaning *of no*
          significance, trifling.
       parātus, -ūs (m.): *food and utensils for the dinner table.*
684   **ūnicus, -a, -um:** *one, only one.*
       anser, -eris (m.): *a goose.*

quem dis hospitibus domini mactare parabant;   685
ille celer penna tardos aetate fatigat
eluditque diu tandemque est visus ad ipsos
confugisse deos: superi vetuere necari
'di' que 'sumus, meritasque luet vicinia poenas
inpia' dixerunt; 'vobis inmunibus huius   690
esse mali dabitur; modo vestra relinquite tecta
ac nostros comitate gradus et in ardua montis
ite simul!' parent ambo baculisque levati
nituntur longo vestigia ponere clivo.
tantum aberant summo, quantum semel ire sagitta   695
missa potest: flexere oculos et mersa palude

✦ ✦ ✦

685   **dis:** variant form of *deīs*.
      domini: i.e., *dominus et domina*, Philemon and Baucis.
      mactō, -āre, -āvī, -ātum: *to kill, slay, sacrifice.*
686   **penna, -ae (f.):** *feather, wing.* This line has a nice balance to it—the subject and verb embrace an adjective and noun pair. The SPONDEES slow the line, reflecting the meaning.
687   **ēlūdō, -ere, -sī, -sum:** *to elude, avoid capture.*
688   **confugiō, -ere, -fūgī:** *to flee to (someone) for safety.*
689   **luō, -ere, -ī:** *to pay (as a penalty).*
690   **inpia:** piety was at the very heart of Roman religion and society. It was manifested in the close observance of the rites required for proper balance and relations with the gods. Adherence to these duties promoted cohesion among families and obedience to the state. Conversely, impiety incurred the wrath of the gods and social instability.
      inmūnis, -e: *free from, exempt.*
692   **comitō, -āre, -āvī, -ātum:** *to follow.*
      arduum, -ī (n.): *high elevation.*
694   **nītor, -tī, -sus:** *to strive, move with difficulty, exert oneself.* The heavily SPONDAIC line mimics the plodding exertion of the old couple as they climb the mountain.
      vestīgium, -ī (n.): *footprint, footstep.*
      clīvus, -ī (m.): *slope, incline.*
695   **tantum...quantum:** *just so far...as.*
696   **mergō, -ere, mersī, mersum:** *to flood, inundate;* here, the perfect passive participle as an adjective.
      palūs, -ūdis (f.): *a swamp.*

cetera prospiciunt, tantum sua tecta manere,
dumque ea mirantur, dum deflent fata suorum,
illa vetus dominis etiam casa parva duobus
vertitur in templum: furcas subiere columnae,   700
stramina flavescunt aurataque tecta videntur
caelataeque fores adopertaque marmore tellus.
talia tum placido Saturnius edidit ore:
'dicite, iuste senex et femina coniuge iusto
digna, quid optetis.' cum Baucide pauca locutus   705
iudicium superis aperit commune Philemon:
'esse sacerdotes delubraque vestra tueri
poscimus, et quoniam concordes egimus annos,
auferat hora duos eadem, nec coniugis umquam

✦   ✦   ✦

698 **suorum:** modifies a missing noun; probably refers to their people,
     i.e., their friends and neighbors.
699 **dominis:** dative with *parva.*
700 **subeō, -īre, -ivī, -itum:** *to replace.*
701 **strāmen, -inis (n.):** *straw thatch.*
     flāvescō, -ere: *to become golden.*
702 **foris, foris (f.):** *door, double door.*
     adoperiō, -īre, -uī, -tum: *to cover over.*
     marmor, -oris (n.): *marble.*
703 **talia:** *the following.*
     Sāturnius, -a, -um: a patronymic for Jupiter.
     ēdō, -ere, ēdidī, ēditum: *to utter, to deliver a message.* In spite of the
     harsh punishment he has just levied on the region, Jupiter
     speaks to the old couple in a calm voice befitting his divine
     presence.
705 **locutus:** perfect participle of a deponent verb, which will have an
     active meaning in English.
706 **aperiō, -īre, -uī, -tum:** *to reveal, disclose.*
707 **dēlūbrum, -ī (n.):** *temple, shrine.* Here, a poetic plural referring to
     their former cottage.
     tueor, -ērī, tuitus: *to observe, watch over, guard.*
709 **auferat:** the first of three jussive subjunctives embodying their
     request. The others are *videam* and *sim tumulandus* (710).

busta meae videam, neu sim tumulandus ab illa.'   710
vota fides sequitur: templi tutela fuere,
donec vita data est; annis aevoque soluti
ante gradus sacros cum starent forte locique
narrarent casus, frondere Philemona Baucis,
Baucida conspexit senior frondere Philemon.   715
iamque super geminos crescente cacumine vultus
mutua, dum licuit, reddebant dicta 'vale' que
'o coniunx' dixere simul, simul abdita texit
ora frutex: ostendit adhuc Thyneius illic
incola de gemino vicinos corpore truncos.   720
haec mihi non vani (neque erat, cur fallere vellent)

✦ ✦ ✦

710 **bustum, -ī (n.):** *tomb.*
    tumulō, -āre, -āvī, -ātum: *to entomb.* Here, a passive periphrastic
        denoting necessity or obligation.
711 **vota...sequitur:** i.e., their request is fulfilled.
    tūtēla, -ae (f.): *guardian, protection.*
712 **solūtus, -a, -um:** *weak.*
714 **frondeō, -ēre:** *to grow foliage.*
    Philemona: a Greek accusative singular ending.
715 **Baucida:** a Greek accusative singular ending.
716 **cacūmen, -inis (n.):** *the tip or top of a tree.* With *crescente* creates a
        strong ALLITERATION.
718 **simul, simul:** the immediate repetition of this word emphasizes
        the extraordinarily close relationship of the elderly couple.
    abditus, -a, -um: *hidden, concealed.*
719 **frutex, -icis (f.):** *green growth.*
    ostendit: with this present tense verb Ovid abruptly brings the
        reader back to present time and to the banquet scene at Lelex's
        house where the story is being recounted.
    adhuc: with this adverb Ovid establishes the *aition* (origin) for this
        passage: to this day the inhabitants of the region still point to
        the twin trees growing side by side.
    Thȳnēius, -a, -um: the inhabitants of Bithynia, a region in north-
        western Asia Minor stretching to the southern coast of the Black
        Sea. Here, it modifies *incola* (720).
720 **gemino...truncos:** the INTERLOCKED WORD ORDER here mimics the
        intertwined tree trunks.
    truncus, -ī (m.): *the trunk of a man or tree.*
721 **neque...vellent:** read *neque erat* [causa] *cur* [me] *fallere vellent.*

narravere senes; equidem pendentia vidi
serta super ramos ponensque recentia dixi
'cura deum di sint, et, qui coluere, colantur.'"

✦ ✦ ✦

722 **vidi:** Ovid has brought us full circle, back to the banquet hall and
to Lelex's own first words (lines 620–622).
723 **serta, -ōrum (n.):** *garlands, wreaths.*
724 **cūra, -ae (f.):** *object of concern, beloved person.* Here, a singular noun
with plural intent.
deum di...coluere, colantur: In a double use of POLYPTOTON, Ovid is
typically playful here, filling this last line of the tale with
variations of these two pairs of words, so essential to the
message of the story.
colo, -ere, -ui, cultum: *worship*

Pygmalion

PYGMALION
Met. X. 238–297

Ovid's Pygmalion is one of the stories told by the singer/poet
Orpheus in an effort to assuage his grief over the loss of his
bride Eurydice. The story follows an account of the
Propoetides who had denied the divinity of Venus. The goddess punished this group of girls by forcing them into prostitu-
tion and later turning them into stone. Pygmalion, an artist, is
so disgusted by the foul activities of these girls that he avoids
all real women. Instead, he creates for himself the ideal
woman out of ivory, a statue of such exquisite beauty that he
falls in love with its perfection. A misogynist, he abhors real,
flesh-and-blood women, and can love only a lifeless image.
At a festival honoring Venus, whom he genuinely reveres, he
wishes silently that his statue come to life. When he returns
home and caresses the ivory, it softens and turns to flesh beneath his hands. Pygmalion gains an ideal wife, and Venus
sanctifies his union with her, a union which produces a child
named Paphos.

An earlier source of a story about a king called Pygmalion
described an arrogant man who defiled a statue of Venus by
attempting to make love to it. Ovid's Pygmalion, however, is
depicted as a moral man, who, revolted by the immoral
Propoetides, is rewarded by the goddess. But at the same time,
when the poet also emphasizes Pygmalion's erotic attraction
for his beautiful statue, he suggests that Pygmalion may not
be quite as pure as he appears.

This tale has through the ages inspired plays, poems, ballets,
operas, and paintings. Although in the Middle Ages the
Pygmalion story was linked to idolatry, narcissism, and mad-
ness, many recent critics perceive in it the transforming power
of art in the hands of a great creative artist. Shakespeare in
The Winter's Tale was fascinated by the idea of changing a
woman's identity. George Bernard Shaw, in his play called
Pygmalion, which is set in nineteenth-century London, and

Lerner and Lowe, creators of *My Fair Lady*, a musical based on Shaw's play, turn their modern Pygamlion, Professor Henry Higgins, into a type of arrogant male superiority, who changes a humble seller of flowers into an upper-class lady as a kind of scientific experiment.

PYGMALION

Met. X. 238–297

"Sunt tamen obscenae Venerem Propoetides ausae
esse negare deam; pro quo sua numinis ira
corpora cum fama primae vulgasse feruntur,   240
utque pudor cessit, sanguisque induruit oris,
in rigidum parvo silicem discrimine versae.

"Quas quia Pygmalion aevum per crimen agentis
viderat, offensus vitiis, quae plurima menti
femineae natura dedit, sine coniuge caelebs   245
vivebat thalamique diu consorte carebat.
interea niveum mira feliciter arte

✦ ✦ ✦

238 **Prōpoetides, -um (f. pl.):** These were young women from
       Amathus, a city in Cyprus sacred to Venus.
239 **quō:** probably a neuter pronoun referring to their foul deed.
240 **vulgō, -āre, -āvī, -ātum:** *to prostitute.*
241 **indūrescō, -esere, -uī:** *to harden, become hard.*
242 **discrīmen, -inis (n.):** *difference, distinction.*
243 **quas:** refers to the Propoetides.
       Pygmaliōn, -ōnis (m.): a legendary king of Cyprus although Ovid
       never refers to him as a king. Here, the nominative singular.
244 **offensus, -a, -um:** *offended, displeased.*
       vitium, -ī (n.): *vice, moral failing.*
       quae...dedit: this clause represents an egregious instance of a
       generalization based on the behavior of the Propoetides.
245 **caelebs, -libis:** *unmarried (male), bachelor.* The juxtaposition of this
       adjective with *coniuge* graphically sets forth the dilemma of this
       story. Pygmalion, a hater of women, wants and needs a
       woman.
246 **thalamus, -ī (m.):** *bedroom, marriage chamber.*
       consors, -rtis (f.): *partner.*
247 **niveus, -a, -um:** *white, snowy-white.* This adjective connotes a cold
       white, emblematic of the lifeless beauty Pygmalion has created.
       The HYPERBATON here helps to create suspense.
       mira...arte: like Daedalus, Pygmalion crafts a metamorphosis of
       his own.
       fēlīciter (adv.): *successfully.*

sculpsit ebur formamque dedit, qua femina nasci
nulla potest, operisque sui concepit amorem.
virginis est verae facies, quam vivere credas,   250
et, si non obstet reverentia, velle moveri:
ars adeo latet arte sua. miratur et haurit
pectore Pygmalion simulati corporis ignes.
saepe manus operi temptantes admovet, an sit
corpus an illud ebur, nec adhuc ebur esse fatetur.   255
oscula dat reddique putat loquiturque tenetque
et credit tactis digitos insidere membris
et metuit, pressos veniat ne livor in artus,
et modo blanditias adhibet, modo grata puellis

✦   ✦   ✦

248   **sculpō, -ere, -psī, -ptum:** *to carve.*
       ebur, -oris (n.): *ivory.*
       qua: an unusual ablative; translate *with which.*
249   **concipiō, -ere, -cēpī, -ceptum:** *to conceive, to fall (in love).*
250   **credas:** the poet's address to the reader makes the story more
       vivid.
251   **obstō, -āre, -stitī, -stātum:** *to stand in the way, block the path.*
       reverentia, -ae (f.): *awe, shyness, modesty.* This refers to the feelings
       of the statue, as if it were alive.
252   **ars adeo latet arte sua:** ASSONANCE; this phrase, an ANTITHESIS, is
       applicable to Ovid's own work. It has become proverbial of
       art which is so skillful it makes its products appear to be
       works of nature.
       hauriō, -īre, hausī, haustum: *to consume, drink.*
253   **ignes:** in poetry this word often refers to the fire of love.
254   **an...an:** *whether...or.*
257   **insīdō, -ere, -sēdī, -sessum:** *to sink in, become embedded.*
258   **līvor, -ōris (m.):** *bluish coloring, bruise.*
259   **blanditia, -ae (f.):** *flattery, compliment, endearing comment.*
       adhibeō, -ēre, -uī, -itum: *to apply.*
       modo, modo: the ANAPHORA here creates a sense of immediacy and
       makes the activity more vivid.

munera fert illi conchas teretesque lapillos   260
et parvas volucres et flores mille colorum
liliaque pictasque pilas et ab arbore lapsas
Heliadum lacrimas; ornat quoque vestibus artus,
dat digitis gemmas, dat longa monilia collo,
aure leves bacae, redimicula pectore pendent: 265
cuncta decent; nec nuda minus formosa videtur.
conlocat hanc stratis concha Sidonide tinctis

✦ ✦ ✦

260   **munera:** it was a standard practice of the elegiac lover to present
      his *puella* with gifts of this same sort.
      concha, -ae (f.): *shell.* This noun stands in apposition to *munera* as
      do the next six accusative nouns: *lapillos,* 260, *volucres,* 261,
      flores, 261, *liliaque,* 262, *pilas,* 262, and *lacrimas,* 263.
      teres, -etis: *smooth, rounded.* The POLYSYNDETON here and through-
      out this description isolates each element, drawing attention
      to the different items, and helps to move the lines along.
      lapillus, -ī (m.): *small stone.*
261   **volucris, -cris (f.):** *a bird.*
262   **līlium, -ī (n.):** *a lily.* Note that DIASTOLE lengthens the *-que* and
      emphasizes the POLYSYNDETON.
      pīla, -ae (f.): *ball, sphere.*
      lābor, -ī, lāpsus: *to drip.*
263   **Hēliades, -um (f. pl.):** daughters of the sun god, Helios and
      Clymene, sisters of Phaethon. They were changed into poplar
      trees and their tears of mourning for the loss of their brother
      became amber.
264   **gemma, -ae (f.):** *jewel, gem.*
      monīle, -is (n.): *a necklace.*
265   **bāca, -ae (f.):** *a pearl.*
      redimīculum, -ī: *a band, wreath, garland.*
266   **cunctus, -a, -um:** *all, every.*
      nec…videtur: LITOTES.
267   **strātum, -ī (n.):** *coverlet, throw.*
      concha Sidonide: refers to a shellfish indigenous to the waters off
      Sidon, a Phoenician city, from which came a rare purple dye.
      Sidon was synonomous with the production of dye hence the
      concha Sidonide came to stand for the color purple—rare and
      regal. This whole phrase, *stratis…tinctis,* forms a CHIASMUS.
      tingō, -ere, -nxī, -nctum: *to dye, stain.*

adpellatque tori sociam adclinataque colla
mollibus in plumis, tamquam sensura, reponit.
"Festa dies Veneris tota celeberrima Cypro   270
venerat, et pandis inductae cornibus aurum
conciderant ictae nivea cervice iuvencae,
turaque fumabant, cum munere functus ad aras
constitit et timide 'si, di, dare cuncta potestis,
sit coniunx, opto,' non ausus 'eburnea virgo'   275
dicere Pygmalion 'similis mea' dixit 'eburnae.'
sensit, ut ipsa suis aderat Venus aurea festis,

✦ ✦ ✦

268   **adclīnō, -āre, -āvī, -ātum:** *to lean or rest on.*
       colla: Ovid frequently uses the plural for singular parts of the
           body.
269   **repōnō, -ere, -posuī, -positum:** *to lay to rest.*
270   **dies:** although most commonly masculine (especially in prose),
           here, and frequently in poetry, feminine.
       Cyprus, -ī (f.): an island in the eastern Mediterranean Sea known
           for its worship of Venus.
271   **pandus, -a, -um:** *curved, bent, bowed*
       indūcō, -ere, -dūxī, -ductum: *to cover, spread on or over.*
       aurum: a Greek accusative with the passive participle *inductae* to
           describe the material used for the gilding.
272   **concidō, -ere, -ī:** *to fall, collapse.*
       īciō, -ere, īcī, ictum: *to strike, beat.*
       nivea: another use of the color of cold snow associated with purity
           as in 247.
       cervix, -vīcis (f.): *the neck, back of the neck.*
       iuvenca, -ae (f.): *a cow, heifer.*
273   **tūs, tūris (n.):** *incense.*
       fūmō, -āre, -āvī, -ātum: *to give off smoke.*
       mūnus, -eris (n.): *ritual duty.*
274   **constō, -āre, -stitī:** *to take up a position; to stand up.*
275   **eburneus, -a, -um:** *of ivory.*
276   **similis:** HYPERBATON creates a sense of the hesitancy Pygmalion
           feels in speaking his true wish.
       eburnus, -a, -um: *of ivory.*
277   **sensit:** the subject here is the same as that in the next clause—
           Venus.

vota quid illa velint et, amici numinis omen,
flamma ter accensa est apicemque per aera duxit.
ut rediit, simulacra suae petit ille puellae   280
incumbensque toro dedit oscula: visa tepere est;
admovet os iterum, manibus quoque pectora temptat:
temptatum mollescit ebur positoque rigore
subsidit digitis ceditque, ut Hymettia sole
cera remollescit tractataque pollice multas   285
flectitur in facies ipsoque fit utilis usu.
dum stupet et dubie gaudet fallique veretur,
rursus amans rursusque manu sua vota retractat.

✦ ✦ ✦

278   **vōtum, -ī (n.):** *prayer, vow, oath.*
279   **ter** (adv.): *three times.* The number three is always significant and
       often implies divine intervention. Here, since Venus is present
       at her own festival, it signifies her direct response.
       apex, apicis (m.): *a tip of a flame.* Here, *apicemque duxit* is best
       translated "and the flame lept up."
       āēr, āeris (m.): *the air.*
280   **simulācrum, -ī (n.):** *an image, statue.*
       simulacra suae...puellae: the reference to the statue as well as the
       girl anticipates the transformation.
       petit: the abrupt shift to the present tense makes the following
       description of the miracle more vivid.
281   **incumbō, -ere, -cubuī:** *to lie on.*
       tepeō, -ēre: *to be warm, tepid.* Often used of the passion of love.
283   **mollescō, -ere:** *to become soft.*
       rigor, -ōris (m.): *stiffness, rigidity.*
284   **subsīdō, -ere, -sēdī:** *to give way.*
       ut: introduces a SIMILE comparing the softening statue to beeswax.
       Hymettia: modifies *cera*, 285. This is the adjectival form of
       Hymettus, a mountain near Athens that was known for its
       honey.
285   **tractō, -āre, -āvī, -ātum:** *to handle, manage.*
       pollex, -icis (m.): *the thumb.*
286   **faciēs, -eī (f.):** *shape.*
288   **amans:** here, the noun, not the participle.
       sua vota: refers to those things he had wished for and prayed for,
       i.e., that his statue become a wife.
       retractō, -āre, -āvī, -ātum: *to handle, feel for a second time.*

corpus erat! saliunt temptatae pollice venae.
tum vero Paphius plenissima concipit heros   290
verba, quibus Veneri grates agat, oraque tandem
ore suo non falsa premit dataque oscula virgo
sensit et erubuit timidumque ad lumina lumen
attollens pariter cum caelo vidit amantem.
coniugio, quod fecit, adest dea, iamque coactis   295
cornibus in plenum noviens lunaribus orbem
illa Paphon genuit, de qua tenet insula nomen."

✦   ✦   ✦

289   **temptatae pollice:** nearly the same phrase as used in the SIMILE in
        285.
        saliō, -īre, -uī, -tum: *to leap*, i.e., to pulse.
        vēna, -ae (f.): *blood vessel, vein.*
290   **Paphius, -a, -um:** *of or pertaining to the city of Paphos on the island of
        Cyprus.*
        concipiō, -ere, -cēpī, -ceptum: *to form, produce, conceive.*
        hērōs, -ōos (m.): *a hero.*
291   **grātēs, -ium (f. pl.):** *thanks*; a variation of the more common *gratias
        agere* meaning *to give thanks.*
292   **non falsa:** *genuine*; LITOTES for emphasis.
293   **ērubescō, -ere, -buī:** *to blush with shame or modesty.* Pygmalion's
        statue, full of modesty, blushes, unlike the Propoetides who,
        because of their vileness, lost the ability to blush, 241. This
        reference to modesty at the end of the story is reminiscent of the
        statue's *reverentia* in 251.
        lumen: here meaning *eye.*
294   **attollō, -ere:** *to lift up, raise.*
295   **coniugium, -ī (n.):** *marriage.*
296   **cornibus:** with *coactis* describes the phases of the moon.
        lūnāris, -e: *of or pertaining to the moon.*
297   **illa:** refers to the ivory statue which is now a woman.
        Paphos, -ī (m., f.): *the child of Pygmalion.* By tradition a son who
        became the founder of the Cyprian city of Paphos which was
        sacred to Venus. Ovid ends his tale with an aition (origin) of
        how the city got its name.
        gignō, -ere, genuī, genitum: *to give birth to.*
        qua: the gender of this relative pronoun is problematic as it should
        refer to the masculine Paphos. Some texts prefer *quo.*

TRANSLATION QUESTIONS
AND ANSWERS

To provide further help in translation, the following section offers a series of questions accompanied by answers for all of the Latin passages. These questions prompt you to think about the syntactical arrangement of words in a given line or lines. They are designed to aid translation and are a means by which you may read and interpret the poems on your own. They have been placed apart from the Latin passages so that they are secondary, rather than primary, guides for reading the text. Since these questions do provide training in the thought process necessary for meaningful translation, we strongly suggest that those who use them think through the questions on their own before consulting the answers.

ABBREVIATIONS

abl.	=	ablative
abs.	=	absolute
acc.	=	accusative
adj.	=	adjective
conj.	=	conjunction
dat.	=	dative
decl.	=	declension
fem.	=	feminine
gen.	=	genitive
inf.	=	infinitive
masc.	=	masculine
nom.	=	nominative
pl.	=	plural
prep.	=	preposition
sing.	=	singular
voc.	=	vocative

AMORES I. 1

2 **edere** - complementary inf. dependent on what verb?
materia - scan the line. What case is this noun?
modis - what case and why?

3 **risisse** - what tense inf. and how is it used here?

Cupido - what case is this name?

4 **surripuisse** - what tense inf. and how is it used here?

6 **Pieridum** - what case?
vates - what case?

7 **arma** - nom. or acc.?

9 **Cererem** - what type of acc.?

10 **arva** - what case and why?

coli - what verb form is this and why?

11 **crinibus** - abl. dependent on which word in the line?

12 **Marte movente** - what kind of a construction is this noun / present participle pair?
lyram - what type of acc.?

13 **nimium** - what part of speech?

14 **ambitiose** - scan the line. What is the quantity of the final -*e*? What case is this adj.?

---

2 **edere** - dependent on *parabam*, 1.
materia - abl. with *conveniente* forming an abl. abs.
modis - dat. with *conveniente*.

3 **risisse** - perfect active complementary inf. used with *dicitur*, 4.
Cupido - nom. subject of *dicitur*, 4.

4 **surripuisse** - perfect active complementary inf. also with *dicitur*.

6 **Pieridum** - gen. pl. with *turba*.
vates - nom. subject of *sumus*.

7 **arma** - acc. direct object of *praeripiat*.

9 **Cererem** - subject in indirect statement.

10 **arva** - acc. subject in an indirect statement functioning here exactly as *Cererem* does in 9.
coli - present passive inf. of a 3rd conjugation verb here used in another indirect statement.

11 **crinibus** - depends on *insignem*.

12 **Marte movente** - an abl. abs.

lyram - direct object of *movente*.

13 **nimium** - adverb.

14 **ambitiose** - the final -*e* is short, making this the voc. adj. addressing Cupid.

15   **an** - what is its function in this question?

tuum - why neuter?
est - where is the subject for this verb?
Heliconia - why neuter pl.?

17   **cum** - prep. or conj.?

18   **proximus ille** - why masc. sing.?

20   **puer** - what case and why?

longas . . . comas - why is this construction acc.?

21   **questus eram** - active or passive?

cum - prep. or conj.?

24   **quod** - what word in this line is the antecedent?

28   **cum** - prep. or conj.?

29   **cingere** - what verb form is this and how is it used here?
litorea - what case? Modifies what noun in this line?

flaventia tempora - what type of acc.?

30   **Musa** - what case and why?

emodulanda - what verb form is this and what does it express?

---

15   **an** - used to introduce the second part of a double question (the first part being implied) expressing surprise or disbelief.
tuum - agrees with *quod*.
est - take *quod ubique* as the subject.
Heliconia - modifies the irregular neuter pl. form *tempe*.

17   **cum** - conj. introducing a temporal indicative clause.

18   **proximus ille** - masc. sing. agreeing with *versu*, 17.

20   **puer** - nom. standing in apposition to *materia* (10) as is *puella* of this same line.
longas . . . comas - a Greek acc. used of the part of the body affected.

21   **questus eram** - deponent verb; passive form, active meaning.
cum - conj. introducing a temporal clause.

24   **quod** - the very last word in the line is the antecedent.

28   **cum** - prep. with an abl. adj. and noun.

29   **cingere** - the present passive imperative used reflexively.
litorea - abl. modifying *myrto* which, as a plant, is a 2nd decl. fem. noun.
flaventia tempora - another Greek acc. used with the part of the body affected. A direct object of the passive *cingere* used reflexively.

30   **Musa** - voc. case of direct address with the imperative *cingere*, 29.
emodulanda - future passive participle used to express necessity or obligation.

AMORES I. 3

1	**quae** - where is the antecedent?	1	**quae** - the antecedent is *puella* at the end of the line.
	me - what case and why?		**me** - acc. object of the deponent verb *praedata est*.
3	**tantum** - adj. or adverb?	3	**tantum** - adverb.
	amari - what kind of inf.?		**amari** - present passive inf.
4	**audierit** - what tense?	4	**audierit** - a future perfect indicative.
7	**magna** - what noun nearby does this adj. modify?	7	**magna** - modifies *nomina*, 8.
10	**sumptus** - what case is this noun?	10	**sumptus** - acc. pl. 4th decl. direct object of *temperat*.
13	**nulli** - what case?	13	**nulli** - dat. with *cessura*.
	cessura - what part of speech?		**cessura** - future active participle agreeing with *fides*.
	fides - what case and why?		**fides** - another nom. appositive to *Phoebus* (11), *comitesque* (11), *repertor* (11), and *Amor* (12).
17	**tecum** - abl. of accompaniment with which verb?	17	**tecum** - abl. of accompaniment with *vivere*, 18.
	quos - where is the antecedent?		**quos** - antecedent is *annos*.
	dederint - where is the subject?		**dederint** - subject is *fila*.
18	**teque dolente** - what case are this pronoun and participle?	18	**teque dolente** - abl. abs.
19	**materiem felicem** - why acc.?	19	**materiem felicem** - an appositive to the direct object *te*.
20	**causa** - scan the line. What case is this noun and on what adj. in this line does it depend?	20	**causa** - abl. with *digna*.
21	**carmine** - what use of the abl. has no prep.?	21	**carmine** - abl. of means or instrument.
22	**quam...ave** - what is missing from this clause?	22	**quam...ave** - supply a missing nom. *ea (she whom)* for the antecedent of *quam*.
23	**quaeque** - why fem.?	23	**quaeque** - agrees with *vecta*.
24	**virginea** - scan the line to determine the quantity of all the final -*as*. What case is this adj. and what noun does it modify?	24	**virginea** - abl. sing. modifying *manu*.

AMORES I. 9

2	**Attice** - what case? **mihi** - why dat.?	2	**Attice** - voc. **mihi** - dat. with *credo*.
3	**quae** - what case and what is the antecedent? **bello** - what case and why? **Veneri** - why dat.?	3	**quae** - nom. subject of *est*. Its antecedent is *aetas*. **bello** - dat. with *habilis*, an adj. of fitness. **Veneri** - dat. with *convenit*.
5	**quos** - what is the antecedent? **petiere** - what type of perfect?	5	**quos** - antecedent is *animos*. **petiere** - a gnomic perfect used of a general truth.
6	**hos** - what is the antecedent for this demonstrative pronoun?	6	**hos** - antecedent is *animos*.
9	**est** - which nom. is the subject?	9	**est** - either nom. will work as subject.
10	**exempto fine** - what kind of a construction?	10	**exempto fine** - abl. abs. describing the conditions under which the lover will follow his mistress.
11	**duplicataque** - modifies what noun in the next line?	11	**duplicataque** - modifies *flumina*, 12.
12	**flumina** - direct object of what verb?	12	**flumina** - a second object of *in*, 11.
13	**freta** - acc. direct object of which verb? **tumidos** - modifies what noun?	13	**freta** - acc. direct object of the future active participle *pressurus*. **tumidos** - modifies *Euros*.
14	**verrendis...aquis** - what case?	14	**verrendis...aquis** - dat. with *apta*.
15	**miles** - why nom.?	15	**miles** - one of two alternative appositives to *quis* (the other being *amans*).
17	**speculator** - why nom.?	17	**speculator** - predicate nom.
18	**hoste** - appositive with which word in this line?	18	**hoste** - appositive with *rivale*.
19	**ille** - refers to which of the two antecedents—the soldier or the lover? Where is the verb it goes with? **hic** - refers to whom? Where is the verb it goes with?	19	**ille** - refers to the soldier. It is the subject of *obsidet*, 20. **hic** - refers to the lover. It too is a subject of *obsidet*, 20.
20	**hic** - refers to whom? **at ille fores** - to whom does it refer?	20	**hic** - refers to the soldier. **at ille fores** - refers to the lover.

22 **caedere** - complementary inf. with which verb?

22 **caedere** - a second complmentary inf. with *profuit*, 21.

23 **Threicii** - modifies what noun? What case is this adj.? **ceciderunt** - scan the line to determine the quantity of the vowels. What is the first principle part of this verb? What is its subject?

23 **Threicii** - modifies *Rhesi*, gen. with *agmina*. **ceciderunt** - from *cado*. Its subject is *agmina*.

24 **capti...equi** - what case?

24 **capti...equi** - voc. pl.

25 **maritorum** - gen. with which word in this line? **somnis** - what case and why? **utuntur** - where is the subject?

25 **maritorum** - gen. with *somnis*. **somnis** - abl. with *utuntur*. **utuntur** - subject is *amantes*.

26 **sopitis hostibus** - what kind of a construction? **movent** - where is the subject for this verb?

26 **sopitis hostibus** - abl. abs. **movent** - subject is *amantes*, 25.

27 **custodum** - gen. pl. with which word in the line? **transire** - what is the function of this inf.? **manus** - what case and why?

27 **custodum** - gen. pl. with *manus*. **transire** - subject of a missing *est*, 28. **manus** - acc. pl. direct object of *transire*.

vigilumque - gen. pl. with which noun? **catervas** - acc. pl. direct object of which verb?

vigilumque - gen. pl. with *catervas*. **catervas** - a second direct object of *transire*.

28 **militis** - gen. sing. with which word in this line? **miseri** - modifies which nouns in this line? **opus** - what verb must be supplied to make this a predicate nom.?

28 **militis** - gen. with *opus*. **miseri** - modifies both *militis* and *amantis*. **opus** - supply *est* to create a predicate nom.

31 **desidiam** - why acc.?

amorem - why acc.?

31 **desidiam** - appositive to *amorem*. **amorem** - direct object of *vocabat*.

34 **Argeas** - refers to whom? Modifies which noun in this line? **Troes** - what case?

34 **Argeas** - refers to the Greeks. Modifies *opes*. **Troes** - voc. pl.

36 **quae** - what is the antecedent and what is the function of this relative pronoun?

36 **quae** - the antecedent is *uxor* and it is the subject of *daret*.

37 **ducum** - what case?
    visa Priameide - what kind of a construction?
38 **Maenadis** - gen. with which noun?
42 **mollierant** - where is the pl. subject for this verb?
43 **impulit** - where is the nom. subject for this verb?
    formosae...puellae - why gen.?
44 **iussit** - what are the subject and direct object for this verb?
45 **vides** - what word must be supplied to make the direct object complete?

37 **ducum** - gen. pl.
    visa Priameide - abl. abs. with *obstipuisse*.
38 **Maenadis** - gen. with *comis*.
42 **mollierant** - *lectus* and *umbra* are the subjects.
43 **impulit** - *cura* is the subject.

    formosae...puellae - objective gen. with *cura*.
44 **iussit** - take *cura* (43) as subject and *ignavum* (43) as direct object.
45 **vides** - supply an assumed *me* with *agilem*.

AMORES I. 11

1 **colligere** - inf. dependent on which word in the next line?
   ponere - inf. dependent on which word in the next line?
2 **docta** - modifies which noun in this line?
   ancillas - why acc.?
   habenda - what kind of participle? What does it express? What other word in the line does it modify?
   Nape - what case?
3 **cognita** - modifies which word nearby?
4 **utilis** - adj. with which word nearby?
   dandis...notis - what case and why? What form is *dandis*?
5 **dubitantem...Corinnam** - why acc.?
   hortata - what kind of participle? With what word does it agree?

1 **colligere** - inf. dependent on *docta*, 2.
   ponere - inf. dependent on *docta*, 2.
2 **docta** - modifies *Nape*.

   ancillas - acc. with *inter*.
   habenda - future passive participle used to express obligation or necessity, and modifying *Nape*.
   Nape - voc.
3 **cognita** - modifies *Nape*, 2.
4 **utilis** - predicate adj. with *cognita*. Supply a missing *esse*.
   dandis...notis - dat. case with *ingeniosa. Dandis* is the future passive participle.
5 **dubitantem...Corinnam** - direct object of *hortata*.
   hortata - perfect participle of *hortor* which, because deponent, has an active meaning. It modifies *Nape*, 2.

7 **accipe** - what verb form is this?
et - conj. introducing what verb?
ad dominam - prepositional phrase with which verb?
peraratas...tabellas - acc. direct object of which verb? What form is *peraratas*?

8 **perfer** - what verb form is this?
obstantes... moras - acc. direct object of which verb? What form is *obstantes*?
sedula - modifies which word?

9 **silicum** - what case?
venae - what case?

10 **ordine** - what kind of abl.?

12 **signa** - nom. or acc.?

13 **si quaeret** - what type of conditional clause? What is the understood subject?

vivere - where is the subject for this inf.?

14 **cetera** - scan the line carefully to determine the quantity of all the final -*as* in this line. What case is this pl. noun?
blanda - what case and what noun does it modify?
cera - what case is this noun?
notata - which noun in this line does this adj. modify?

16 **continuo** - adverb or verb?

17 **legentis** - what case? What word must this participle modify?

18 **futura** - what case and gender?

---

7 **accipe** - imperative sing.

et - conj. introducing *perfer*, 8.

ad dominam - prepositional phrase with *perfer*, 8.
peraratas...tabellas - direct object of both *accipe* and *perfer*. *Peraratas* is the perfect passive participle used as an adj.

8 **perfer** - imperative sing.

obstantes...moras - direct object of *pelle*. *obstantes* is the present active participle.
sedula - modifies *Nape*, 2.

9 **silicum** - gen. pl. with *venae*.
venae - nom. pl.

10 **ordine** - abl. of comparison.

12 **signa** - acc. direct object of *tuere*.

13 **si quaeret** - a future-more-vivid conditional clause with both verbs in the future indicative. Assume *ea*.
vivere - supply an acc. *me* as a subject for indirect discourse.

14 **cetera** - neuter acc. pl. direct object of *fert*.

blanda - abl. fem. sing. modifying *manu*.
cera - nom. fem. sing.
notata - modifies *cera*.

16 **continuo** - adverb with *legat*.

17 **legentis** - gen. sing. dependent on *oculos* and *frontem* but modifying a missing *eius* referring to Corinna.

18 **futura** - neuter acc. pl.

19 **nec mora** - what verb must be supplied to complete the meaning here?
perlectis - what case, what verb form, and modifies what missing noun?

20 **cum** - conj. or prep.?

21 **versus** - what case?

22 **margine in extremo** - prepositional phrase with which other word in this line?
meos - modifies what nearby noun?

25 **ego** - where is the verb this nom. governs?
redimire - inf. dependent on what other verb?
tabellas - acc. direct object of what verb?

27 **Veneri** - dat. with which word in this clause?
sibi - this reflexive pronoun refers to whom?

---

19 **nec mora** - supply *sit* as a missing iussive subjunctive.

perlectis - abl. pl. of the perfect passive participle modifying a missing *tabellis*.

20 **cum** - conj. introducing a temporal clause.

21 **versus** - acc. pl. direct object of *comprimat*.

22 **margine in extremo** - with *rasa*.

meos - modifies *oculos*, 21.

25 **ego** - governs *morer*, 26.

redimire - inf. object of *morer*, 26.
tabellas - acc. direct object of *redimire* and of *ponere*, 26.

27 **Veneri** - dat. indirect object of *dedicat*, 28.
sibi - refers to the subject, *Naso*. Take with *fidas*.

AMORES I. 12

1 **flete** - what verb form is this?
tristes - what case is this adj. and what noun does it modify?

2 **posse** - where is the subject for this inf. in indirect statement?

3 **vellet** - where is the subject for this verb?

5 **missa** - why fem.?

6 **cautius** - adverb with which verb in this couplet?

7 **ite** - what type of verb form?

---

1 **flete** - imperative pl.
tristes - nom. pl. modifying *tabellae*.

2 **posse** - supply a missing *eam* for the subject.

3 **vellet** - *Nape* (4) is the subject.

5 **missa** - modifies *Nape*, 4.

6 **cautius** - adverb with *transire*, 5.

7 **ite** - present active imperative addressing the tablets.

9 **quam** - what is the nearest fem. sing. noun to serve as antecedent for this relative pronoun? Why is it in the acc. case?

longae - agrees with which word in this line and why gen.?

collectam - what kind of a participle and with which word in the line does it agree?

11 **at** - conj. introducing which verb?

tamquam - adverb with which verb in this line?

13 **triviis** - what kind of abl.?

inutile lignum - what case?

14 **praetereuntis** - what verb form is this and how is it used here?

15 **illum** - acc. direct object of which verb in this couplet?

16 **habuisse** - what tense and type of inf.?

17 **illa** - modifies which noun in this line?

18 **carnifici** - note the decl. What case is this noun and why?

illa - refers to what noun?

19 **illa** - what is the antecedent for this pronoun and what case is it?

20 **tulit** - what is the subject for this verb?

21 **his** - dat. or abl.?

23 **aptius** - what degree of adverb is this?

hae...cerae - what case?

24 **quas** - what is the antecedent of this relative pronoun?

9 **quam** - antecedent is *cera*, 8. This relative pronoun is the direct object of *misit*, 10.

longae - agrees with *cicutae* and dependent on *flore*.

collectam - perfect passive participle agreeing with *quam*.

11 **at** - conj. introducing *rubebas*.

tamquam - adverb with *medicata*.

13 **triviis** - abl. of place without a prep., as often in poetry.

inutile lignum - voc.

14 **praetereuntis** - the present active participle used as an adj. modifying *rotae*.

15 **illum** - acc. direct object of *convincam*, 16.

16 **habuisse** - perfect active infinitive in an indirect statement after *convincam*.

17 **illa** - modifies *arbor*.

18 **carnifici** - dat. indirect object of *praebuit*.

illa - refers to *arbor*, 17.

19 **illa** - antecedent is *arbor* (17), and it is the nom. subject of *dedit*.

20 **tulit** - subject is still *illa*, 19.

21 **his** - dat. indirect object with both *commisi* and *dedi*, 22.

23 **aptius** - comparative adverb.

hae...cerae - nom. pl.

24 **quas** - antecedent is *hae cerae*, 23.

27   **vos** - what case and why?

    rebus - what kind of abl. without a prep.?

    duplices - what case and why?

27   **vos** - acc. pl. direct object of *sensi* and subject of missing inf. *esse*.
    rebus - abl. of place where without a prep., as often in poetry.
    duplices - acc. standing in apposition to *vos*.

AMORES III. 15

1   **quaere** - what verb form is this?

    mater - what case?

3   **quos** - where is the masc. pl. antecedent for this pronoun?
    alumnus - why nom.?

4   **dedecuere** - what verb form is this?

7   **Mantua** - what case?
    Vergilio - what case and why?
    Verona Catullo - what verb is missing from this phrase?

8   **dicar gloria** - what word is needed to complete the meaning of this phrase?

9   **quam** - what is the antecedent for this relative pronoun?
    coegerat - which word in this line is the subject?

10   **cum** - what is the function of this word in its clause?

    manus - what case?

11   **aliquis spectans hospes** - what case are all three?
    Sulmonis aquosi - what case?

12   **moenia** - what case and why?

    quae - what is the antecedent for this relative pronoun?

1   **quaere** - imperative sing. addressing the *tenerorum mater Amorum*.
    mater - voc. sing.

3   **quos** - antecedent is *elegis*, 2.

    alumnus - appositive to *ego*.

4   **dedecuere** - 3rd person pl. perfect active alternate form.

7   **Mantua** - nom.
    Vergilio - abl. with *gaudet*.

    Verona Catullo - supply another *gaudet*.

8   **dicar gloria** - supply an understood *esse*.

9   **quam** - antecedent is *gentis*, 8.

    coegerat - subject is *sua libertas*.

10   **cum** - a conj. introducing a temporal *cum*-clause with its verb in the indicative.
    manus - acc. pl.

11   **aliquis spectans hospes** - nom.
    Sulmonis aquosi - gen. dependent on *moenia*, 12.

12   **moenia** - acc. direct object of *spectans*, 11.
    quae - antecedent is *moenia*, 12.

13 **tantum** - modifies which noun in this line?
dicet - what tense and where is the subject for this verb?
potuistis - where is the subject for this verb?

14 **estis** - what is the subject for this verb?
magna - what gender, case, and number and why?

15 **puerique** - why gen.?
Amathusia - what case is this adj.?
culti - what case? Modifies which noun in this line?

18 **pulsanda** - what verb form and what does it express?

magnis...equis - what case?

19 **imbelles elegi** - what case?
genialis Musa - what case?
valete - what verb form is this?

---

13 **tantum** - modifies *poetam*.

dicet - future active indicative. The subject is *hospes*, 11.
potuistis - subject is *moenia*, 12.

14 **estis** - subject is *moenia*, 12.

magna - neuter, acc., pl. modifying *quae* (13) and, by extension, *moenia* (12).

15 **puerique** - gen. with *parens*.
Amathusia - voc. sing. modifying *parens*.
culti - gen. sing. modifying *pueri*.

18 **pulsanda** - the future passive participle expressing obligation or necessity.
magnis...equis - dat. of agent.

19 **imbelles elegi** - voc. pl.
genialis Musa - voc. sing.
valete - imperative pl.

APOLLO AND DAPHNE
Met. I. 452–567

454 hunc - pronoun referring to whom?

455 adducto...nervo - what construction does this noun/participle pair form?
flectentem - modifies what pronoun?
cornua - what case and why?

456 lascive - what case?

458 dare...dare - both complementary inf. with what verb?
certa - modifies what noun?

459 prementem - modifies what acc. noun in the next line?

462 adsere - what verb form?

463 figat - what is its subject?

465 deo - which case—dat. or abl.?
tua gloria nostra - scan the line. Which of these words is abl. and why?

466 eliso percussis aere pennis - what kind of a construction do these four words form?

467 umbrosa - scan line. What case is this adj. and what does it modify?

468 sagittifera - case? Modifies what other word in this line?
duo - case? Modifies what word in the line?

469 amorem - why acc.?

472 hoc - refers to which arrow?

illo - refers to what?

475 latebris - abl. dependent on what word in the next line?

---

454 hunc - antecedent is *Cupidinis*, 453.

455 adducto...nervo - abl. abs. with the present participle *flectentem*.
flectentem - modifies *hunc* (454), i.e., Cupid.
cornua - neuter acc. pl. direct object of *flectentem*.

456 lascive - voc.

458 dare...dare - both complementary inf. with *possumus*.
certa - modifies *vulnera*. The expression *certa vulnera* must be taken with both inf. phrases.

459 prementem - modifies *Pythona*, 460.

462 adsere - sing. imperative.

463 figat - subject is *arcus*, 464.

465 deo - dat. after *cedunt*.
tua gloria nostra - *nostra* is abl. of comparison here.

466 eliso percussis aere pennis - an abl. abs. with an abl. of means/instrument embedded.

467 umbrosa - abl. modifying *arce*.

468 sagittifera - fem. abl. sing. modifying *pharetra*.
duo - neuter acc. pl. modifying *tela*.

469 amorem - to be taken as direct object of both verbs, *fugat* and *facit*.

472 hoc - neuter acc. sing. meaning *the latter*.
illo - *the former* (arrow).

475 latebris - abl. pl. dependent on *gaudens*, 476.

476 exuviis - why abl.?

gaudens - what word does this nom. present participle modify?

478 aversata - how can this perfect passive participle have an acc. direct object?

479 viri - why gen.?

480 sint - why subjunctive?

483 crimen - what case and why?

illa - refers to whom?
taedas - why acc.?
exosa - active or passive?

485 inque - to be taken with which abl. in the line?
patris - possessive gen. with which other word in the line?

486 perpetua - what case and why?

487 virginitate - why abl.?
ante - prep. or adverb?
Dianae - gen. or dat.?

488 te - how does this acc. personal pronoun function grammatically in the sentence?

493 quas - what is the antecedent for this relative pronoun?

---

476 exuviis - another abl. pl. dependent on *gaudens*.
gaudens - modifies *altera* (Daphne).

478 aversata - deponent participle—passive form, active meaning.

479 viri - gen. sing. to be taken with both *impatiens* and *expers*.

480 sint - subjunctive in an indirect question introduced with *quid*.

483 crimen - acc. sing., 2nd direct object of *exosa*, this one in the simile.
illa - Daphne.
taedas - acc. object of *exosa*.
exosa - an adj. formed from a perfect participle. *Odi* and its compounds have forms in the perfect that are present in meaning; its perfect participle can have either an active or passive meaning—here, present active.

485 inque - with *cervice*.

patris - with *cervice*.

486 perpetua - abl. modifying *virginitate*, 487.

487 virginitate - abl. after *frui*.
ante - adverb.
Dianae - dat.

488 te - acc. pronoun subject in an indirect statement with *esse vetat*, 489. The indirect statement is easier to see if reworded: *iste decor vetat te esse quod optas*.

493 quas - antecedent is *facibus*.

498 igne - abl. dependent on what other word in the line?
micantes - modifies what word in the next line?
499 similes - modifies what other word in the line?
quae - antecedent?
500 est - where is the subject?

503 revocantis - refers to whom?
506 penna - what case?
fugiunt - what are its subjects?

507 quaeque - what gender and what case of which pronoun is this?
508 laedi - what verb form is this?

509 crura - nom. or acc.?
510 aspera - what case and why?
514 temeraria - what case?

516 servit - what are its subjects?

518 concordant - where is the subject?
519 certa - modifies what noun in the line?
sagitta - what case?
520 quae - what is the antecedent?
524 prosunt - where is the subject for both occurrences of this verb?
530 auctaque - what verb form is this?
fuga - difficult to tell because of the elision but what case must this noun be in?

498 igne - dependent on *micantes*.

micantes - modifies *oculos*, 499.
499 similes - modifies *oculos*.

quae - antecedent is *oscula*.
500 est - subject is the perfect active inf. *vidisse*.
503 revocantis - refers to Apollo.
506 penna - abl. with *trepidante*.
fugiunt - its subjects are: *agna* and *cerva* (505), *columbae* (506), and *quaeque* (507).
507 quaeque - fem. nom. pl. of *quisque*.
508 laedi - present passive inf. after *indigna*.
509 crura - acc.
510 aspera - predicate nom.
514 temeraria - voc. referring to Daphne.
516 servit - subjects are *Delphica tellus* (515), *Claros, Tenedos, Patarea regia*.
518 concordant - subject is *carmina*.
519 certa - modifies *sagitta*.

sagitta - nom.
520 quae - antecedent is *sagitta*.
524 prosunt - subject of both is *artes*.

530 auctaque - 4th principal part of *augeō* with *est*.
fuga - abl. of means/instrument.

533 **Gallicus** - modifies what nom. noun in the line?
535 **similis** - what case and why?

540 **qui** - refers to whom?
543 **viribus adsumptis** - what kind of a construction?
548 **finita** - scan line to determine the case. Of what construction is this participle a part?
553 **hanc** - refers to what/whom?

   positaque - scan the line. What case, gender, and why?
   dextra - why fem.?
558 **habebunt** - where is the pl. subject for this verb?

559 **laure** - what case?
564 **intonsis** - modifies which noun in the line?
   capillis - why abl.?
566 **factis...ramis** - what type of construction?

533 **Gallicus** - modifies *canis*.

535 **similis** - nom. modifying *alter*.
540 **qui** - *he who*, i.e., Apollo.
543 **viribus adsumptis** - abl. abs.

548 **finita** - abl. with *prece*; abl. abs.

553 **hanc** - refers to Daphne in her new appearance as the laurel.
   positaque - fem. abl. agreeing with *dextra* in an abl. abs.
   dextra - assume *manu*.
558 **habebunt** - the three nom. nouns in the next line are the subjects for this verb.
559 **laure** - voc.
564 **intonsis** - modifies *capillis*.

   capillis - abl. with *iuvenale*.
566 **factis...ramis** - an abl. abs. in embracing word order.

PYRAMUS AND THISBE
Met. IV. 55–166

55 alter - refers to which of the two possible antecedents: Pyramus or Thisbe?

56 altera - who is its antecedent?
quas - refers to what fem. pl. noun in this line?

57 domos - what gender and case?
dicitur - which nom. sing. noun in the next line is the subject of this verb?
altam - modifies what word in the next line?

61 vetuere, potuere - which tense?

62 ambo - what case, gender, and number?

63 loquuntur - what class of verb is this?

64 tegitur - what is the noun subject for this verb?

tectus - which participle is this and which word is it modifying?

65 fissus erat - look for the nom. subject for this verb in the next line. What is it?
rima - scan the line. What is the quantity of the final vowel?
duxerat - What is the only possible nom. subject for this verb?

66 utrique - modifying which other word in the line?

67 vitium - this is an acc. case direct object of which verb?

55 alter - Pyramus, masc. sing.

56 altera - Thisbe, fem. sing.
quas - antecedent is *puellis*. Translate this parenthetical clause after *praelata puellis*.

57 domos - fem. with 2nd decl. acc. pl. ending.
dicitur - subject is *Semiramis*.

altam - modifies *urbem*, 58.

61 vetuere, potuere - 3rd person pl. perfect active alternate forms for *-erunt*.

62 ambo - nom. masc. pl. Declined like *duo, duae, duo*.

63 loquuntur - deponent verb, therefore pass. form but act. meaning.

64 tegitur - *ignis* functions as subject of both verbs in this line.
tectus - perfect pass. participle modifying *ignis*.

65 fissus erat - subject is *paries*, 66.

rima - ends in a long *-a*, therefore abl.

duxerat - subject is *paries*, 66.

66 utrique - dat. adj. modifying *domui*.

67 vitium - *vidistis*, 68.

notatum - perfect participial adj. modifying which noun in this line?

68 **quid** - which case, nom. or acc.?

69 **tutae** - which noun is this modifying and what case is it in?

72 **captatus** - perfect participle to be taken with which noun?

73 **amantibus** - what case and why?

74 **iungi** - what is the voice of this inf.?

76 **tibi** - dat. case with which verb in this phrase?

nos - what is the function of this acc. pronoun?

77 **amicas -** what part of speech, adj. or noun?

78 **talia** - what gender, case, and number?
diversa - scan the line. What is the quantity of the final syllable in this word? Which noun is it modifying?

80 **suae** - which noun in the previous line does this adj. modify?

83 **coiere -** scan the line. What is the quantity of the vowels? What verb form is this?

84 **multa** - what case and why?

questi - what verb does this come from and how can it be used with an active meaning?

91 **visa** - modifies which other fem. nom. sing. noun in the line?

92 **aquis -** what case?

notatum - modifies *vitium*.

68 **quid** - acc.

69 **tutae** - nom. fem. pl. modifying *blanditiae*, 70.

72 **captatus** - modifies *anhelitus*.

73 **amantibus** - dat. used with a compound verb.

74 **iungi** - pass. inf.

76 **tibi** - take with *debere* but could apply equally as well with *fatemur*.
nos - subject of *debere*.

77 **amicas -** adj. modifying *auris*.

78 **talia** - acc. neuter pl. direct object of the participle *locuti*.
diversa - the final -*a* is long; modifies the fem. abl. sing. *sede*.

80 **suae -** *partique*.

83 **coiere -** the third syllable contains a long -*e*. This verb is formed on the perf. stem with the alternate -*ere* 3rd person pl. perf. act. ending.

84 **multa** - acc. direct object with *questi*.
questi - from *queror*, a deponent verb. Its pass. form has an active meaning.

91 **visa** - modifies *lux*.

92 **aquis -** the dat. used to express place to which in poetry.

93　**callida** - which other nom. sing. noun in the line is this modifying?
　　versato cardine - what construction do these two words form?
94　**adopertaque** - what is this participle modifying?
95　**dictaque** - which fem. noun in this line does it modify?
96　**recenti** - abl. adj. modifying what abl. noun in the next line?
97　**caede** - why abl.?
99　**quam** - what is the antecedent in the previous clause for this relative pronoun, and why is it acc.?
103　**inventos** - which noun in the next line does this participial adj. modify?
105　**egressus** - what nom. sing. noun to be found in the next few lines does this perfect participle modify?
106　**certa** - modifies which noun in the previous line?
107　**vero** - modifies what noun?
108　**una duos** - which number goes with which noun in this line?
109　**quibus** - what is the antecedent?
　　illa - scan the line to find all the quantities of the *-a* endings. In what case is this word and to whom does it refer?
　　longa - what case is this and which word does it modify?
　　dignissima - what case and why? What case does this adj. govern?
　　vita - what case and why?

93　**callida** - Thisbe.

　　versato cardine - an abl. abs.

94　**adopertaque** - *Thisbe*, 93.

95　**dictaque** - modifies *arbore.*

96　**recenti** - modifies *caede.*

97　**caede** - abl. of cause.
99　**quam** - antecedent is *leaena.* This relative pronoun is the direct object of *vidit*, 100.

103　**inventos** - modifies *amictus,* 104.

105　**egressus** - modifies *Pyramus,* 107.

106　**certa** - modifies *vestigia,* 105.

107　**vero** - modifies *sanguine.*
108　**una duos** - *una* modifies *nox* and *duos* modifies *amantes.*

109　**quibus** - antecedent is *amantes.*
　　illa - nom. sing. subject of the clause—refers to Thisbe, *that other one.*

　　longa - abl. sing. adj. modifying *vita.*
　　dignissima - a predicate adj., nom. case—generally followed by the abl. case.
　　vita - abl. case as expected after *dignissima.*

111 **qui** - what case and to whom does it refer?

119 **quoque** - conj. or relative pronoun?

ferrum - used as direct object not only of *demisit* but also of which other verb?

120 **mora** - what verb is missing here?

122 **vitiato...plumbo** - what case are both of these? What construction do they form?

124 **eiaculatur** - what kind of a verb is it? What is its subject here?

rumpit - what is the subject of this verb?

125 **arborei** - what case and why?

fetus - what decl. does this noun come from? What case is it in?

128 **metu...posito** - what construction do these two words form?

ne - introduces what kind of subjunctive clause?

129 **illa** - refers to whom?

oculis animoque - both represent what kind of abl.?

130 **quantaque** - what other noun in this line does it modify and what case is it?

narrare - inf. object of which of the two verbs in this line?

131 **visa** - scan the line to determine the case. What does this participle modify?

132 **incertam** - why fem.?

pomi - gen. with which flanking word?

---

111 **qui** - nom. subject of *iussi* and *veni*, 112; refers to *ego* (Pyramus), 110.

119 **quoque** - neuter abl. sing. of the relative pronoun. *Ferrum* is the antecedent.
ferrum - direct object for *demisit* and for *traxit*, 120.

120 **mora** - assume *erat*.

122 **vitiato...plumbo** - abl. abs. This phrase also recalls the description of the hole in the wall as a *vitium*, 67.

124 **eiaculatur** - deponent— subject is *fistula*.

rumpit - subject is *fistula*, 122.

125 **arborei** - nom. pl. modifying *fetus*.
fetus - a 4th decl. noun; *-us* ending is nom. pl.

128 **metu...posito** - abl. abs.

ne - introduces a subjunctive adverbial purpose clause.

129 **illa** - refers to Thisbe.
oculis animoque - both are abl. of means or instrument.

130 **quantaque** - modifies *pericula*; both are in the acc., direct objects of the inf. *narrare*.
narrare - object of *gestit*.

131 **visa** - abl. modifying *arbore*.

132 **incertam** - modifies the girl, Thisbe.
pomi - gen. noun with *color*.

haec - why fem.?

133 **tremebunda** - what case and why?

134 **buxo** - what case and why?

136 **exigua** - scan the line. What is the quantity of the final -*a*? What noun does this adj. modify?
cum - prep. or conj.?
summum - what case and how does this word function in the clause?

139 **corpus** - which case and why?

142 **quis** - adj. or pronoun?

144 **exaudi** - what verb form?
145 **oculos...gravatos** - direct object of which verb in the next line?
146 **illa** - to whom does this pronoun refer and what case is it in?

147 **ense** - why abl. case?

151 **miserrima** - what two nouns in the next line does this adj. modify?
152 **tui** - what case is this adj. and what noun does it modify?
quique - refers to whom?
153 **sola** - scan the line in order to determine the quantity of the final -*a*. What case is this adj. and which noun does it modify?

haec - refers to *arbore.*

133 **tremebunda** - acc. adj. agreeing with *membra,* 134, and functioning as the acc. subject of *pulsare* in an indirect statement.

134 **buxo** - abl. of comparison with *pallidiora,* 135.

136 **exigua** - the final -*a* is long. An abl. adj. modifying *aura.*

cum - temporal conj.
summum - neuter nom. agreeing with *aequor,* 135, and functioning as the subject of *stringitur.*

139 **corpus** - acc.—a direct object following the perfect participle of the deponent verb *amplexa.*

142 **quis** - an adj. modifying *casus* even though this form is traditionally the pronoun.

144 **exaudi** - imperative sing.
145 **oculos...gravatos** - direct object of both verbs in 146.

146 **illa** - refers to Thisbe and is abl. which explains the fem. abl. of *visa.* Together these two words form an abl. abs.

147 **ense** - abl. of separation, this one dependent on the adj. *vacuum,* 148.

151 **miserrima** - modifies *causa comesque,* 152.

152 **tui** - a gen. adj. modifying *leti,* 151.
quique - refers to Pyramus.

153 **sola** - because the final -*a* is long this adj. is abl. and modifies *morte* in the previous line.

156 ut - what purpose does this conj. have here?

156 ut - introduces an indirect command expected after the participle *rogati*, 154. In fact the actual substance of the command will be delayed until the next line.

158 ramis - what case and why?

158 ramis - abl. of means or instrument with *tegis*, 159.

159 duorum - what is missing that would make this gen. seem more logical?

159 duorum - supply *miserabilia corpora* before translating *duorum*.

160 pullos; aptos - modify which noun?

160 pullos; aptos - modify *fetus*, 161.

162 aptato . . . mucrone - abl. adj. and noun together function how?

162 aptato . . . mucrone - abl. abs.

163 ferro - what case and why?

163 ferro - dat. after a compound verb.

quod - what is the neuter sing. antecedent for this relative pronoun?

quod - antecedent is *ferro*.

166 requiescit - what is the subject for this verb?

166 requiescit - subject is *quodque rogis superest*.

DAEDALUS AND ICARUS
Met. VIII. 183–235

183 longum - where is the noun this adj. modifies?
perosus - modifies what noun?
184 exilium - what case and why?

tactus - modifies which noun?

185 clausus erat - where is the subject for this verb?
186 obstruat - where is the subject?
190 longam - why acc.?

breviore sequenti - why abl.?

191 crevisse - where is the subject for this inf.?
rustica - modifies which noun in the next line?
193 medias - why fem. pl.?
et - joins which elements of this clause?

imas - why fem.?
194 conpositas - why fem.?

195 ut - introduces what type of clause?
196 sua...pericla - acc. with which word in this line?
se - refers to whom? What case is this pronoun? How does it function in the clause?

197 modo - adv. with which word in its clause?
quas - where is the antecedent for this relative pronoun?

183 longum - modifies *exilium*, 184.
perosus - modifies Daedalus.

184 exilium - acc. direct object of *perosus*.
tactus - modifies *Daedalus*, 183.

185 clausus erat - subject is *Daedalus*, 183.
186 obstruat - subject is *Minos*, 187.
190 longam - direct object of *sequenti*.
breviore sequenti - an abl. abs.
191 crevisse - subject is the *pennas* from 189.
rustica - modifies *fistula*, 192.

193 medias - modifies *pennas*, 189.
et - joins both *lino* and *ceris*, as well as *medias* and *imas* in interlocked word order.
imas - modifies *pennas*, 189.
194 conpositas - modifies *pennas*, 189.
195 ut - introduces a purpose clause.
196 sua...pericla - direct object of *tractare*.
se - refers to Icarus. It is the acc. subject of *tractare* in an indirect statement after *ignarus*.
197 modo - modifies *captabat*, 198.

quas - antecedent is *plumas*, 198.

199 mirabile - what gender, case, and number? What noun does this adj. modify?

200 coepto - what case is this past participle and what noun does it modify?

203 ut - what kind of a clause?

205 si celsior - what verb is missing from this clause?
ignis adurat - what is the missing direct object for this clause?

206 vola - what verb form is this?
te - why acc.?

208 me duce - what case and why?
carpe - what verb form?
pariter - adv. of manner or time?
praecepta - what case and why?
volandi - what verb form?

210 monitus - what case?
maduere - what verb form is this? What is its subject?

212 repetenda - what verb form is this? What case and gender is it?

213 ante - adv. of space or time?
alto - modifies what noun?

214 quae - what is the antecedent for this relative pronoun?
nido - what case and why?

215 sequi - what sort of inf.? What is missing from this construction?

216 suas - modifies which noun in the line?
nati - what case and why?
alas - acc. direct object of which verb?

199 mirabile - neuter acc. sing. modifying *opus*, 200.

200 coepto - dat. with the compound verb *inposita est*; here modifying a missing *operi*.

203 ut - introduces an indirect command with *moneo*, 204.

205 si celsior - supply a missing *ibis*.
ignis adurat - supply another *pennas* as a direct object.

206 vola - imperative sing.
te - direct object of *iubeo*, 207, and subject of *spectare*.

208 me duce - abl. abs.

carpe - imperative sing.
pariter - adv. of time.

praecepta - acc. pl. direct object of *tradit*, 209.
volandi - gen. sing. of the gerund.

210 monitus - acc. pl. with *inter*.
maduere - 3rd person pl. perfect active alternate form. Its subject is *genae*.

212 repetenda - future passive participle; acc. neuter pl. modifying *oscula*, 211.

213 ante - adv. of space.
alto - modifies *nido*, 214.

214 quae - antecedent is *ales*, 213.

nido - abl. of place from which with *ab alto*, 213.

215 sequi - an inf. in indirect statement. The subject, Icarus, is missing.

216 suas - modifies *alas*.

nati - gen. with *alas*.
alas - direct object of both *movet* and *respicit*.

217 **hos** - acc. pl. direct object of which verb?
aliquis - subject of which verbs?

218 **innixus** - modifies which noun in this line?

220 **Iunonia** - modifies what noun in the next line?
laeva - modifies what noun in the next line?

222 **melle** - why abl.?

223 **audaci** - modifies which word in this line?
volatu - why abl.?

224 **caelique** - why gen.?

225 **altius** - adj. or adv.?

226 **vincula** - what case and why?

228 **remigioque** - what case and why?

229 **oraque** - what case and why?

patrium - what noun does this adj. modify?
nomen - what case and why?

230 **aqua** - what case and why?

235 **dicta** - what verb form is missing to make this clause complete?

217 **hos** - direct object of *vidit*, 219, and also of *credidit*, 220.
aliquis - subject of *captat* (217), *vidit* and *obstipuit* (219), and *credidit* (220).

218 **innixus** - modifies both *pastor* and *arator*.

220 **Iunonia** - modifies *Samos*, 221.
laeva - modifies *parte*, 221.

222 **melle** - abl. with *fecunda*.

223 **audaci** - modifies *volatu*.

volatu - abl. with *gaudere*.

224 **caelique** - gen. with *cupidine*.

225 **altius** - adv. modifying *egit*.

226 **vincula** - acc. pl. standing in apposition to *ceras*, the direct object of *mollit*.

228 **remigioque** - abl. with *carens*.

229 **oraque** - neuter nom. pl. subject of *excipiuntur*, 230.
patrium - modifies *nomen*.

nomen - acc. sing. direct object of *clamantia*.

230 **aqua** - abl. of agent with the passive *excipiuntur*.

235 **dicta** - supply a missing *est* to complete the perfect passive verb governed by *tellus*.

PHILEMON AND BAUCIS
Met. VIII. 616–724

617 **animo** - what case and why?

aevo - what case and why?

618 **finem** - why acc.?

potentia - why nom.?

619 **peractum est** - where is the subject for this passive verb?

620 **quoque** - what is the quantity of the first vowel in this word? What does that reveal about its meaning?

621 **collibus…Phrygiis** - what case and why?

circumdata - modifies which nearby noun? What verb form is this?

622 **me** - acc. direct object of which verb?

623 **quondam** - adv. modifying which word in this line?
regnata - modifies which noun?

625 **celebres** - modifies what noun?

mergis…palustribus - what case and why?

627 **positis…alis** - what kind of a construction does this participle/noun pair form?
caducifer - modifies which word in the line?

628 **mille** - modifies which noun in the line?
locum requiemque - what case and why?

629 **mille** - modifies which noun in this line?

---

617 **animo** - abl. of specification with *maturus*.
aevo - another abl. of specification with *maturus*.

618 **finem** - acc. direct object of *habet*, 619.
potentia - subject of *est* and *habet*, 619.

619 **peractum est** - subject is *quicquid superi voluere*.

620 **quoque** - the first syllable is long making this the relative abl. pronoun with an enclitic *-que*. It functions as a conj. introducing a relative clause of purpose.

621 **collibus…Phrygiis** - abl. of place without the prep., as often in poetry.
circumdata - modifies *quercus*, 620. Perfect passive participle of *circumdo*, used as an adj.

622 **me** - direct object of *misit*, 623.

623 **quondam** - modifies *regnata*.

regnata - modifies *arva*.

625 **celebres** - modifies *undae*, nom. pl. in apposition to *stagnum*.
mergis…palustribus - abl. with *celebres*.

627 **positis…alis** - abl. abs.

caducifer - modifies *Atlantiades*.

628 **mille** - modifies *domos*.

locum requiemque - acc. objects of *petentes*.

629 **mille** - modifies *serae*.

una - modifies what missing noun?

recepit - what is the missing direct object for this verb?

631 **aetate** - what case and why?

633 **paupertemque** - acc. direct object of which verb?

634 **levem** - modifies which noun nearby?

639 **membra** - what case and why?
relevare - where is the subject for this inf.?

640 **cui** - why dat.?

644 **faces ramaliaque** - acc. direct objects of which verbs?

tecto - what type of abl.?

645 **parvo...aeno** - what case and why?

646 **quodque** - where is the antecedent for this relative pronoun?

647 **truncat** - who is the subject for this verb?
foliis - what type of abl.?
furca - what case is this noun and why?
ille - what function does this nom. pronoun have?

649 **diu** - modifies which verb in the line?

650 **exiguam** - modifies which nearby noun?
sectamque - why fem.? What verb form?
ferventibus undis - what case and why?

657 **hunc** - refers to what?
non - negates what verb?

---

una - supply *domus*.

recepit - supply a missing *eos* as a direct object.

631 **aetate** - abl. of quality modified by *parili*.

633 **paupertemque** - direct object of both *fatendo* and *ferendo*, (634) as well as of *effecere* (634).

634 **levem** - modifies *paupertem*, (633) but only as the direct object of *effecere*.

639 **membra** - acc. pl. direct object of *relevare*.
relevare - supply a missing *eos*.

640 **cui** - dat. with the compound verb *superiniecit*.

644 **faces ramaliaque** - direct objects of *detulit*, *minuit*, and *admovit*, 645.
tecto - abl. of separation with *detulit*, 645.

645 **parvo...aeno** - dat. after the compound verb *admovit*.

646 **quodque** - antecedent is *holus*, 647.

647 **truncat** - subject is *Baucis*, 640.

foliis - abl. of specification.
furca - abl. of means / instrument.
ille - indicates a change of subject to Philemon.

649 **diu** - modifies *servato*.

650 **exiguam** - modifies *partem*, 649.
sectamque - modifies *partem*, 649.

ferventibus undis - abl. of means or instrument.

657 **hunc** - refers to the *lecto*, 656.
non - negates *consuerant*, 658.

tempore festo - what type of abl.?

659 **lecto...saligno** - what case and why?

660 **adcubuere** - what verb form?

662 **parem** - modifies what noun?

663 **aequatam** - modifies what noun?
tersere - what verb form is this and what is its subject?

664 **hic** - adj., adv., or pronoun?
baca - what case and why?

665 **conditaque** - scan the line carefully to determine the quantity of all the final -*as*. What case is this participle and what other word does it modify?
liquida - what case?

corna - difficult to tell because of the elision but what case must this noun be?

666 **intiba** - what case and why?

radix - what case and why?

massa - what case and why?

667 **ovaque** - what case and why?

acri - modifies which noun in this line?
versata - modifies which noun in this line? What verb form?

668 **fictilibus** - what type of abl.?

caelatus - modifies which noun in the next line?
eodem - modifies what nearby noun?

669 **fabricataque** - modifies which noun nearby?

tempore festo - abl. of time when.

659 **lecto...saligno** - abl. with *indignanda*.

660 **adcubuere** - alternate 3rd person pl. perfect active form.

662 **parem** - modifies a missing *pedem*.

663 **aequatam** - modifies a missing *mensam*.
tersere - 3rd person pl. perfect active alternate form. Its subject is *mentae virentes*.

664 **hic** - adv.
baca - nom. subject (1st) of *ponitur*.

665 **conditaque** - neuter nom. pl. modifying *corna*.

liquida - fem. abl. sing. modifying *faece*.
corna - neuter nom. pl., 2nd subject of *ponitur*, 664.

666 **intiba** - neuter nom. pl., 3rd subject of *ponitur*, 664.
radix - fem. nom. sing., 4th subject of *ponitur*, 664.
massa - fem. nom. sing., 5th subject of *ponitur*, 664.

667 **ovaque** - neuter nom. pl., 6th subject of *ponitur*, 664.
acri - modifies *favilla*.

versata - modifies *ova*. Perfect passive participle as an adj.

668 **fictilibus** - abl. of place without the prep.
caelatus - modifies *crater*, 669.

eodem - modifies *argento*, 669.

669 **fabricataque** - modifies *pocula*, 670.

670 **qua** - adv. or relative pronoun?
671 **foci** - what case and why?
  misere - what verb tense?

672 **nec** - negative with which word in this line?
673 **paulum seducta** - refers to what?

678 **accessere** - what verb tense?

679 **haustum** - modifies which noun in this line? What verb form?

680 **succrescere** - what verb form is this?

681 **manibus supinis** - abl. with which verb?
682 **concipiunt** - where are the subjects for this verb?

685 **dis** - what case and why?

686 **ille** - refers to whom?
  penna - what case?

  tardos - refers to whom?

  aetate - why abl.?

687 **eluditque diu** - what is missing from this clause?
688 **superi...necari** - what is missing from this clause?

690 **inpia** - modifies which word in the previous line?
  vobis - why dat.?

  inmunibus - why dat.?

  huius - modifies which noun in the next line? Why gen.?
691 **dabitur** - what is the subject for this verb?
695 **sagitta** - what case and why?

---

670 **qua** - adv.
671 **foci** - nom. subject of *misere*.
  misere - 3rd person pl. perfect active alternate form.
672 **nec** - with *longae*.

673 **paulum seducta** - refers to the *vina*, 672.

678 **accessere** - 3rd person pl. perfect active form.
679 **haustum** - modifies *cratera*, a Greek masc. sing. acc. Perfect passive participle used as an adj.

680 **succrescere** - present active inf. with *vina* as subject in an indirect statement.

681 **manibus supinis** - abl. with *concipiunt*, 682.
682 **concipiunt** - subjects are *Baucis...timidusque Philemon*.

685 **dis** - dat. pl. indirect object of *mactare*.
686 **ille** - refers to the *anser*, 684.
  penna - abl. of specification with *celer*.
  tardos - acc. direct object of *fatigat* referring to Baucis and Philemon.
  aetate - another abl. of specification, this time with *tardos*.

687 **eluditque diu** - supply an *eos*.

688 **superi...necari** - supply an *eum* referring to the goose as an acc. subject for the inf.
690 **inpia** - modifies *vicinia*, 689.

  vobis - indirect object of *dabitur*, 691.
  inmunibus - predicate dat. after *esse*, 691.
  huius - modifies *mali*, 691; gen. with *inmunibus*.
691 **dabitur** - used impersonally.

695 **sagitta** - nom. sing. subject of *potest*, 696.

696 flexere - what verb form?
mersa - what case? Modifies what word in the next line?
697 tantum - adj. or adv.?
manere - what verb form?

698 ea - what case?

699 dominis...duobus - what case and why?
700 subiere - what verb form?
701 videntur - how many subjects control this verb?

704 iuste - what case? Modifies which noun in the line?
705 Baucide - what case and why?
pauca - what gender, case, and why?
locutus - agrees with which noun in the next line?
706 commune - what case and why?

709 auferat - what tense and mood, and why?
nec - introduces what type of clause?
711 vota - what case and why?

tutela - what case and why?

712 annis aevoque - why abl.?
soluti - modifies what?

713 starent - why imperfect subjunctive?
714 Philemona - what case and why?

Baucis - what case and why?

715 Baucida - what case and why?

716 crescente cacumine - what type of expression do these two abls. form?

696 flexere - 3rd pl. perfect active.
mersa - neuter acc. pl. modifying *cetera*, 697.
697 tantum - adv.
manere - present inf. in indirect statement with *prospiciunt*
698 ea - neuter acc. pl. direct object of *mirantur*.
699 dominis...duobus - dat. with *parva*.
700 subiere - 3rd pl. perfect active.
701 videntur - take *tecta* (701), *fores* and *tellus* (702), all as subjects.
704 iuste - masc. voc. sing. modifying *senex*.
705 Baucide - abl. with *cum*.
pauca - neuter acc. pl. direct object of *locutus*.
locutus - agrees with *Philemon*, 706.
706 commune - neuter acc. sing. agreeing with *iudicium*.
709 auferat - present subjunctive in a wish, optative.
nec - introduces a negative purpose clause.
711 vota - neuter acc. pl. direct object of *sequitur*.
tutela - predicate nom.
712 annis aevoque - abl. of cause.
soluti - modifies the unexpressed subject, *they*.
713 starent - in a *cum* circumstantial clause, as is *narrarent*, 714.
714 Philemona - a Greek acc. ending; direct object of *conspexit*, 715.
Baucis - nom. subject of *conspexit*, 715.
715 Baucida - a Greek acc. ending; direct object of *conspexit*.
716 crescente cacumine - abl. abs.

717 **mutua** - modifies what word?
718 **abdita** - what case? Modifies which word in the next line?
721 **vellent** - why imperfect subjunctive?

723 **recentia** - why neuter acc. pl.?

724 **sint, colantur** - why subjunctives?

717 **mutua** - modifies *dicta*.
718 **abdita** - acc. pl. modifying *ora*.
721 **vellent** - subjunctive in an indirect question dependent on an imperfect indicative verb—*erat*.
723 **recentia** - a second participle modifying *serta*.
724 **sint, colantur** - jussive subjunctives.

PYGMALION
Met. X. 243–297

238 Venerem - why acc.?

239 sua - what case and why?

ira - what case and why?

242 versae - what is missing from this verb form?

243 quas - what case and why?

agentis - what case is this participle and what noun does it modify?

244 quae - what is the antecedent for this relative pronoun? How is it used here?
plurima - what gender, case, number, and why?

menti - what case and why?

245 femineae - adj. or noun? What case and why?
natura - what case and why?

246 thalami - what case and why?

consorte - why abl.?

247 niveum - what nearby noun does this adj. modify?
mira - what case and what does this adj. modify?

248 femina - what case?

249 nulla - what case? Modifies which noun?

250 virginis...verae - why gen.?

credas - why subjunctive?

---

238 Venerem - subject of *esse* in an indirect statement with *negare*, 239.

239 sua - acc. modifying *corpora*, 240.

ira - abl. of means/instrument.

242 versae - supply a missing *sunt*.

243 quas - acc. direct object of *viderat*, 244.

agentis - an acc. pl. participle modifying *quas*.

244 quae - antecedent is *vitis*; direct object of *dedit*, 245.

plurima - neuter acc. pl. modifying *quae*, and by extension *vitiis*.

menti - dat. sing. indirect object of *dedit*, 245.

245 femineae - adj., dat. sing. modifying *menti*, 244.

natura - nom. subject of *dedit*.

246 thalami - gen. object of *consorte*.

consorte - abl. of separation with *carebat*.

247 niveum - modifies *ebur,,*; direct object of *scuplsit*, 248.

mira - abl. case modifying *arte*.

248 femina - nom. subject of *potest*, 247.

249 nulla - nom. modifying *femina*, 248.

250 virginis...verae - gen. of quality.

credas - potential subjunctive.

251 **obstet** - why subjunctive?

velle - dependent on what other verb?

252 **adeo** - adv. or verb?
arte sua - why abl.?

254 **manus** - what case and number?
operi - what case and why?
an sit - why subjunctive?

256 **oscula** - direct object of which verbs in this line?
reddique - what type of inf.? Where is its subject?

257 **tactis** -modifies what noun?
insidere - where is the subject for this inf.?
membris - what case and why?

258 **veniat** - why subjunctive?

259 **grata** - modifies what noun in 260?
puellis - why dat.?

260 **illi** - refers to whom? What case?

265 **aure** - why abl.?

267 **conlocat** - who is the subject?

hanc - refers to whom?
stratis - why abl.?

268 **adclinataque colla** - neuter direct object of which verb?

269 **sensura** - what verb form is this?

270 **tota** - what is the quantity of the final syllable?

celeberrima - what degree is this adj., what case is it, and what word does it modify?

251 **obstet** - the protasis of a future-less-vivid clause.
velle - dependent on *credas*, 250, in an indirect statement.

252 **adeo** - adv.
arte sua - abl. of means/instrument.

254 **manus** - acc. pl. direct object of *admovet*.
operi - dat. after *admovet*.
an sit - indirect question.

256 **oscula** - direct object of *dat* and subject of *reddi*.
reddique - present passive inf. used in an indirect statement after *putat*; subject is *oscula*.

257 **tactis** - modifies *membris*.
insidere - subject is *digitos*.

membris - dat. after *insideres*.

258 **veniat** - subjunctive in a clause of fearing introduced by the *ne* which follows.

259 **grata** - modifies *munera*, 260.

puellis - dat. after *grata*.

260 **illi** - refers to the statue; dat. indirect object of *fert*.

265 **aure** - abl. of place from which with *pendent*, as is *pectore*.

267 **conlocat** - subject is *he* (Pygmalion).
hanc - refers to the statue.
stratis - abl. of place where.

268 **adclinataque colla** - direct object of *reponit*, 269.

269 **sensura** - neuter acc. pl. future active participle modifying *colla*, 268.

270 **tota** - the final syllable is long—an abl. adj. modifying *Cypro*.
celeberrima - superlative degree, fem. nom. sing., modifying *dies*.

271 **pandis...cornibus** - what case and why?
inductae - modifies what noun?

272 **nivea** - what is the quantity of the final syllable?

273 **cum** - conj. or prep.?
munere - why abl.?
functus - active or passive? Modifes which noun?

274 **constitit** - where is the subject?
di - what case?

275 **sit** - why subjunctive?

276 **dicere** - complement to what verb?
similis - modifies what noun?

mea - modifies which noun in his prayer?

277 **suis...festis** - why dat.?

278 **vota** - scan the line to determine the gender, case, and number of this noun. What is its function in the clause?
quid - what are the gender, case, and number of this relative pronoun?
illa - modifies what noun?
velint - what mood and why?

280 **rediit** - what verb form is this?

281 **incumbens** - what verb form? Whom does it modify?

271 **pandis...cornibus** - dat. with *inductae*.
inductae - modifies *iuvencae*, 272.

272 **nivea** - final syllable is long —an abl. adj. modifying *cervice*.

273 **cum** - conj.
munere - abl. with *functus*.
functus - passive participle of a deponent verb, which translates actively. Modifies *Pygmalion*, 276.

274 **constitit** - subject is *Pygmalion*, 276.
di - voc. pl. of *deus*.

275 **sit** - an optative subjunctive

276 **dicere** - to be taken with *non ausus*, 275.
similis - modifies *coniunx*, 275.
mea - modifies *coniunx*, 275.

277 **suis...festis** - dat. case after a compound verb.

278 **vota** - neuter nom. pl. subject of *velint*.

quid - neuter acc. sing. direct object of *velint*.

illa - modifies *vota*.
velint - subjunctive used in an indirect question introduced by *sensit*, 277.

280 **rediit** - the syncopated perfect active indicative used in a simple temporal clause.

281 **incumbens** - present participle modifying the subject *ille*.

282 **os** - scan the line. What is the quantity of the *o*? What word is this?

283 **temptatum** - what word in this line does this past participle modify?

284 **subsidit** - where is the subject?
digitis - what case and why?

ceditque - what is the subject?

285 **tractata** - modifies what noun?
multas - modifies what noun in the next line?

287 **fallique** - what type of verb form?

290 **plenissima** - modifies what noun in the next line?

291 **agat** - why subjunctive?

oraque - what gender, case, and number?

292 **falsa** - modifies what noun?

293 **sensit** - what has the subject changed to?

tumidumque...lumen - what case and why?

295 **coniugio** - what case?

quod - what is the antecedent?
coactis - modifies what noun in the next line? Forms what type of construction?

296 **lunaribus** - modifies what noun in the line?

297 **Paphon** - what case?

---

282 **os** - the *o* is long making this the noun *os, oris.*

283 **temptatum** - modifies *ebur,* nom. case.

284 **subsidit** - *ebur* (283) is the subject.
digitis - dat. after a compound verb.
ceditque - subject is *ebur,* 283.

285 **tractata** - modifies *cera.*

multas - modifies *facies,* 286.

287 **fallique** - present passive inf. in an indirect statement after *veretur.* Assume an understood *se* for its subject.

290 **plenissima** - modfies *verba,* 291.

291 **agat** - a relative clause of purpose.
oraque - neuter acc. pl. direct object of *premit,* 292.

292 **falsa** - modifies *ora,* 291.

293 **sensit** - the subject for the last three verbs in this sentence has changed to *virgo,* 292.
tumidumque...lumen - acc. sing. direct object of the present participle *attollens,* 294.

295 **coniugio** - dat. with the compound verb *adest.*
quod - antecedent is *coniugio.*
coactis - modifies *cornibus,* 296, and forms an abl. abs.

296 **lunaribus** - modifies *cornibus,* therefore part of the abl. abs.

297 **Paphon** - acc. sing. direct object of *genuit.*

METRICAL TERMS

Caesura—a natural break in the hexameter line where a word end occurs within a metrical foot. In Ovid, this is often in the third foot in a hexameter line. Some hexameter lines contain double caesurae, one in the second and one in the fourth foot. Caesurae usually correspond to pauses or breaks in the meaning. Caesurae are traditionally indicated by two vertical lines: ||.

Third foot caesura:

$$— \quad \cup \quad \cup | — \cup \quad \cup | — \quad ||$$

Met. I. 527: *Tum quoque visa decens:* ||

$$—| — — \ | \ — \quad \cup \ \cup | — \ —$$

nudabant corpora venti

Second and fourth foot caesurae:

$$— \quad \cup \quad \cup | — || \ —| — \quad \cup \ \cup | — \qquad ||$$

Met. I. 505: *nympha, mane!* || *Sic agna lupum,* ||

$$—| — \quad \cup \ \cup | — —$$

sic cerva leonem

Dactyl—a long syllable, followed by two short syllables — $\cup\cup$.

Diaeresis—coincidence of word end and the end of a metrical foot. It may occur in any foot of a hexameter line; it is the regular break in a pentameter line.

$$— \cup \ \cup | \ — \cup \cup | — \ || \ — \ \cup \cup | — \cup \quad \cup | —$$

Amores I. 1.2: *edere, materia* || *conveniente modis.*

Diastole—the lengthening of a syllable regularly short.

Elegiac couplet—the meter of Latin love elegy. It consists of a dactylic hexameter line followed by a pentameter line.

Elision—the suppression or dropping of a final vowel, dipthong, or vowel plus *m* before a word beginning with an initial vowel or *h*:

$$—\cup\cup|\ —\quad —|—\ ||—\ \cup\cup|—\ \cup\ \cup|—$$

Amores I. 1.4: *dicitur atque **unum** surripuisse pedem.*

Hexameter—a metrical line of six feet (dactyls and spondees are interchangeable, except for the fifth foot, which is usually a dactyl and the sixth foot which is always a spondee).

Ictus—metrical stress which falls on the first syllable in the foot. When this corresponds with the natural stress (accent) of a word, the syllable receives greater emphasis.

Pentameter—a metrical line of five feet divided into two halves. The first half consists of two feet, which may be either dactyls or spondees, followed by a half foot that is always a single long syllable (two-and-a-half feet). The caesura between the two halves coincides with a diaeresis. The second half of the line always contains two dactyls followed by a single long syllable (two-and-a-half feet).

$$—\cup\cup\ |—\cup\cup\ |—|\ |—\cup\cup\ |—\cup\cup\ |—$$
$$\updownarrow\qquad\updownarrow$$
$$—\ —\ |—\ —\ |—|\ |—\cup\cup\ |—\cup\cup\ |—$$

Spondee—a metrical foot with two long syllables (either by nature or by position); indicated as — —.

Syncope—loss of a short vowel or a syllable within a word.

Amores I. 3.6: *accipe, qui pura **norit** amare fide!*

Systole—the shortening of a syllable regularly long.

FIGURES OF SPEECH

Allegory—an extended narrative that suggests an implied meaning in addition to the one stated on the surface; for example, the story of Daedalus and Icarus might be viewed as an illustrative story about excessive mortal pride.

Alliteration—repetition of initial sounds in two or more words.

Met. VIII. 716: *iamque super geminos crescente cacumine vultus*

Anaphora—repetition of a word at the beginning of phrases or clauses.

Amores I. 3.5: ***Accipe**, per longos tibi qui deserviat annos;*
*   **accipe**, qui pura norit amare fide!*

Antithesis—an opposition of ideas in a balanced grammatical structure.

Met. I. 469: *...**fugat hoc, facit illud** amorem*

Apostrophe—addressing a person or abstraction as if present.

Met. I. 488: *ille quidem obsequitur, sed **te** decor iste quod **optas***
*   esse vetat, votoque **tuo tua** forma repugnat:*

Assonance—juxtaposition of similar sounds (usually vowels) in a series of words.

Amores I. 3.14: ***nu**daque simplicitas **purpureusque pu**dor.*

Asyndeton—the omission of a conjunction.

Met. I. 512–14: *...non incola montis, **(et)***
*   non ego sum pastor, **(et)** non hic armenta gregesque*
*   horridus observo.*

Chiasmus—an arrangement of words in an ABBA pattern.

Met. VIII. 187: *omnia possideat, non possidet aera Minos.*
                        A   B   B   A

Ellipsis—the omission of a word or words necessary for the sense.

Amores I. 9.20: *...hic portas frangit, at ille (frangit) fores.*

Enjambment—a line which continues into the next without a grammatical break.

Met. I. 517–18: *...per me, quod eritque fuitque*
                    estque, patet; per me concordant carmina nervis.

Golden Line—a line with a verb in the center and two pairs of words in interlocked word order on each side of the verb.

Met. VIII. 638: *summissoque humiles intrarunt vertice postes*
                            A   B   A   B

Hendiadys—using **two** nouns connected by a conjunction to express **one** idea:

Amores I. 9.42: *mollierant animos lectus et umbra meos*

Hyperbaton—a significant distortion of normal word order.

Met. VIII. 229–30: *oraque caerulea patrium clamantia nomen*
                        excipiuntur aqua, ...

Hyperbole—exaggeration for rhetorical effect.

Met. I. 460: *stravimus innumeris tumidum Pythona sagittis.*

Hysteron proteron—a reversal of the natural order of ideas.

Met. VIII. 696–97: *...flexere oculos et mersa palude*
                        cetera prospiciunt, tantum sua tecta manere,

Interlocked word order (Synchesis)—the arrangement of a group of words to form an ABAB pattern (often used to emphasize the closeness of the words to one another).

Amores I. 12.24: *quas **aliquis duro cognitor ore** legat*
A   B   A   B

Irony—purposeful discrepancy for rhetorical effect between an assertion and intended or understood meaning.

Met. VIII. 668–70: *. . . post haec caelatus **eodem** sistitur **argento** crater fabricatque fago pocula, . . .*

Litotes—affirming something by stating its opposite with a negative.

Met. IV. 122: ***non aliter quam** cum vitiato fistula plumbo*

Metaphor—an implied comparison suggesting a likeness between two things.

Amores I. 9.1: ***militat** omnis **amans,** et habet sua **castra** Cupido*

Metonymy—use of one noun for another that is closely related.

Met. I. 483: *illa velut crimen **taedas** exosa **iugales***

Onomatopoeia—use of sounds that reflect meaning.

Met IV. 70: ***murmure** blanditiae **minimo** transire solebant.*

Oxymoron—the use of seemingly contradictory words in the same phrase.

Met. X. 287: *dum stupet et **dubie gaudet** fallique veretur,*

Personification—treating something inanimate as if human.

Amores III. 15.19–20: ***imbelles elegi,** genialis Musa, **valete,** post mea mansurum fata superstes opus.*

Pleonasm—use of unnecessary and additional words to express an idea.

Met. X. 283–84: *temptatum **mollescit** ebur positoque rigore*

Polyptoton—the use of the same word in different inflexional forms in the same sentence.

Met. VIII. 724: *cura **deum di** sint, et, qui, **coluere, colantur***

Polysyndeton—use of more conjunctions than are necessary.

Met. VIII. 665–66: *condita**que** in liquida corna autumnalia faece*
            *intiba**que et** radix **et** lactis massa coacti*

Prolepsis—introduction of a word before it is naturally appropriate.

Met. VIII. 197–98: *ore renidenti modo, **quas** vaga moverat aura,*
            *captabat **plumas***

Simile—a comparison between two similar things; introduced by *velut, ut, or sic.*

Met. VIII. 213: *ante volat comitique timet, **velut ales**, ab alto*

Synchesis—see **Interlocked word order**.

Synechdoche—use of the part of something to represent the whole of it.

Met. IV. 86: *cumque domo exierint, urbis quoque **tecta** relinquant,*

Transferred epithet—an adjective used to characterize one thing or person applied to another that is closely associated with it for emphasis.

Met. VIII. 676: *et de **purpureis** conlectae **vitibus** uvae,*

Tricolon Crescendo—three examples in an ascending order of size or importance.

Amores I. 11.9: *nec silicum venae nec durum in pectore ferrum*
nec tibi simplicitas ordine maior adest.

Zeugma—the linking of two words by a single verb thereby creating a paradoxical clash because one subject or object is literal and the other abstract or figurative.

Met. IV.129: *illa redit iuvenemque oculis animoque requirit,*

HIGH-FREQUENCY WORD LIST

The following list contains words which occur **five** or more times in the Ovid AP passages.

ā, ab - (+ abl.) from
accipiō, -ere, -cēpī, -ceptum - to receive, accept
ad - (+ acc.) to, at; by the light of
aes, aeris (n.) - money, pay
āiō - to say, assert; reply
alter...alter - the one...the other
amans, -ntis (m., f.) - lover
amō, -āre, -āvī, -ātum - to love; to fall in love
amor, -ōris (m.) - love, love affair
aqua, -ae (f.) - water, sea
arbor, -oris (f.) - tree
arma, -ōrum (n. pl.) - arms, weapons; fighting, war
ars, -tis (f.) - skill, art
at (conj.) - at least, but, yet; while, whereas
atque (conj.) - and in fact, and what is more, and indeed, and even
aura, -ae (f.) - breeze, air
aut (conj.) - or
aut...aut - either...or
bellum, -ī (n.) - war
carmen, -minis (n.) - poetry, song
cēra, -ae (f.) - wax, beeswax
certus, -a, -um - accurate, precise, sure
color, -ōris (m.) - color
corpus, -oris (n.) - body
cum - (conj.) when; (prep. + abl.) with, along with
deus, -ī (m.) - god, deity

dīcō, -ere, dixī, dictum - to say; to appoint, fix
digitus, -ī (m.) - finger; toe
dō, dare, dedī, datum - to give; to allow; to cause to go
dum (conj.) - while
dux, -cis (m.) - general, leader
ē, ex - (+ abl.) from
ebur, -oris (n.) - ivory
ego - I
eō, īre, i(v)ī, itum - to go
et (conj.) - and; also; even
et...et - both...and; also
faciō, -ere, fēcī, factum - to make, do; bring about, inspire; to act; to reveal; to see that
fallō, -ere, fefellī, falsum - to deceive, trick; to fail; to while away, beguile
ferō, ferre, tulī, lātum - to tell, relate; to carry, bear, bring
ferus, -a, -um - fierce, wild
fugiō, -ere, -ī, -itum - to flee
habeō, -ēre, -uī, -itum - to have, possess; to hold
hic, haec, hoc - this, the latter
hostis, -is (m.) - enemy
iaceō, -ēre, -uī, -tum - to lie down, lie; to be overthrown
iam (adv.) - now
ignis, -is (m.) - fire, star
ille, illa, illud - that, the former; he, she
in - (+ acc.) over, affecting; for, towards; into; among; (+ abl.) in, on

inquam, inquit - to say
ipse, -a, -um - oneself, itself
lacertus, -ī (m.) - upper arm
legō, -ere, lēgī, lectum - to choose, select, pick out; to read
locus, -ī (m.) - place; open land
longus, -a, -um - long, tall
loquor, -quī, -cūtus - to speak
magnus, -a, -um - great, large
manus, -ūs (f.) - hand; armed force, band
medius, -a, -um - middle, middle of; between; in half, half; medium, moderate
meus, -a, -um - my
mīles, -itis (m.) - soldier
miser, -era, -erum - wretched, miserable
modo (adv.) - just now, recently, lately; just, only
multus, -a, -um - much
nātus, -ī (m.) - son
nec - and...not; not even
nimium (adv.) - excessively, extremely, very much
nōmen, -minis (n.) - name, family name, fame, reputation
nōn (adv.) - not
noster, -tra, -trum - our
novus, -a, -um - new, unfamiliar
nox, -ctis (f.) - night
nūdus, -a, -um - bare, pure, open, simple; naked, unclothed
nullus, -a, -um - no one, nobody, nothing; no; insignificant, trifling
oculus, -ī (m.) - eye
omnis, -e - each, every, all
opus, -eris (n.) - task, undertaking, work, job; need
ordō, -dinis (m.) - order; class, rank; a linear arrangement

ōs, ōris (n.) - face; mouth
osculum, -ī (n.) - mouth, lips; kiss
pārens, -entis (m., f.) - ancestor, parent
pater, -tris (m.) - father
pectus, -oris (n.) - chest, breast
penna, -ae (f.) - wing, feather
per - (+ acc.) through, throughout
perdō, -ere, -idī, -itum - to waste one's effort or time; to destroy
pēs, pedis (m.) - foot, metrical foot
petō, -ere, -īvī, -ītum - to seek, look for; to seek the hand of in marriage, to court
placeō, -ēre, -uī, -itum - (+ dat.) to be pleasing or acceptable
pōnō, -ere, posuī, positum - to put, place, arrange; to lay aside, abandon
possum, posse, potuī - to be able
puella, -ae (f.) - girl, young woman
puer, -ī (m.) - boy
quī, quae, quod - who, which
quis, quid - who? what?
quoque (adv.) - also, too
rāmus, -ī (m.) - branch
relinquō, -ere, -liquī, -lictum - to leave behind
saepe (adv.) - often
sed (conj.) - but
semper (adv.) - always
sentiō, -īre, sensī, sensum - to feel, sense
sī (conj.) - if
sīc (adv.) - thus, in this way, in like manner

sub - (+ abl.) under, underneath; at the base of; (+ acc.) at the base of, just at

sum, esse, fuī, futūrus - to be

suus, -a, -um - his, her, its, their

tabella, -ae (f.) - writing tablet

tamen (adv.) - nevertheless

tangō, -ere, tetigī, tactum - to touch, come in contact with

temptō, -āre, -āvī, -ātum - to try, attempt; to handle, touch, feel

teneō, -ēre, -uī, -tum - to hold, have; to catch

timidus, -a, -um - fearful, apprehensive, timid

tōtus, -a, -um - the whole of

tū - you *(sing.)*

tuus, -a, -um - your *(sing.)*

unda, -ae (f.) - body of flowing water, river; water

ūnus, -a, -um - one; alone

ut (conj.) - just as, like; when; in order that; since

vacuus, -a, -um - empty, unattached, free, unoccupied

vel (conj.) - either...or; at any rate

veniō, -īre, vēnī, ventum - to come

verbum, -ī (n.) - word

vestis, -is (f.) - clothing; cloth

virgō, -inis (f.) - maiden

volō, velle, voluī - to wish for; to wish

vōs - you *(pl.)*

vulnus, -eris (n.) - wound, injury

GLOSSARY

Words marked with a ~ are also listed in the High-Frequency Word List.

ā (interj.) - ah!

~ā, ab - (+ abl.) from

abditus, -a, -um - hidden, concealed

abdūco, -dūcere, -dūxi, - ductum - to carry off

abeō, -īre, -iī, -itum - to change, be transformed into

absum, -esse, āfuī, āfūtūrus - to be missing; to be away from

absūmō, -ere, -sumpsī, -sumptum - to use up, squander, spend

ac (conj.) - and

accēdō, -ere, -cessī, -cessum - to follow in accordance; to be added

accendo, -ere, -di, -censum - to light, ignite; (pass.) to flare up

accingō, -ere, -cinxī, -cinctum - to gird, equip

~accipiō, -ere, -cēpī, -ceptum - to receive, accept

accommodō, -āre, -āvī, -ātum - to fasten on, fit

acer, -eris (n.) - maple wood

ācer, ācris, ācre - vigorous, energetic

Achillēs, -is (m.) - Achilles, Greek hero of the Trojan War

acūtus, -a, -um - pointed, sharp

~ad - (+ acc.) to, at; by the light of

adclīnō, -āre, -āvī, -ātum - to lean or rest on

adcumbō, -ere, -cubuī, -cubitum - to recline at table

addūco, -ere, -dūxi, -ductum - to pull taut

adeō, -īre, -iī, -itum - to approach

adeō (adv.) - especially, extremely, to such a degree

adflō, -āre, -āvī, -ātum - to breathe onto, blow onto

adhibeō, -ēre, -uī, -itum - to apply

adhūc (adv.) - already; yet, as yet, still

adimō, -ere, -ēmī, -emptum - to take away

adiuvō, -āre, -iūvī, -iūtum - to help, assist

admittō, -ere, -mīsī, -missum - to give loose rein to, release, let go

admoveō, -ēre, -mōvi, -mōtum - to move or place near to

adnuō, -ere, -uī, -ūtum - to nod; to nod in approval

adoleō, -ēre, -uī, adultum - to burn

adoperiō, -īre, -uī, -tum - to cover over

adpellō, -āre, -āvī, -ātum - to call, address, name

adserō, -ere, -uī, -tum - to lay claim to

adspergō, -ginis (f.) - sprinkling, splashing, scattering

adspiciō, -ere, -spexī, -spectum - to observe, behold, catch sight of

adsum, -esse, -fui, -fūtūrus - to be present

adulter, -erī (m.) - adulterer

adūrō, -ere, -ussī, -ustum - to burn, scorch

adversus, -a, -um - opposing, obstructing, standing in the way

aedēs, -is (f.) - temple, sanctuary

aemula, -ae (f.) - a female imitator

aēnum, -ī (n.) - a pot or cauldron made of bronze

aequō, -āre, -āvī, -ātum - to make level

aequor, -oris (n.) - calm, flat surface of the sea

aequus, -a, -um - like, equal; ex aequo - equally

āēr, āeris (m.) - air

~aes, aeris (n.) - money, pay

aestuō, -āre, -āvī, -ātum - to
seethe; to blaze

aetās, -ātis (f.) - age

aethēr, -eris (m.) - air, sky

aevum, -ī (n.) - lifetime, experience, years of age

affectō, -āre, -āvī, -ātum - to
aspire to, attempt

agilis, -e - active, busy

agitō, -āre, -āvī, -ātum - to shake,
brandish

agmen, -minis (n.) - army

agna, -ae (f.) - ewe lamb

agō, -ere, ēgī, actum - to lead,
drive; to deliver, give; spend
(time) quid agam - how am I?

~āiō - to say, assert, reply

āla, -ae (f.) - wing

albus, -a, -um - white, clear,
colorless

āles, -itis (m.) - large bird

aliquis, aliquid - someone,
something

aliter (adv.) - otherwise, differ-
ently

alligō, -āre, -āvī, -ātum - to tie,
fasten

altē (adv.) - at a great height

~alter...alter - the one...the other

altus, -a, -um - high; deep

alumnus, -ī (m.) - a "son" in the
sense of a product of a particular environment

alveus, -ī (m.) - a hollowed-out
vessel, dish

~amans, -ntis (m., f.) - lover

Amathusius, -a, -um - of or
pertaining to a town on Cyprus,
sacred to Venus

ambiguum, -ī (n.) - uncertainty,
doubt

ambitiōsus, -a, -um - vain,
ambitious, conceited

ambō, -ae, -ō - both, the two

amīca, -ae (f.) - mistress

amictus, -ūs (m.) - cloak

amīcus, -a, -um - friendly, loving

~amō, -āre, -āvī, -ātum - to love,
fall in love

~amor, -ōris (m.) - love, love affair

amplector, -ī, -plexus - to embrace

an (conj.) - or, or rather; whether

an...an - whether...or

ancilla, -ae (f.) - female slave

Andromachē, -ēs (f.) -
Andromache, wife of Hector

anhēlitus, -ūs (m.) - gasp, panting

anīlis, -e - of or pertaining to an
old woman

anima, -ae (f.) - soul, life; breath

animal, -ālis (n.) - animal

animus, -ī (m.) - courage, spirit,
morale; mind, soul

annus, -ī (m.) - year

ansa, -ae (f.) - a handle

anser, -eris (m.) - goose

ante (adv.) - previously, once; in
front, ahead (prep. + acc.)
before, in front of

antrum, -ī (n.) - cave

anus, -ūs (f.) - an old woman

anxius, -a, -um - anxious, worried,
troubled

Āonius, -a, -um - of Aonia,
Boeotian; of or connected with
the Muses, poetic

aperiō, -īre, -uī, -tum - to reveal,
disclose

apex, apicis (m.) - a tip of a flame

apis, -is (f.) - bee

Apollineus, -a, -um - of or
pertaining to Apollo

aptō, -āre, -āvī, -ātum - to fit, put
into position

aptus, -a, -um - (+ dat.) appropriate, fitting, suited

~aqua, -ae (f.) - water, sea

aquila, -ae (f.) - eagle

aquōsus, -a, -um - watery, wet

āra, -ae (f.) - altar

arātor, -ōris (m.) - ploughman

aratrum, -ī (n.) - plow

~arbor, -oris (f.) - tree

arboreus, -a, -um - of or pertaining to trees, arboreal

arcus, -ūs (m.) - bow

ardeō, -ēre, arsī, arsum - to burn, be inflamed
arduum, -ī (n.) - high elevation
arduus, -a, -um - tall, lofty
ārea, -ae (f.) - open space out-of-doors
argentum, -ī (n.) - silver
Argēus, -a, -um - Greek
āridus, -a, -um - dry
arista, -ae (f.) - harvest
~arma, -ōrum (n. pl.) - arms, weapons; fighting, war
armātus, -a, -um - armed
armentum, -ī (n.) - herd
~ars, -tis (f.) - skill, art
artus, -ūs (m.) - limb of a tree or body; a joint of the body
arvum, -ī (n.) - field, ploughed land; territory, country
arx, -cis (f.) - summit, peak
asper, -era, -erum - wild, rough, harsh
aspiciō, -ere, -spexī, -spectum - to look at, gaze upon, observe
~at (conj.) - at least, but, yet; while, whereas
āter, ātra, ātrum - black, dark-colored, stained
Atlantiadēs, -ae (m.) - Mercury, a grandson of Atlas
~atque (conj.) - and in fact, and what is more, and indeed, and even
Atrīdēs, -ae (m.) - a male descendant of Atreus, king of Argos and Mycenae; usually used of Agamemnon
attenuō, -āre, -āvī, -ātum - to enfeeble, lessen, weaken
Atticus, -ī (m.) - Atticus
attollō, -ere - to lift up, raise
attonitus, -a, -um - dazed, astounded
auctor, -ōris (m.) - founder, author, originator
auctus, -a, -um - increased in intensity
audax, -ācis - bold, confident

audeō, -ēre, ausus - to go so far as to, dare, have the courage
audiō, -īre, -īvī, -ītum - to hear
auferō, -ferre, abstulī, ablātum - to carry away, carry off
augeō, -ēre, auxī, auctum - to increase, augment, strengthen
Augustus, -ī (m.) - Caesar Augustus, emperor
Augustus, -a, -um - of or pertaining to the emperor Augustus
~aura, -ae (f.) - breeze, air
aurātus, -a, -um - golden
aureus, -a, -um - golden
auris, -is (f.) - ear
Aurōra, -ae (f.) - Aurora, goddess of the dawn
aurum, -ī (n.) - gold
auspicium, -ī (n.) - portent, fortune, luck
~aut (conj.) - or
aut...aut - either...or
autumnālis, -e - autumnal
avārus, -a, -um - greedy, avaricious, miserly
avēna, -ae (f.) - stem, stalk
āversor, -ārī, -ātus - to turn away from in disgust, reject
avis, avis (f.) - bird
āvius, -a, -um - distant, remote
Babylōnius, -a, -um - Babylonian
bāca, -ae (f.) - olive; pearl
baculum, -ī (n.) - walking stick, staff
Baucis, -idis (f.) - Baucis, wife of Philemon
~bellum, -ī (n.) - war
bellus, -a, -um - pretty, beautiful
bene (adv.) - well
bicolor, -ōris - having two colors
bicornis, -e - having two prongs
blanditia, -ae (f.) - flattery, compliment, endearing comment
blandus, -a, -um - charming, seductive, carressing
bonus, -a, -um - good, worthy, reliable

Boōtēs, -ae (m.) - Bootes, a constellation

bōs, bovis (m., f.) - bull, cow

brācchium, -ī (n.) - arm

brevis, -e - short

Brīsēis, -idos (f.) - Briseis, Achilles' slave and concubine

būbō, -ōnis (m.) - the horned owl

bustum, -ī (n.) - tomb

buxus, -ī (f.) - boxwood

cacūmen, -cūminis (n.) - the tip or top of a tree

cadō, -ere, cecidī, cāsum - to fall down

cādūcifer, -erī (m.) - Mercury, the bearer of the caduceus.

caedēs, -is (f.) - slaughter, killing

caedō, -ere, cecīdī, caesum - to kill, murder, slaughter

caelebs, -libis - unmarried male, bachelor

caelicola, -ae (m., f.) - an inhabitant of heaven

caelō, -āre, -āvī, -ātum - to engrave, emboss

caelum, -ī (n.) - sky, heaven

caeruleus, -a, -um - blue, greenish blue

caleō, -ēre, -uī - to be hot or warm

callidus, -a, -um - clever, resourceful

Calymnē, -ēs (f.) - an island off the coast of Asia Minor

campus, -ī (m.) - field

candidus, -a, -um - glistening

canis, canis (m.) - dog, hound

canistrum, -ī (n.) - a basket

canna, -ae (f.) - a small reed

canō, -ere, cecinī, cantum - to sing, tell of, relate

cantō, -āre, -āvī, -ātum - to sing, celebrate in song

capillus, -ī (m.) - hair

capiō, -ere, cēpī, captum - to capture, contain

Capitōlium, -ī (n.) - the Capitoline Hill

captīvus, -a, -um - captured, hunted

captō, -āre, -āvī, -ātum - to seek out; try to catch

captus, -a, -um - captured

caput, -itis (n.) - head

cardō, -inis (m.) - hinge

careō, -ēre, -uī, -itum - (+ abl.) to be lacking

cāricus, -a, -um - carian, a type of fig

cariōsus, -a, -um - decayed, withered

~carmen, -minis (n.) - poetry, song

carnifex, -ficis (m.) - executioner

carpō, -ere, -sī, -tum - to pass over, pursue one's way

cārus, -a, -um - beloved, dear

casa, -ae (f.) - cottage

castra, -ōrum (n. pl.) - camp

cāsus, -ūs (m.) - misfortune, event

caterva, -ae (f.) - band, squadron, troop

Catullus, -ī (m.) - Catullus

causa, -ae (f.) - cause, reason, inspiration

causor, -ārī, -ātus - to plead as an excuse or reason

cautus, -a, -um - cautious

cavus, -a, -um - hollow, concave

cēdō, -ere, cessī, cessum - to yield, give way; to be inferior

celeber, -bris, -bre - crowded, populous, festive

celer, -eris, -ere - swift

celsus, -a, -um - high, lofty

~cēra, -ae (f.) - wax, beeswax

Cerēs, -eris (f.) - Ceres, goddess of open fields and agriculture

certē (adv.) - at any rate, at least; certainly, without a doubt

~certus, -a, -um - accurate, precise, sure

cerva, -ae (f.) - deer

cervix, -īcis (f.) - neck

cēterus, -a, -um - the rest of, remaining

cicūta, -ae (f.) - poisonous hemlock (*conium maculatum*) cingō, -ere, cinxī, cinctum - to gird, encircle, surround, bind

cinis, -eris (m.) - ashes, embers

circumdō, -are, -edī, -atum - (+ abl.) to surround, encircle

cithara, -ae (f.) - lyre

citus, -a, -um - rapid, speedy

clāmō, -āre, -āvī, -ātum - to shout

Claros, -ī (f.) - Claros, a small town, sacred to Apollo, on the central coast of Asia Minor

clārus, -a, -um - loud, shrill

claudō, -ere, -sī, -sum - to close, shut

clāvus, -ī (m.) - nail

clīvus, -ī (m.) - slope, incline

coactus, -a, -um - curdled

coctilis, -e - of baked bricks

coeō, -īre, -iī, -itum - to come together, unite

coepī, coepisse, coeptum - to begin

coerceō, -ēre, -uī, -itum - to restrain, restrict, control, bind up

cognitor, -ōris (m.) - attorney

cognitus, -a, -um - known to be

cognoscō, -ere, -nōvī, -nitum - to recognize

cōgō, -ere, coēgī, coactum - to force, compel; to bring together

colligō, -ere, -lēgī, -lectum - to gather together, collect

collis, -is (m.) - hill, mountain

collum, -ī (n.) - neck

colō, -ere, -uī, cultum - to till, cultivate; to worship

~color, -ōris (m.) - color

columba, -ae (f.) - dove

columna, -ae (f.) - column, pillar

coma, -ae (f.) - hair

comes, -itis (m., f.) - companion

comitō, -āre, -āvī, -ātum - to follow

commendō, -āre, -āvī, -ātum - to recommend, make agreeable or attractive

committō, -ere, -mīsī, -missum - to entrust

commūnis, -e - shared, common

cōmō, -ere, -psī, -ptum - to adorn, arrange

complector, -i, -plexus - to embrace

complexus, -ūs (m.) - embrace

compōnō, -ere, -posuī, -positum - to compose, put together

comprimō, -ere, -pressī, -pressum - to pack closely or densely, squeeze

comptus, -a, -um - adorned

concha, -ae (f.) - shell

concidō, -ere, -ī - to fall, collapse

concipiō, -ere, -cēpī, -ceptum - to produce, form; to conceive

concordō, -āre, -āvī, -ātum - to agree, harmonize

concors, -cordis - agreeing, harmonious

concutiō, -ere, -cussī, cussum - to shake

conditus, -a, -um - preserved

condō, -ere, -idī, -itum - to inter, lay to rest

confugiō, -ere, -fūgī - to flee to for safety

congestus, -a, -um - piled up

coniugium, -ī (n.) - marriage

coniunx, -iugis (f./m.) - wife, bride; husband

conligō, -ere, -lēgī, -lectum - to gather together, collect

conlocō, -āre, -āvī, -ātum - to place, position, arrange

conpescō, -ere, -uī - to quench

conplector, -i, -plexus - to embrace

conpōnō, -ere, -posuī, -positum - to place together

conprendō, -ere, -dī, -sum - to seize, catch hold of

conscius, -ī (m.) - accomplice, conspirator

consenescō, -ere, -senuī - to grow old

consors, -rtis (f.) - partner

conspiciō, -ere, -spexī, -spectum - to see, witness

constō, -āre, -stitī - to take up a position; to stand up

consuescō, -ere, -suēvī, -suētum - to be in the habit of, become accustomed to

consūmō, -ere, -psī, -ptum - to consume, devour

contentus, -a, -um - content, satisfied

conterminus, -a, -um - nearby, adjacent

contiguus, -a, -um - adjacent, neighboring

contingō, -ere, -tigi, -tactum - to come about, happen

continuō (adv.) - forthwith, immediately, without delay

contrā - (+ acc.) on the opposite side; (adv.) to the opposite side

cōnūbium, -ī (n.) - the rite of marriage

conveniens, -entis - (+ dat.) fitting, appropriate, consistent

conveniō, -īre, -vēnī, -ventum - to be suitable or adapted for; to come together, meet

convincō, -ere, -vīcī, -victum - to prove, demonstrate

Corinna, -ae (f.) - Corinna

corniger, -era, -erum - having horns

cornū, -ūs (n.) - horn, bow

cornum, -ī (n.) - a cornelian cherry

~corpus, -oris (n.) - body

Corsicus, -a, -um - of or belonging to the island of Corsica off the western coast of Italy

cortex, -icis (m.) - outer bark of a tree

crātēr, -ēris (m.) - a mixing bowl for wine

crēdibilis, -e - capable of being believed, credible, likely

crēdō, -ere, -idī, -itum - to believe, trust

crescō, -ere, crēvī, crētum - to grow, increase; arise

Crētē, -ēs (f.) - the island of Crete

crīmen, -minis (n.) - reproach, blame; evil thing

crīnis, crīnis (m.) - hair, tresses

cruentō, -āre, -āvī, -ātum - to stain with blood

cruentus, -a, -um - bloody

cruor, -ōris (m.) - blood; bloodshed; gore

crūs, crūris (n.) - lower leg, shin

crux, crucis (f.) - wooden frame or cross on which criminals were hanged or impaled

cultus, -a, -um - refined, sophisticated, elegant, revered

~cum - (conj.) when; (prep. + abl.) with, along with

cunctus, -a, -um - all; every

cupīdō, -dinis (f.) - desire, longing

Cupīdō, -dinis (m.) - Cupid

cupiō, -ere, -īvī, -ītum - to desire

cur (adv.) - why?

cūra, -ae (f.) - care, anxiety, worry; object of concern, beloved person

cūrō, -āre, -āvī, -ātum - to bother with, care about

currō, -ere, cucurrī, cursum - to run, fly quickly

cursus, -ūs (m.) - running, rushing

curvāmen, -minis (n.) - curvature, arc

cuspis, -pidis (f.) - spear, lance; sharp point, tip

custōdia, -ae (f.) - defence, guard

custōs, -ōdis (m., f.) - watchman, doorkeeper

Cyprus, -ī (f.) - the island of Cyprus

Cytherēa, -ae (f.) - Venus

Daedalus, -ī (m.) - Daedalus, builder of the labyrinth in Crete and father of Icarus

damnōsus, -a, -um - ruinous, destructive,

Daphnē, -ēs (f.) - Daphne, daughter of the river god Peneus; loved by Apollo and changed into a laurel tree

daps, dapis (f.) - feast, meal

dē - (+ abl.) from

dea, -ae (f.) - goddess

debeō, -ēre, -uī, -itum - to owe, be indebted to

decens, -entis - graceful, attractive

decet, -ēre, -uit - to be right, fitting, proper; to be becoming or appropriate

decor, -ōris (m.) - beauty, good looks

dēdecet, -ēre, -uit - to disgrace, dishonor

dēdicō, -āre, -āvī, -ātum - to dedicate

dēferō, -ferre, -tulī, -lātum - to bring down, carry down

dēfleō, -ēre, -ēvī, -ētum - to lament, feel sorrow

dēlicia, -ae (f.) - pleasure, delight

Dēlius, -iī (m.) - Apollo

Dēlos, -ī (f.) - Delos, an island in the Aegean

Delphicus, -a, -um - of or connected to Delphi

dēlūbrum, -ī (n.) - temple, shrine

dēmissus, -a, -um - low, close to the ground

dēmittō, -ere, -mīsī, -missum - to thrust, drive

dēmō, -ere, -psī, -ptum - to remove, take away

densus, -a, -um - thick, dense

dēpōnō, -ere, -posuī, -positum - to lay aside, get rid of; to allay

dēprendō, -ere, -ī, -prensum - to catch, discover

dēserō, -ere, -uī, -tum - to withdraw, desert, abandon

dēserviō, -īre - to serve zealously, devote oneself

dēsīdia, -ae (f.) - idleness, inactivity, leisure

dēsidiōsus, -a, -um - idle, lazy

dēsinō, -ere, -si(v)ī, -situm - to cease, stop, desist

dēsultor, -ōris (m.) - a circus rider who leaps from horse to horse

~deus, -ī (m.) - god, deity

dēvoveō, -ēre, -vōvī, -vōtum - to curse

dexter, -tra, -trum - right, righthand

Diāna, -ae (f.) - Diana, twin sister to Apollo, virgin goddess of woodlands

~dīcō, -ere, dixī, dictum - to say; to appoint, fix

diēs, -ēī (f.) - day

difficilis, -e - troublesome

~digitus, -ī (m.) - finger; toe

dignus, -a, -um - worthy

dīmittō, -ere, -mīsī, -missum - to direct oneself to; to let go

dīmoveō, -ēre, -mōvī, -mōtum - to move about

dīrus, -a, -um - dreadful, awful

discēdō, -ere, -cessī, -cessum - to depart, go away

discinctus, -a, -um - easygoing, undisciplined

discrīmen, -inis (n.) - difference, distinction

dispār, -ris - unequal, dissimilar

diū (adv.) - for a long time

dīvellō, -ere, -vulsī, -vulsum - to tear apart, tear open, tear in two

dīversus, -a, -um - differing, distinct

~dō, dare, dedī, datum - to give; to allow, cause to go

doctus, -a, -um - expert, skilled

dolens, -entis - grieving, sorrowing

dolor, -ōris (m.) - pain, grief

domina, -ae (f.) - mistress

dominus, -ī (m.) - master, owner

domō, -āre, -āvī, -ātum - to boil soft

domus, -ī (f.) - house, home, household

dōnec (conj.) - as long as

dōnō, -āre, -āvī, -ātum - to give as a gift, grant

dubitō, -āre, -āvī, -ātum - to hesitate; to doubt

dubius, -a, -um - uncertain

dūcō, -ere, dūxī, ductum - to lead; to shape, develop, mold

~dum (conj.) - while

duo, -ae, -o - two

duplex, -plicis - twofold, deceitful, duplicitous

duplicō, -āre, -āvī, -ātum - to double in size or amount

dūrus, -a, -um - stubborn, hard; unsympathetic, uncaring, dull

~dux, -cis (m.) - general, leader

~ē, ex - (+ abl.) from

~ebur, -oris (n.) - ivory

eburneus, -a, -um - of ivory

eburnus, -a, -um - of ivory

ecce (interj.) - behold! look!

ēdō, -ere, -idī, -itum - to publish; produce, put forth; to deliver a message, utter

efficiō, -ere, -fēcī, -fectum - to cause to be, become

effūsus, -a, -um - loose, flowing

~ego - I

ēgredior, -ī, -gressus - to go out, leave

ei (interj.) - oh!

ēiaculor, -ārī, -ātus - to shoot forth

elegī, -ōrum (m. pl.) - elegiac verses

ēlīdō, -ere, -lisī, -lisum - to expel, force out, drive out

ēlūdō, -ere, -lūsī, -lūsum - to elude, avoid capture

ēmicō, -āre, -āvī, -ātum - to spurt, shoot forth

ēmodulor, -ārī, -ātum - to sing in rhythm

enim (conj.) - indeed, truly

ensis, -is (m.) - sword

~eō, īre, i(v)ī, itum - to go

eōdem (adv.) - to the same place

ephēmeris, -idos (f.) - a record book, daybook, diary

epulae, -ārum (f. pl.) - feast, banquet

eques, -itis (m.) - a member of the equestrian order

equidem (adv.) - truly, indeed

equus, -ī (m.) - horse

ergo (adv.) - therefore, for that reason

ērigō, -ere, -rexī, -rectum - to raise oneself

eripiō, -ere, -ripuī, -reptum - to snatch, pluck

errō, -āre, -āvī, -ātum - to wander about

ērubescō, -ere, -buī - to blush with shame or modesty

ērudiō, -īre, -īvī, -ītum - to teach, instruct

~et (conj.) - and; also; even

et...et - both...and

etiam (adv.) - even; likewise; indeed

etsī (conj.) - even if, although

Eurus, -ī (m.) - Eurus, the east wind

exaudiō, -īre, -īvī, -ītum - to hear, listen

excēdō, -ere, -cessī, -cessum - to go away, pass out of, depart

excipiō, -ere, -cēpī, -ceptum - to accept, receive

exeō, -īre, -iī, -itum - to go out; emerge

exhorreō, -ēre - to shudder

exiguus, -a, -um - small, slight

exilium, -ī (n.) - exile

eximō, -ere, -ēmī, -emptum - to take away, banish

exitium, -ī (n.) - destruction, ruin

exōsus, -a, -um - hating, despising

expallescō, -ere, -paluī - to turn pale

experiens, -ntis - active

expers, -pertis - (+ gen.) lacking experience or knowledge, free from

extendō, -ere, -dī, -tum - to stretch out, thrust out

exterō, -ere, -trīvī, -trītum - to wear down, trample on

exterreō, -ēre, -uī, -itum - to terrify, frighten

extinguō, -ere, -tinxī, -tinctum - to die, perish

extrēmus, -a -um - farthest, outermost

exuviae, -ārum (f. pl.) - spoils

fabricō, -āre, -āvī, -ātum - to work, fashion, shape

fabrīlis, -e - of or belonging to a metalworker, skilled; fabricated

fābula, -ae (f.) - gossip, scandal, myth, story

faciēs, -iēī (f.) - appearance, looks shape; beauty

~faciō, -ere, fēcī, factum - to make, do; to bring about, inspire; to act; to reveal, to see that

faex, -cis (f.) - the dregs or sediment of any liquid, particularly of wine; brine

fāgineus, -a, -um - of the beech tree

fāgus, -ī (f.) - beech tree

~fallō, -ere, fefellī, falsum - to deceive, trick; to fail; to while away, beguile

falsus, -a, -um - false, not genuine

fama, -ae (f.) - reputation

famulus, -ī (m.) - servant, attendant

fateor, -ērī, fassus - to profess, agree; acknowledge

fatīgō, -āre, -āvī, -ātum - to exhaust, tire out

fātum, -ī (n.) - destiny, death, end

favilla, -ae (f.) - ashes of a fire

favus, -ī (m.) - honeycomb

fax, facis (f.) - torch, firebrand

fēcundus, -a, -um - fertile, fruitful

fēlīciter (adv.) - successfully

fēlix, -īcis - fruitful, fertile

fēmina, -ae (f.) - woman

fēmineus, -a, -um - female, feminine, womanly

fera, -ae (f.) - wild animal

~ferō, ferre, tulī, lātum - to tell, relate; to carry, bear, bring

ferreus, -a, -um - iron-like, hard-hearted, unfeeling

ferrum, -ī (n.) - iron, steel; blade, sword

~ferus, -a, -um - fierce, wild

fervens, -ntis - hot, fresh; boiling, bubbling

festum, -ī (n.) - holiday, festival

festus, -a, -um - (+ *dies*) holiday

fētus, -ūs (m.) - fruit or product of a plant

fictilis, -e - earthenware, pottery

fidēs, -ēī (f.) - good faith, honesty, honor

fīdus, -a, -um - faithful, loyal

fīgō, -ere, -xī, -xum - to pierce, run through; to fix, fasten, lodge

figūra, -ae (f.) - shape, appearance

fīlia, -ae (f.) - daughter

fīlius, -ī (m.) - son

fīlum, -ī (n.) - yarn, thread

findō, -ere, fidī, fissum - to split

fīniō, -īre, -īvī, -ītum - to finish, end

fīnis, fīnis (m.) - boundary, remotest limit

fīō, fierī - to become, be made

fistula, -ae (f.) - pipe, tube; pan-pipe

flāmen, -minis (n.) - wind, breeze

flamma, -ae (f.) - flame

flāvens, -entis - yellow, golden

flāvescō, -ere - to become golden

flāvus, -a, -um - fair-haired, blonde; yellow

flectō, -ere, flexī, flectum - to bend

fleō, -ēre, -ēvī, -ētum - to weep, weep for

flētus, -ūs (m.) - weeping, tears

flōs, -ōris (m.) - flower, blossom

flūmen, -minis (n.) - river

flūmineus, -a, -um - of or associated with a river

focus, -ī (m.) - hearth, fireplace

folium, -ī (n.) - leaf of a plant

fons, -ntis (m.) - spring of water

forāmen, -minis (n.) - hole, aperture

forās (adv.) - out-of-doors

foris, foris (f.) - door, double door

forma, -ae (f.) - appearance; good looks, beauty

formōsus, -a, -um - beautiful

fors, -tis (f.) - chance, luck

forte (adv.) - by chance, accidentally

fortis, -e - strong, courageous, brave, powerful

fortiter (adv.) - vigorously, powerfully, with great force

foveō, -ēre, fōvī, fōtum - to make warm

frangō, -ere, frēgī, fractum - to break, smash

fretum, -ī (n.) - strait, sea

frīgus, -oris (n.) - cold, chill

frondeō, -ēre - to grow foliage

frons, -dis (f.) - foliage, leafy boughs

frons, -tis (f.) - forehead, brow

fruor, -ī, -ctus - to enjoy

frutex, -icis (f.) - green growth

fuga, -ae (f.) - flight, fleeing

fugax, -ācis - running away, fleeing

~fugiō, -ere, -ī, -itum - to flee

fugō, -āre, -āvī, -ātum - to cause to flee, drive away, repel

fulgeō, -ēre, fulsī - to glisten, gleam

fulica, -ae (f.) - waterfowl, coot

fūmō, -āre, -āvī, -ātum - to give off smoke

funēbris, -e - deadly, funereal

fungor, -ī, functus - to perform, observe

furca, -ae (f.) - a length of wood with a forked end

furtīvus, -a, -um - clandestine, secret

galea, -ae (f.) - helmet

Gallicus, -a, -um - of Gaul

garrulus, -a, -um - loquacious, talkative, wordy

gaudeō, -ēre, gāvīsus - to rejoice; to be pleased

gelidus, -a, -um - icy cold

geminus, -a, -um - double; pair of, twin

gemma, -ae (f.) - jewel, gem

gena, -ae (f.) - cheek

gener, -erī (m.) - son-in-law

genialis, -e - creative, festive

genitor, -ōris (m.) - father; ancestor

gens, -tis (f.) - race, group of people

genu, -ūs (n.) - knee

gerō, -ere, gessī, gestum - to wage; to bear, carry

gestāmen, -minis (n.) - load, burden

gestiō, -īre, -īvī - to desire eagerly, want, be anxious to

gignō, -ere, genuī, genitum - to give birth to

gloria, -ae (f.) - glory

gradus, -ūs (m.) - step

graphium, -ī (n.) - stylus

grātēs, -ium (f. pl.) - thanks

grātus, -a, -um - welcome; pleasant, attractive

gravis, grave - heavy, weighty; important; hard to capture

gravō, -āre, -āvī, -ātum - to make heavy, weigh down

grex, gregis (m.) - flock

~habeō, -ēre, -uī, -itum - to have, possess; to hold

habilis, -e - suitable, fit

habitābilis, -e - inhabitable

habitō, -āre, -āvī, -ātum - to live, dwell

hāc (adv.) - on this side; **hāc fāciō** - to be on a side

haereō, -ēre, haesī, haesum - to cling; to be brought to a standstill; to be perplexed, hesitate

harundō, -dinis (f.) - reed; shaft of an arrow, arrow

haud (adv.) - not

hauriō, -īre, hausī, haustum - to swallow up, consume; to drink in, draw in

haustus, -ūs (m.) - a drawn quantity of liquid, drink

Hector, -oris (m.) - Hector, son of Priam, prince of Troy

Hēliades, -um (f. pl.) - daughters of the sun god Helios

Helicē, -ēs (f.) - the constellation Ursa Major

Helicōnius, -a, -um - of Helicon

herba, -ae (f.) - plant, herb

hērēs, -ēdis (m.) - heir, successor

hērōs, -ōos (m.) - hero
hesternus, -a, -um - yesterday's
heu (interj.) - alas
~hic, haec, hoc - this, the latter
hīc (adv.) - here, in this place
hinc (adv.) - from this place; on this side
hodiē (adv.) - today
holus, -eris (n.) - vegetable (i.e., cabbage, turnip)
honestus, -a, -um - honorable
honor, -ōris (m.) - honor, mark of esteem, glory
hōra, -ae (f.) - hour, time
horridus, -a, -um - rough in manners, rude, uncouth; hairy
hortor, -ārī, -ātus - to encourage
hortus, -ī (m.) - garden
hospes, -itis (m.) - visitor, stranger, guest; (adj.) of or pertaining to a guest
~hostis, -is (m.) - enemy
hūc (adv.) - here, to this place
humilis, -e - humble, lowly
humus, -ī (f.) - earth, ground
Hymēn (m.) - the god of marriage, wedding
Hymettius, -a, -um - of or pertaining to Mt. Hymettus near Athens, famous for its honey
~iaceō, -ēre, -uī, -tum - to lie down, lie; to be overthrown
~iam (adv.) - now
ibi (adv.) - there, in that place
Īcarus, -ī (m.) - Daedalus's son
iciō, -ere, īcī, ictum - to strike, beat
ictus, -ūs (m.) - blow, stroke, thrust
īdem, eadem, idem - the same
ideō (adv.) - for that reason
ignārus, -a, -um - unaware, ignorant, unfamiliar, unknown, blind
ignāvus, -a, -um - lazy, sluggish
~ignis, -is (m.) - fire, star
ignōtus, -a, -um - unfamiliar, unknown
īlia, -ium (n. pl.) - the gut, groin

illāc (adv.) - by that way
~ille, illa, illud - that, the former; he, she
illīc (adv.) - there, in that place
illinc (adv.) - on the other side
imbellis, -e - not suited to warfare, unwarlike
imber, -bris (m.) - rain
imitor, -ārī, -ātus - to imitate, resemble
immundus, -a, -um - unclean, foul, impure
impediō, -īre, -īvī, -ītum - to hinder, impede
impellō, -ere, -pulī, -pulsum - to push forward, urge on
īmus, -a, -um - the lowest, bottommost
~in - (+ acc.) over, affecting; for, towards; into; among; (+ abl.) in, on
incertus, -a, -um - disarranged, not fixed; not sure, uncertain
incola, -ae (m., f.) - inhabitant
increpō, -āre, -uī, -itum - to make a loud rattle, clang, noise
incubō, -āre, -uī, -itum - to throw oneself upon
incumbō, -ere, -cubuī - to lean over or on; to lie on
inde (adv.) - therefore, and so
indignor, -ārī, -ātum - to consider as unworthy or improper
indignus, -a, -um - not deserving, unworthy
indūcō, -ere, -dūxī, -ductum - to cover, spread on or over
indūrescō, -esere, -uī - to harden, become hard
inermis, -e - unarmed, defenceless
iners, -rtis - lazy, feeble
infāmis, -e - infamous, disgraced
infēlix, -icis - unhappy, ill-fated, unlucky
inferior, -ius - lower, bottom, second
infestus, -a, -um - hostile
ingeniōsus, -a, -um - clever

ingenium, -ī (n.) - character, spirit, nature

ingrātus, -a, -um - ungrateful, thankless

inhaereō, -ēre, -haesī, -haesum - to stick, cling, attach, grasp

inhibeō, -ēre, -uī, -itum - to restrain, check, stop

inīquus, -a, -um - resentful, discontented

inlinō, -ere, -lēvī, -litum - to smear, coat

inmensus, -a, -um - boundless, immense, huge

inmineō, -ēre - to be poised over

inmūnis, -e - (+ gen.) free from, exempt

innītor, -ī, -nixus - to lean on, rest on

innumerus, -a, -um - countless, innumerable,

innuptus, -a, -um - unmarried

inornātus, -a, -um - not adorned, dishevelled, unarranged

inpār, -ris - unequal

inpatiens, -ntis - impatient

inpediō, -īre, -īvī, -ītum - to hinder, impede

inpellō, -ere, -pulī, -pulsum - to push, drive, set in motion

inperfectus, -a, -um - unfinished, incomplete

inpiger, -gra, -grum - quick, energetic, tireless

inpius, -a, -um - impious, irreverent, undutiful

inpleō, -ēre, -ēvī, -ētum - to fill up

inpōnō, -ere, -posuī, -positum - to place on

inpulsus, -ūs (m.) - thrust, blow

~inquam, inquit - to say

inquīrō, -ere, -quisīvī, -sītus - to inquire, ask

inrītō, -āre, -āvī, -ātum - to provoke, arouse

insānus, -a, -um - frenzied, mad, insane

insequor, -sequī, -secūtus - to pursue

insīdō, -ere, -sēdī, -sessum - to sink in, become embedded

insignis, -e - outstanding, remarkable, distinguished

instar (n.) - (+ gen.) according to, like

instruō, -ere, -xī, -ctum -to instruct, equip, outfit

insula, -ae (f.) - island

inter - (+ acc.) among; between

intereā (adv.) - meanwhile

intibum, -ī (n.) - chicory or endive

intonsus, -a, -um - unshorn, uncut

intrō, -āre, -āvī, -ātum - to go into, enter

inūtilis, -e - useless

invādō, -ere, -vāsī, -vāsum - to attack, set on

inveniō, -īre, -ī, -tum - to discover

inventum, -ī (n.) - discovery, invention

invideō, -ēre, -vīdī, -vīsum - to refuse, be unwilling

invidus, -a, -um - envious, malevolent

Īō (f.) - Io

~ipse, -a, -um - oneself, itself

īra, -ae (f.) - anger, rage, wrath

īrātus, -a, -um - angry, furious

is, ea, id - he, she, it; this, that

iste, -a, -ud - that of yours

ita (adv.) - thus, in this way

iter, -ineris (n.) - journey, passage

iterum (adv.) - again, another time

iubeō, -ēre, iussi, iussum - to order, bid, command

iūdicium, -ī (n.) - decision, pronouncement

iugālis, -e - nuptial, matrimonial

iūgerum, -ī (n.) - a measurement of land equal approximately to two-thirds of an acre

iugōsus, -a, -um - hilly, mountainous

iungo, -ere, -xi, -ctum - to join (in marriage)

Iūnōnius, -a, -um - of or pertaining to Juno

Iuppiter, Iovis (m.) - Jupiter
iūs, iūris (n.) - authority, jurisdiction, power, right
iustus, -a, -um - just, fair
iuvenālis, -e - youthful
iuvenca, -ae (f.) - heifer, cow
iuvencus, -ī (m.) - young bull
iuvenis, -e - young
lābor, -ī, lāpsus - to slip, slide; to drip
labor, -ōris (m.) - labor, toil, hardship, task
labōrō, -āre, -āvī, -ātum - to be anxious, worried, distressed
lac, -ctis (n.) - milk
~lacertus, -ī (m.) - upper arm
lacrima, -ae (f.) - tear
laedō, -ere, laesī, laesum - to harm, injure
laetus, -a, -um - joyful
laevus, -a, -um - left, lefthand
laniō, -āre, -āvī, -ātum - to tear, mangle
lapillus, -ī (m.) - small stone, gem
lascīvus, -a, -um - naughty, unrestrained, mischievous
lassō, -āre, -āvī, -ātum - to tire, exhaust
lātē (adv.) - over a large area, widely
latebra, -ae (f.) - hiding place
lateō, -ēre, -uī - to hide; to take refuge; to be concealed, lie hidden
Latius, -a, -um - Roman
lātus, -a, -um - broad, wide
laudō, -āre, -āvī, -ātum - to praise
laurea, -ae (f.) - the laurel/bay tree
laurus, -ī (f.) - foliage of the laurel (bay) tree; the laurel tree
laus, -dis (f.) - praise, glory
lea, -ae (f.) - lioness
leaena, -ae (f.) - lioness
Lebinthos, -ī (f.) - an island off the east coast of Greece
lectus, -ī (m.) - bed, couch
~legō, -ere, lēgī, lectum - to choose, select, pick out; to read

leō, -ōnis (m.) - lion
lepus, -oris (m.) - hare
lētum, -ī (n.) - death
levis, -e - light, not ponderous
leviter (adv.) - lightly
levō, -āre, -āvī, -ātum - to lift off, remove; to relieve, support
lex, lēgis (f.) - law, rule; **sine lege** - in disorder, unruly
liber, -brī (m.) - inner bark of a tree
lībertās, -tātis (f.) - liberty
lībrō, -āre, -āvī, -ātum - to level, balance
licet, -ēre, -uī, -itum - it is permitted, one may; (conj.) although
lignum, -ī (n.) - wood, firewood
līlium, -ī (n.) - lily
līmen, -minis (n.) - threshold, doorstep
līmes, -mitis (m.) - path, track
līnum, -ī (n.) - thread, string
liquidus, -a, -um - liquid, fluid
lītoreus, -a, -um - of the seashore
littera, -ae (f.) - letter
līvor, -ōris (m.) - bluish coloring, bruise
~locus, -ī (m., n. pl.) - place, open land
~longus, -a, -um - long, tall
~loquor, -quī, -cūtus - to speak
luctus, -ūs (m.) - grief, mourning
lūdō, -ere, lūsi, lūsum - to trick, deceive
lūmen, -minis (n.) - light, brilliance; eye
lūna, -ae (f.) - moon
lūnāris, -e - of or pertaining to the moon
lūnō, -āre, -āvī, -ātum - to curve, bend
luō, -ere, -ī - to pay as a penalty, amend for
lupus, -ī (m.) - wolf
lustrō, -āre, -āvī, -ātum - to move through or around, roam
lūsus, -ūs (m.) - playing, sporting
lux, lūcis (f.) - light of day, **sub luce** - at dawn

Lyaeus, -ī -(m.) - Bacchus
lyra, -ae (f.) - lyre, lute
mactō, -āre, -āvī, -ātum - to kill, slay, sacrifice
madefaciō, -ere, -fēcī, -factum - to soak, drench
madeō, -ēre, -uī - to grow wet
Maenas, -adis (f.) - female worshipper of Bacchus, Bacchante, Maenad
magis (adv.) - more
~magnus, -a, -um - great, large
maior, -ius - greater, larger
malum, -ī (n.) - evil, wickedness
mālum, -ī (n.) - an apple
malus, -a, -um - wicked
mandō, -āre, -āvī, -ātum - to order, command
māne (adv.) - early in the day, morning
maneō, -ēre, -sī, -sum - to remain, stay
Mantua, -ae (f.) - the city of Mantua in the north of Italy
~manus, -ūs (f.) - hand; armed force, band
margō, -inis (m.) - margin
marītus, -ī (m.) - husband
marmor, -oris (n.) - marble
Mars, -tis (m.) - Mars, god of war
massa, -ae (f.) - heap, lump, mass
māter, -tris (f.) - mother
māteria, -ae (f.) - material, subject-matter
māteriēs, -iēi (f.) - material, subject-matter
mātūrus, -a, -um - mature, experienced,
medicīna, -ae (f.) - medicine
medicō, -āre, -āvī, -ātum - to dye
medium, -ī (n.) - a neutral or undecided state
~medius, -a, -um - middle, middle of; between; in half, half, medium, moderate
medulla, -ae (f.) - marrow
mel, mellis (n.) - honey
melior, -ius - better, finer, superior
melius (adv.) - better, more fittingly

membrum, -ī (n.) - part of the body; limb of tree or body
meminī, -isse - to remember
mens, -tis (f.) - mind; inclination
mensa, -ae (f.) - table
menta, -ae (f.) - mint
mereō, -ēre, -uī, -itum - to earn
mergō, -ere, -rsī, -rsum - to flood, inundate
mergus, -ī (m.) - sea bird, gull
meritus, -a, -um - deserving, just
mēta, -ae (f.) - turning post, goal
metuō, -ere, -uī -ūtum - to fear, be afraid
metus, -ūs (m.) - fear
~meus, -a, -um - my
micō, -āre, -āvī - to flash, glitter, glisten
~mīles, -itis (m.) - soldier
mīlitia, -ae (f.) - military service
mīlitō, -āre, -āvī, -ātum - to serve as a soldier, be a soldier
mille (n.) - (indecl.) a thousand
Minerva, -ae (f.) - Minerva, the goddess associated with handicrafts (particularly spinning) and war
minimus, -a, -um - smallest, very small, least
ministerium, -ī (n.) - duty, office, work
ministra, -ae (f.) - an assistant
minium, -ī (n.) - bright red dye, cinnabar
minor, -us - smaller
Mīnōs, -ōis (m.) - Minos, king of Crete
minuō, -ere, -uī, -ūtum - to make smaller
minus (adv.) - less, to a smaller degree
mīrābilis, -e - wondrous, extraordinary
mīror, -ārī, -ātus - to wonder at, be surprised
mīrus, -a, -um - remarkable, extraordinary, wondrous
misceō, -ēre, -uī, mixtum - to mix together, blend

~**miser, -era, -erum** - wretched, miserable

miserābilis, -e - pitiable

miserandus, -a, -um - wretched, pitiable

mittō, -ere, mīsī, missum - to let go, set free; send, shoot

mixtus, -a, -um - mixed

moderātē (adv.) - gently, in a restrained manner

modicus, -a, -um - moderate in size

~**modo** (adv.) - just now, recently, lately; just, only

modus, -ī (m.) - measure, meter, rhythm

moenia, -ium (n. pl.) - defensive walls encircling a town

mollescō, -ere - to become soft

molliō, -īre, -īvī, -ītum - to soften, weaken

mollis, -e - gentle, smooth; soft

moneō, -ēre, -uī, -itum - to advise, recommend

monīle, -is (n.) - necklace

monimentum, -ī (n.) - memorial

monitus, -ūs (m.) - warning, advising

mons, -tis (m.) - mountain, mountainous country

mora, -ae (f.) - delay

morior, -ī, mortuus - to die

moror, -ārī, -ātus - to delay, wait; to hold back

mors, -tis (f.) - death

morsus, -ūs (m.) - bite

mortālis, -e - mortal, human

mōrum, -ī (n.) - the fruit of the mulberry tree

mōrus, -ī (f.) - mulberry tree

mōs, mōris (m.) - character, morals, behavior

moveō -ēre, mōvī, mōtum - to move, strike; rouse

mox (adv.) - soon

mucrō, -ōnis (m.) - tip or point of a sword

multifidus, -a, -um - split, splintered

multum (adv.) - very, greatly

~**multus, -a, -um** - much

mūnus, -eris (n.) - gift, present; ritual duty

murmur, -is (n.) - mutter, whisper

mūrus, -ī (m.) - wall, city-wall

Mūsa, -ae (f.) - Muse

mūtō, -āre, -āvī, -ātum - to change, replace

mūtuus, -a, -um - mutual, reciprocal

myrtus, -ī (f.) - foliage of the myrtle tree

nam (conj.) - for, to be sure

Napē, -ēs (f.) - Nape

narrō, -āre, -āvī, -ātum - to tell, relate

nascor, -ī, nātus - to be born

Nāsō, -ōnis (m.) - Naso, Ovid's cognomen

nāta, -ae (f.) - daughter

nātālis, -e - of or belonging to birth

nātūra, -ae (f.) - nature, natural world

~**nātus, -ī (m.)** - son

nē (conj.) - lest, in order that...not; do not

~**nec** - and...not; not even

necō, -āre, -āvī, -ātum - to kill, put to death

negō, -āre, -āvī, -ātum - to say not; to deny

nempe (conj.) - to be sure, no doubt, certainly

nemus, -oris (n.) - wood, sacred grove

nepōs, -ōtis (m., f.) - grandson, granddaughter

neque (conj.) - and...not

nēquīquam (adv.) - in vain

nervus, -ī (m.) - string of a musical instrument or bow

nesciō, -īre, -īvī, -ītum - not to know, to be unfamiliar with; **nescio quis** - some, little, insignificant

neu (conj.) - nor

nēve (conj.) - and that...not

nex, necis (f.) - death

nīdus, -ī (m.) - nest

niger, -gra, -grum - black, dark-colored

nimbus, -ī (m.) - cloudburst, rainstorm

nimis (adv.) - too much, excessively, too

~**nimium** (adv.) - excessively, extremely, very much

nimius, -a, -um - too much, too great

Ninus, -ī (m.) - Ninus, king of Assyria and second husband to Semiramis

nisi (conj.) - if not

nītor, -tī, -sus - to strive, move with difficulty, exert oneself

nitor, -ōris (m.) - brilliance, brightness, splendor, elegance

niveus, -a, -um - white, snowy-white

nix, nivis (f.) - snow

nocens, -ntis - guilty

nocturnus, -a, -um - nightly, of the night

nolō, nolle, noluī, - not to want or wish

~**nōmen, -minis (n.)** - name, family name, fame, reputation

nōminō, -āre, -avī, -ātum - to name, call by name

~**nōn** (adv.) - not

nōndum (adv.) - not yet

nōs - we

noscō, -ere, nōvī, nōtum - to learn

~**noster, -tra, -trum** - our

nota, -ae (f.) - note, mark

nōtitia, -ae (f.) - acquaintance

notō, -āre, -āvī, -ātum - to mark, inscribe, scratch; to notice

nōtus, -a, -um - famous, well-known

novem - (indecl.) nine

noviens (adv.) - nine times

novissimus, -a, -um - last, final

novitās, -tātis (f.) - novelty, strange phenomenon

novō, -āre, -āvī, -ātum - to make or devise as new

~**novus, -a, -um** - new, unfamiliar

~**nox, -ctis (f.)** - night

nūdō, -āre, -āvī, -ātum - to make naked, expose

~**nūdus, -a, -um** - bare, pure, open, simple; naked, unclothed

~**nullus, -a, -um** - no one, nobody, nothing; no; insignificant, trifling

nūmen, -minis (n.) - divine power, divinity

numerus, -ī (m.) - number, rhythm, measure, meter

nunc (adv.) - now, at this time

nūper (adv.) - recently

nūtriō, -īre, -īvī, -ītum - to encourage, foster

nūtus, -ūs (m.) - nod

nux, -cis (f.) - nut

nympha, -ae (f.) - demi-goddess spirit of nature, nymph; unmarried girl

oblinō, -ere, -lēvī, -litum - to besmear, make dirty

obscūrus, -a, -um - dim, dark

obscēnus, -a, -um - polluted, foul, ill-omened

obsequor, -sequī, -secūtus - to comply, gratify, humor

observō, -āre, -āvī, -ātum - to watch over, guard

obsideō, -ēre, -sēdī, -sessum- to occupy, beseige,

obstipescō, -ere, -stipuī - to be amazed, astonished

obstō, -āre, -stitī, -stātum - to stand in the way, block the path

obstruō, -ere, -xī, -ctum - to block, obstruct

obtūsus, -a, -um - blunt, dull

obvius, -a, -um - opposing, confronting

occupō, -āre, -āvī, -ātum - to seize, occupy

ōcior, ōcius - swifter, faster

~**oculus, -ī (m.)** - eye

ōdī, odisse, ōsum - to hate, dislike

odōrātus, -a, -um - sweet-smelling, fragrant

offensus, -a, -um - offended, displeased

officium, -ī (n.) - duty
ōlim (adv.) - a long time ago
ōmen, -minis (n.) - omen
~omnis, -e - each, every, all
onus, -eris (n.) - burden
opifer, -era, -erum - aid-bringing, helper
opifex, -ficis (m.) - craftsman, artisan
ops, opis (f.) - (sing.) aid, help, military strength; (pl.) wealth
optō, -āre, -āvī, -ātum - to desire, wish for
~opus, -eris (n.) - task, undertaking, work, job; need
ōrāculum, -ī (n.) - oracular power, divine utterance
orbis, -is (m.) - globe, world
~ordō, -dinis (m.) - order; class, rank; a linear arrangement
Oriens, -ntis (m.) - the East
Ōrīōn, -onis (m.) - the constellation Orion
ornō, -āre, -āvī, -ātum - to adorn, decorate, attire
ōrō, -āre, -āvī, -ātum - to pray, beseech, beg
~ōs, ōris (n.) - face; mouth
os, ossis (n.) - bone
~osculum, -ī (n.) - mouth, lips; kiss
ostendō, -ere, -tendī, -tentum - to show, point out
ōtium, -ī (n.) - leisure
ōvum, -ī (n.) - egg
paciscor, -ī, pactus - to agree upon
pactum, -ī (n.) - agreement
Paeān, -nis (m.) - Apollo, as healer; a hymn or praise addressed to Apollo
Paelignus, -a, -um - of the Paelignian region in central Italy
pāgina, -ae (f.) - page
pallidus, -a, -um - pale, lacking color
palma, -ae (f.) - fruit of the palm, a date
palūs, -ūdis (f.) - swamp, floodwater

paluster, -tris, -tre - marshy
pandus, -a, -um - curved, bent, bowed
Paphius, -a, -um - of or pertaining to the city of Paphos on Cyprus
Paphos, -ī (m.) - the child of Pygmalion
pār, paris - equal
parātus, -ūs (m.) - preparation
parcus, -a, -um - thrifty, frugal
~pārens, -entis (m., f.) - ancestor, parent
pāreō, -ēre, -uī, -itum - to obey
pariēs, -etis (m.) - wall
parilis, -e - similar, like
pariter (adv.) - in the same manner, likewise; at the same time, simultaneously
Parnāsus, -ī (m.) - Parnasus, a mountain in Greece at the base of which is Delphi, sacred to both Apollo and the Muses.
parō, -āre, -āvī, -ātum - to prepare
Paros, -ī (f.) - Paros, an island in the Aegean Sea
pars, -tis (f.) - part, portion; side
parvus, -a, -um - small
passus, -ūs (m.) - pace, stride
pastor, -ōris (m.) - shepherd
Patarēus, -a, -um - of or related to Patara, a coastal city in southern Asia Minor with an oracle of Apollo
pateō, -ēre, -uī - to be visible or revealed; to be open
~pater, -tris (m.) - father
patior, -tī, passus - to allow, permit
patrius, -a, -um - of or pertaining to a father
patulus, -a, -um - broad
paucus, -a, -um - few
paulātim (adv.) - little by little, by degrees
paulum (adv.) - a little bit, to a small extent
pauper, -eris - poor, scanty
paupertās, -tātis (f.) - poverty
paveō, -ēre - to be frightened

~**pectus, -oris (n.)** - chest, breast, heart

pelagus, -ī (n.) - open sea

pellō, -ere, pepulī, pulsum - to fend off, drive away, repel; to strike, beat

Pelopēius, -a, -um - of or pertaining to the Peloponnesian peninsula

penātēs, -ium (n. pl.) - the household gods

pendeō, -ēre, pependī - to hang, hang down, fall

Pēnēis, -idos - descended from the river god Peneus

Pēnēius, -a, -um - of or connected with the river god Peneus

penitus (adv.) - thoroughly, completely

~**penna, -ae (f.)** - wing, feather

~**per** - (+ acc.) through, throughout

peragō, -ere, -ēgī, -actum - to carry out, perform

perārō, -āre, -āvī, -ātum - to plow through, inscribe

percipiō, -ere, -cēpī, -ceptum - to catch hold of

percutiō, -ere, -cussī, -cussum - to strike, beat

~**perdō, -ere, -idī, -itum** - to waste one's effort or time; to destroy

peremō, -ere, -ī, -ptum - to kill

perennis, -e - lasting, enduring

perferō, -ferre, -tulī, -lātum - to suffer, endure, undergo; carry, convey

perīclum - see **periculum**

perīculum, -ī (n.) - danger

perlegō, -ere, -lēgī, -lectum - to read over, read through

permātūrescō, -ere, -tūruī - to become fully ripe

perōdī, -disse, -sum - to despise, loathe

perpetuus, -a, -um - eternal, everlasting

persequor, -sequī, -secūtus - to follow all the way, accompany

perveniō, -īre, -vēnī, -ventum - to penetrate, extend, reach; to arrive

pervigilō, -āre, -āvī, -ātum - to keep watch all night

~**pēs, pedis (m.)** - foot; metrical foot

pestifer, -era, -erum - deadly, pernicious, pestilential

~**petō, -ere, -īvī, -ītum** - to seek, look for; to seek the hand of in marriage, to court

pharetra, -ae (f.) - quiver

pharetrātus, -a, -um - wearing a quiver

Philēmōn, -onis (m.) - Philemon, husband of Baucis

Phoebē, -ēs (f.) - Diana, twin sister to Apollo

Phoebus, -ī (m.) - Apollo

Phrygia, -ae (f.) - Phrygia, a region in central Asia Minor

pictus, -a, -um - painted

Pīerides, -um (f. pl.) - the Muses, daughters of Pierus

piger, -gra, -grum - sluggish, inactive

pīla, -ae (f.) - ball, sphere

piscis, -is (m.) - fish

Pittheus, -eī (m.) - Pittheus, son of Pelops and grandfather to Theseus

pius, -a, -um - dutiful, conscientious, pious

~**placeō, -ēre, -uī, -itum** - (+ dat.) to be pleasing or acceptable

placidus, -a, -um - agreeable, kindly

plangor, -ōris (m.) - beating, lamentation

plēnus, -a, -um - full

plūma, -ae (f.) - feather

plumbum, -ī (n.) - lead

plūrimus, -a, -um - most plentifully supplied, greatest in amount

plūs, plūris (n.) - more

plūs (adv.) - more

pōculum, -ī (n.) - a drinking cup

poena, -ae (f.) - penalty, punishment

poēta, -ae (m.) - poet
pollex, -icis (m.) - thumb
pompa, -ae (f.) - ceremonial
  procession
pōmum, -ī (n.) - fruit
~pōnō, -ere, posuī, positum - to
  put, place, arrange; to lay aside,
  abandon
pontus, -ī (m.) - sea
porta, -ae (f.) - gate, entryway
poscō, -ere, poposcī - to demand,
  ask for insistently
possideō, -ēre, -sēdī, -sessum - to
  control
~possum, posse, potuī - to be able
post - (+ acc.) after
posterus, -a, -um - next, following
postis, -is (m.) - door jamb, door,
  lintel
postquam (conj.) - after, when
potens, -tis - powerful, mighty,
  influential
potentia, -ae (f.) - power, influence
praebeō -ēre, -uī, -itum - to offer,
  provide
praeceptum, -ī (n.) - teaching,
  piece of advice
praecipitō, -āre, -āvī, -ātum - to
  plunge down, sink
praecordia, -ōrum (n. pl.) - heart,
  chest, breast
praeda, -ae (f.) - prey
praedor, -ārī, -ātus - to take as
  prey, catch
praeferō, -ferre, -tulī, -lātum
  - (+ dat.) to prefer, esteem more
praeripiō, -ere, -ripuī, -reptum
  - to seize, snatch away
praetereō, -īre, -iī, -itum - to pass by
precor, -ārī, -ātus - to pray for,
  implore, beg, beseech
premō, -ere, -ssī, -ssum - to press
  on, push; to cover
prex, precis (f.) - prayer
Priamēis, -idos (f.) - Cassandra,
  daughter of Priam
prīmus, -a, -um - first
prior, -us - first, earlier
prius (adv.) - first

prō - (+ abl.) on account of,
  because of
proavus, -ī (m.) - forefather
probō, -āre, -āvī, -ātum - to
  authorize, sanction, approve
procul (adv.) - far off, at a great
  distance
prōdūcō, -ere, -dūxī, -ductum - to
  bring forth, lead forth
prohibeō, -ēre, -uī, -itum - to
  prevent; to refuse
prōiciō, -ere, -iēcī, -iectum - to
  throw down
prōlēs, -is (f.) - offspring
prōmō, -ere, -psī, -ptum - to bring
  forth, draw forth, produce
prōnus, -a, -um - lying on the face
  or stomach, headlong
properō, -āre, -āvī, -ātum - to
  hasten
Prōpoetides, -um (f. pl.) - young
  women from Cyprus
prospiciō, -ere, -spexī, -spectum
  - to see before one, have a view
prōsum, prōdesse, prōfuī,
  prōfutūrus - to benefit, be
  helpful or useful to
prōtinus (adv.) - forthwith, at
  once, immediately, suddenly
prōveniō, -īre, -vēnī, -ventum - to
  come into being, arise
proximus, -a, -um - next
pruīnōsus, -a, -um - frosty
prūnum, -ī (n.) - a plum
pudor, -ōris (m.) - modesty
~puella, -ae (f.) - girl, young
  woman
~puer, -ī (m.) - boy
pulcher, -ra, -um - beautiful
pullus, -a, -um - dingy, sombre
pulsō, -āre, -āvī, -ātum - to beat,
  strike repeatedly
pulvis, -eris (m.) - dust
purpureus, -a, -um - radiant,
  glowing, blushing; purple,
  crimson
pūrus, -a, -um - pure, unsoiled
putō, -āre, -āvī, -ātum - to think,
  consider; to imagine

Pygmalion, -ōnis (m.)
- Pygmalion, king of Cyprus
Pyramus, -ī (m.) - Pyramus
Pythōn, -ōnis (m.) - a serpent slain
by Apollo
quā (adv.) - where, in which
direction
quam - (rel. adv.) than
quaerō, -ere, quaesīvī, -sītum - to
require, demand; to seek
quantō...tanto (adv.) - by however
much...by just so much
**quantuluscumque, -acumque,
-umcumque** - however small
quantus, -a, -um - how great
quatiō, -ere, quassum - to shake
-que - and;
-que...-que - both...and...
quercus, -ūs (f.) - oak tree; oak
garland
queror, -rī, questus - to complain
~**quī, quae, quod** - who, which
quia (conj.) - because, since
**quīcumque, quaecumque,
quodcumque** - the person who,
whoever, whatever
quid (adv.) - why? for what
reason?
quidem (adv.) - certainly, indeed,
it is true
quinque - five
~**quis, quid** - who? what?
quisque, quaeque, quidque
- each, each one, each thing
quisquis, quidquid - anyone who,
whoever
quō (adv.) - for that reason; in
order that; by which degree, by
how much
quod (conj.) - because; that, the
fact that
quondam (adv.) - once, formerly
quoniam (conj.) - since
~**quoque** (adv.) - also, too
radius, -ī (m.) - ray of light
rādix, -īcis (f.) - root; radish
rādō, -ere, rāsī, -sum - to rub clean,
erase; to graze, scrape, scratch

rāmāle, -is (n.) - branches, twigs
~**rāmus, -ī (m.)** - branch
rapidus, -a, -um - swift-moving
raucus, -a, -um - harsh-sounding,
raucous
recens, -ntis - recent, fresh
recipiō, -ere, -cēpī, -ceptum - to
receive, make welcome
recondō, -ere, -idī, -itum - to close
again
reddō, -ere, -idī, -itum - to deliver;
to give back, return
redeō, -īre, -iī, -itum - to return
redimīculum, -ī (n.) - band,
wreath, garland
redimiō, -īre, -iī, -ītum - to
wreathe, encircle
redoleō, -ēre - to give off a smell,
be fragrant
referō, -ferre, rettulī, relātum - to
bring back, bring out
rēfert, -ferre, -tulīt - it is of
importance
refertus, -a, -um - crammed full
refugiō, -ere, -fūgī - to shrink
from, recoil from
rēgia, -ae (f.) - royal palace, court
regiō, -ōnis (f.) - direction
regnō, -āre, -āvī, -ātum - to reign,
govern, hold sway
regnum, -ī (n.) - kingdom, domain
relevō, -āre, -āvī, -ātum - to
relieve, ease
~**relinquō, -ere, -liquī, -lictum** - to
leave behind
remaneō, -ēre, -sī, -sum - to
remain, stay put
rēmigium, -ī (n.) - oars, wings
remollescō, -ere - to grow soft
again, melt
remoror, -ārī, -ātus - to linger,
delay
removeō, -ēre, -mōvī, -mōtum -
to remove
renīdeō, -ēre - to smile with
pleasure, beam
renovō, -āre, -āvī, -ātum - to
renew

reperiō, -īre, repperī, repertum - to find, discover

repertor, -ōris (m.) - originator, discoverer

repetō, -ere, -īvī, -ītum - to repeat

repleō, -ēre, -ēvī, -ētum - to refill, replenish

repōnō, -ere, -posuī, -positum - to lay to rest

repugnō, -āre, -āvī, -ātum - to resist, fight against

requiēs, -ētis (f.) - (*requiem,* acc.) rest, relaxation

requiescō, -ere, -quēvī, -quētum - to rest, lie at rest

requīrō, -ere, -quīsīvī, -quīsītum - to ask, inquire about; to seek out, look for

rēs, -eī (f.) - matter, thing

rescrībō, -ere, -scrīpsī, -scrīptum - to write back in response

resecō, -āre, -secuī, -sectum - to cut back, trim

resīdō, -ere, -sēdī, -sessum - to fall back, subside

resistō, -ere, -stitī - to halt, pause

respiciō, -ere, -spexī, -spectum - to look back, look around

respondeō, -ēre, -dī, -sum - to answer, reply

restō, -āre, -itī - to linger, remain; to stand firm; to stop

resupīnus, -a, -um - lying on one's back

resurgō, -ere, -surrexī, -surrectum - to rise up again

retractō, -āre, -āvī, -ātum - to handle or feel a second time

retrō (adv.) - backwards

revellō, -ere, -vellī, -vulsum - to remove, tear away

reverentia, -ae (f.) - shyness, awe, modesty

revocō, -āre, -āvī, -ātum - to summon back

Rhēsus, -ī (m.) - Rhesus, a Thracian

rictus, -ūs (m.) - open jaws

rīdeō, -ēre, rīsī, rīsum - to laugh

rigidus, -a, -um - rigid, stiff

rigor, -ōris (m.) - stiffness, rigidity

riguus, -a, -um - irrigated, well-watered

rīma, -ae (f.) - crack

rīvalis, -is (m.) - rival

rōdō, -ere, rōsī, -sum - to eat away, erode

rogō, -āre, -āvī, -ātum - to beg, implore

rogus, -ī (m.) - funeral pyre

Rōma, -ae (f.) - Rome

rostrum, -ī (n.) - snout, muzzle

rota, -ae (f.) - wheel

rubeō, -ēre - to turn red

rubor, -ōris (m.) - redness

rudis, -e - crude, rough

rūgōsus, -a, -um - wrinkled

rumpō, -ere, rūpī, ruptum - to burst, break through

rūpēs, -is (f.) - rocky cliff

rursus (adv.) - in addition, besides

rūs, rūris (n.) - countryside

rusticus, -a, -um - rustic, crude, unrefined

sacer, -cra, -crum - sacred, holy

sacerdōs, -ōtis (m., f.) - priest, priestess

saeculum, -ī (n.) - generation

~saepe (adv.) - often

saepēs, -is (f.) - hedge

saevus, -a, -um - wild, savage, untamed

sagitta, -ae (f.) - arrow

sagittifer, -era, -erum - loaded with arrows, arrow-bearing

salignus, -a, -um - willow wood

saliō, -īre, -uī, -tum - to jump, leap

salūs, -ūtis (f.) - safety

Samos, -ī (f.) - an island in the eastern Mediterranean Sea

sānābilis, -e - curable

sanguis, -guinis (m.) - blood, bloodline

sanguinulentus, -a, -um - blood red

satis (adv.) - enough

Sāturnius, -a, -um - of Saturn, i.e., Jupiter

scelerātus, -a, -um - wicked, accursed, impious

scindō, -ere, scicidī, scissum - to split, rend, tear apart

sciō, -īre, -īvī, -ītum - to know

scrībō, -ere, -psī, -ptum - to write

sculpō, -ere, -psī, -ptum - to carve

secō, -āre, -cuī, -ctum - to cut

secundus, -a, -um - second

~sed (conj.) - but

sedeō, -ēre, sēdī, sessum - to sit

sēdēs, -is (f.) - house, dwelling

sedīle -is (n.) - seat

sēducō, -ere, -dūxī, -ductum - to move away, draw apart

sēdulus, -a, -um - attentive, persistent, zealous

segnis, -e - inactive, sluggish

semel (adv.) - once, a single time

Semīramis, -idis (f.) - Semiramis, a Syrian queen

~semper (adv.) - always

senecta, -ae (f.) - old age

senectūs, -ūtis (f.) - old age

senex, senis - old

senīlis, -e - old, aged

senior, -ius - older

~sentiō, -īre, sensī, sensum - to feel, sense

sentis, -is (m.) - bramble, briar

sepeliō, -īre, -īvī, sepultum - to bury, entomb

sepulcrum, -ī (n.) - tomb, grave

sequor, -quī, -cūtus - to follow; to come next in order

sera, -ae (f.) - a crossbar for locking a door

sermō, -ōnis (m.) - talk, conversation

serpens, -entis (f., m.) - snake, serpent

serta, -ōrum (n. pl.) - garlands, wreaths

sērus, -a, -um - late, after the expected time

servō, -āre, -āvī, -ātum - to guard; save, keep

serviō, -īre, -īvī, -ītum - to be devoted or subject to; to serve

sex - six

~sī (conj.) - if

~sīc (adv.) - thus, in this way, in like manner

siccō, -āre, -āvī, -ātum - to dry, dry up

siccus, -a, -um - dry

Sīdonis, -idis - of or pertaining to Sidon, a town on the Phoenician coast known for its puple dyeing process

sīdus, -eris (n.) - constellation, star

signum, -ī (n.) - signal, sign for action; military standard

silens, -entis - silent

silex, -icis (m.) - hard rock or stone; flint

silva, -ae (f.) - forest, woodland

similis, -e - like, similar

simplicitās, -tātis (f.) - lack of sophistication, frankness

simul (adv.) - together, with one another; at the same time

simulācrum, -ī (n.) - image, statue

simulō, -āre, -āvī, -ātum - to pretend, simulate

sincērus, -a, -um - unblemished

sine - (+ abl.) without

sinō, -ere, sīvī, situm - to permit, allow to take place

sinuōsus, -a, -um - having a bowed form, curved

sistō, -ere, stetī, statum - to set, set down

sitis, -is (f.) - thirst

situs, -ūs (m.) - neglect, disuse

sōbrius, -a, -um - sober, not intoxicated

socius, -a, -um - of or pertaining to a partner, kindred, companionable, fellow

sōl, sōlis (m.) - sun

soleō, -ēre, -itus - to be accustomed to

solitus, -a, -um - usual, accustomed

solum, -ī (n.) - earth, soil

sōlus, -a, -um - alone, only

solūtus, -a, -um - loose, unfastened, undone; weak

somnus, -ī (m.) - sleep, sleepiness

sōpītus, -a, -um - sleepy

sopōrō, -āre, -āvī, -ātum - to put to sleep

sordidus, -a, -um - grimy, dirty, unwashed

soror, -ōris (f.) - sister

spargō, -ere, sparsī, sparsum - to scatter, strew

spatior, -ārī, -ātus - to walk about

speciēs, -iēī (f.) - appearance, impression

spectō, -āre, -āvī, -ātum - to look at, observe

speculātor, -ōris (m.) - scout, spy

spērō, -āre, -āvī, -ātum - to hope for, look forward to; to expect

spēs, -eī (f.) - hope, expectation

spīculum, -ī (n.) - tip, point; arrow

splendidus, -a, -um - bright, shining

sponda, -ae (f.) - the frame of a bed or couch

spons, -ntis (f.) - will, volition

spūmō, -āre, āvī, -ātum - to foam, froth

stāgnum, -ī (n.) - pool

statuō, -ere, -uī, -ūtum - to make up one's mind, decide

sterilis, -e - futile

sternō, -ere, strāvī, strātum - to strew, lay low, spread over an area, throw down

stīpes, -itis (m.) - tree trunk; woody branch

stipula, -ae (f.) - stubble

stīva, -ae (f.) - the shaft of a plow handle

stō, stāre, stetī, stātum - to stand

strāmen, -inis (n.) - straw thatch

strātum, -ī (n.) - coverlet, throw

strēnuus, -a, -um - restless, keen

strīdō, -ere, -ī - to make a high-pitched sound; to whistle, shriek, hiss

stringō, -ere, -nxī, strictum - to touch lightly, graze; to unsheath

strix, -igis (f.) - a screech owl

stupeō, -ēre, -uī - to be amazed, stunned, dazed

~sub - (+ abl.) under, underneath; at the base of; (+ acc) at the base of, just at

subditus, -a, -um - situated beneath

subeō, -īre, -īvī, -itum - to spread upwards; to replace

sūbiciō, -ere, -iēcī, -iectum - to harness, put under the control of

subscrībō, -ere, -scripsī, -scriptum - to write below

subsīdō, -ere, -sēdī - to give way

succinctus, -a, -um - having one's clothes bound up with a girdle or belt

succrescō, -ere, -ēvī - to grow up as a replacement, to be supplied anew

sufferō, -ferre, sustulī, sublātum - to hold up, sustain weight

suffundō, -ere, -fūdī, -fūsum - to pour into, overspread; to color, redden, blush

sui - himself, herself, itself, themselves

Sulmō, -ōnis (m.) - Sulmo, in the province of Paelignia; the town of Ovid's birth

~sum, esse, fui, futūrus - to be

summittō, -ere, -mīsī, -missum - to lower

summus, -a, -um - greatest; highest

sumptus, -ūs (m.) - expenditure

super - (+ acc.) over

superbus, -a, -um - haughty, proud, arrogant

superī, -ōrum (m. pl.) - those inhabiting the heavens, the heavenly deities

superiniciō, -ere, -iniēcī, -iniectum - to throw over a surface

superstes, -itis - surviving after death

supersum, -esse, -fuī -futūrus - to remain, be left over

supīnus, -a, -um - turned palm upwards

suppleō, -ēre, -ēvī, -ētum - to fill up

surgō, -ere, surrexī, surrectum - to rise up

surrigō, -ere, surrexī, surrectum - to rise up

surripiō, -ere, -rripuī, -rreptum - to steal

sūs, suis (m., f.) - pig, sow

suscitō, -āre, -āvī, -ātum - to rouse, restore

suspendium, -ī (n.) - hanging

suspendō, -ere, -ī, -pensum - to hang, suspend

sustineō, -ēre, -uī - to endure, tolerate

~suus, -a, -um - his, her, its, their

~tabella, -ae (f.) - writing tablet

tābescō, -ere, tābuī - to melt gradually

tabula, -ae (f.) - account book

tacitus, -a, -um - silent, quiet

taeda, -ae (f.) - torch made of pine wood

tālis, -e - such

tam (adv.) - so, so very

~tamen (adv.) - nevertheless

tamquam (conj.) - as if

tandem (adv.) - at last, finally

~tangō, -ere, tetigī, tactum - to touch, come in contact with

tantum (adv.) - only, merely, just; tantum...quantum - just so far...as

tantus, -a, -um - so great, such a great

tardē (adv.) - slowly

tardus, -a, -um - slow-moving

tectum, -ī (n.) - roof, ceiling; house

tectus, -a, -um - covered with a roof, roofed

tegō, -ere, texī, tectum - to cover, conceal

tellūs, -ūris (f.) - land, country

telum, -ī (n.) - weapon, shaft

temerārius, -a, -um - reckless, thoughtless, rash

Tempē (n. pl.) - (indecl.) a valley known for its pastoral beauty at the foot of Mt. Olympus

temperō, -āre, -āvī, -ātum - to moderate, regulate

templum, -ī (n.) - temple

~temptō, -āre, -āvī, -ātum - to try, attempt; to handle, touch, feel

tempus, -oris (n.) - time; temple of the forehead

tenebrae, -ārum (f. pl.) - darkness

Tenedos, -ī (f.) - an island sacred to Apollo in the Aegean Sea

~teneō, -ēre, -uī, -tum - to have, hold, preserve; to catch

tener, -era, -erum - tender, sensitive; fragile

tenuis, -e - fine, thin, tender

tepeō, -ēre, - to be warm, tepid

tepidus, -a, -um - warm

ter (adv.) - three times

teres, -etis - smooth, rounded

tergeō, -ēre, tersī, tersum - to wipe clean

tergum, -ī (n.) - back

tergus, -oris (n.) - back of an animal

terra, -ae (f.) - earth, ground

tertius, -a, -um - third

testa, -ae (f.) - a fragment of earthenware

textum, -ī (n.) - woven fabric, cloth

thalamus, -ī (m.) - bedroom, marriage chamber

Thisbē, -ēs (f.) - Thisbe

Thrēicius, -a, -um - Thracian

Thȳnēius, -of or pertaining to the region of Bithynia

thyrsus, -ī (m.) - a wand, usually covered with vine leaves, and carried by worshippers of Bacchus

tignum, -ī (n.) - timber, rafter

tilia, -ae (f.) - the lime (linden) tree

timeō, -ēre, -uī - to fear, be afraid

~timidus, -a, -um - fearful, apprehensive, timid

timor, -ōris (m.) - fear, dread

tingō (tinguo), -ere, -nxī, -nctum - to wet, soak; to dye, stain

tollō, -ere, sustulī, sublātum - to pick up; to raise up

torpor, -ōris (m.) - numbness, heaviness

torus, -ī (m.) - cushion, bed

tot - (indecl.) so many

totiens (adv.) - so often

~tōtus, -a, -um - the whole of

tractō, -āre, -āvī, -ātum - to handle, manage

trādō, -ere, -idī, -itum - to deliver, hand over

trahō, -ere, traxī, tractum - to drag, draw; to influence

trāiciō, -ere, -iēcī, -iectum - to transfix, pierce

transeō, -īre, -īvī, -itum - to cross, pass through

transitus, -ūs (m.) - passage

tremebundus, -a, -um - trembling, quivering

tremō, -ere, -uī - to tremble

tremulus, -a, -um - quivering, shaking

trepidō, -āre, -āvī, -ātum - to tremble, throb, quiver

tristis, -e - unfriendly, dismal, sorrowful

triumphus, -ī (m.) - the procession held in Rome to honor a victorious general

trivium, -ī (n.) - crossroad, meeting point of three roads

Trōs, -ōis (m.) - Trojan

truncō, -āre, -āvī, -ātum - to strip off foliage

truncus, -ī (m.) - a trunk

~tū - you (sing.)

tueor, -ērī, tuitus - to observe, watch over, guard

tum (adv.) - then, at that moment

tumidus, -a, -um - swollen, swelling

tumulō, -āre, -āvī, -ātum - to entomb

tumulus, -ī (m.) - grave

turba, -ae (f.) - crowd of followers, attendants, troop

turbō, -inis (m.) - whirlwind

turpis, -e - loathsome, repulsive, shameful

tūs, tūris (n.) - incense

tūtēla, -ae (f.) - guardian, protection

tūtus, -a, -um - safe, secure

~tuus, -a, -um - your (sing.)

ūber, -eris - plentiful, abundant

ubi (adv.) - where, when

ubīque (adv.) - everywhere, anywhere

ullus, -a, -um - any

ultimus, -a, -um - final, last

ultrā (adv.) - further, beyond that point

ulva, -ae (f.) - rush, marsh grass

umbra, -ae (f.) - shade, darkness, shadow

umbrōsus, -a, -um - shady

umerus, -ī (m.) - shoulder

umquam (adv.) - never, ever (with nec)

ūnā (adv.) - at the same time

~unda, -ae (f.) - body of flowing water, river; water

undēnī, -ae, -a - eleven at a time

ūnicus, -a, -um - one, only one

~ūnus, -a, -um - one; alone

urbs, -is (f.) - city

urna, -ae (f.) - urn

ūrō, -ere, ussī, ustum - to burn, inflame with passion

usque (adv.) - all the way

usus, -ūs (m.) - use, purpose

~ut (conj.) - just as, like; when; in order that; since

uterque, utraque, utrumque - each, each...of the two

ūtilis, -e - useful

ūtor, ūtī, ūsus - (+ abl.) to make use of

ūva, -ae (f.) - a bunch of grapes, grape

uxor, -ōris (f.) - wife

vacō, -āre, -āvī, -ātum - to be empty, unfilled, vacant

~vacuus, -a, -um - empty, unattached, free, unoccupied

vadimōnium, -ī (n.) - a legal term referring to a guarantee that the parties in a suit will appear before the court at an agreed upon date and time

vagus, -a, -um - shifting, moving about

valē, valēte - farewell! good-bye!

vānus, -a, -um - unreliable

vārus, -a, -um - bent outward

vātēs, -is (m.) - poet, prophet

-ve (conj.) - or

vehō, -ere, vexī, vectum - to carry

~vel (conj.) - either...or; at any rate

vēlāmen, -minis (n.) - garment, veil

vellō, -ere, vulsī, -sum - to pull up

vēlō, -āre, -āvī, -ātum - to cover

vēlox, -ōcis - swift, speedy

velut (adv.) - just as, just like, in the same way that

vēna, -ae (f.) - blood vessel, vein

venia, -ae (f.) - justification, excuse, indulgence

~veniō, -īre, vēnī, ventum - to come

venter, -tris (m.) - belly

ventilō, -āre, -āvī, -ātum - to fan, brandish

ventus, -ī (m.) - wind

Venus, -eris (f.) - Venus, goddess sacred to love and lovers

~verbum, -ī (n.) - word

vērē (adv.) - truly, indeed

verēcundus, -a, -um - modest

vereor, -ērī, -itus - to be afraid

Vergilius, -ī (m.) - Vergil

vērō (adv.) - truly, really

Vērōna, -ae (f.) - the city Verona in the north of Italy

verrō, -ere, versum - to pass over, skim, sweep; to row

versō, -āre, -āvī, -ātum - to turn

versus, -ūs (m.) - a line of verse or writing

vertex, -icis (m.) - the top of the head

vertō, -ere, -tī, -sum - to turn into, change

verum (conj.) - but

vērus, -a, -um - real, genuine

vester, -tra, -trum - your (pl.)

vestīgium, -ī (n.) - footprint, sole of a foot, track

~vestis, -is (f.) - clothing; cloth

vetō, -āre, -uī, -itum - to forbid, prohibit

vetus, -eris - old, of a former time, ancient

via, -ae (f.) - journey, march, way

viātor, -ōris (m.) - traveller

vibrō, -āre, -āvī, -ātum - to wave, flutter

vīcīnia, -ae (f.) - proximity

vīcīnus, -a, -um - neighboring, close by

vicis (f.) (gen.) - exchange, interaction; **in vices** - by turns, alternately

victrix, -īcis - victorious

victrix, -īcis (f.) - victorious female

videō, -ēre, vīsī, vīsum - to see, observe, gaze upon; to consider

vigil, -ilis (m.) - sentry, guard

vīlis, -e - worthless, common, ordinary

villa, -ae (f.) - rural dwelling

vincō, -ere, vīcī, victum - to defeat, conquer

vinculum, -ī (n.) - chain, bond

vīnum, -ī (n.) - wine

violentus, -a, -um - violent, aggressive

vir, -ī (m.) - man, husband

vireō, -ēre, -uī - to sprout, show green growth

virgineus, -a, -um - of or relating to a maiden, virgin

virginitās, -tātis (f.) - maidenhood

~virgō, -inis (f.) - maiden

vīs, vīs (f.) - (pl.) strength

viscus, -eris (n.) - innermost parts of the body

vīsō, -ere, -ī - to view

vīta, -ae (f.) - life

vitiō, -āre, -āvī, -ātum - to impair, cause defects in

vītis, -is (f.) - grapevine

vitium, -ī (n.) - defect, fault; vice, moral failing

vītō, -āre, -āvī, -ātum - to avoid
vitta, -ae (f.) - headband
vīvō, -ere, vīxī, vīctum - to live
vix (adv.) - hardly, scarcely
vocō, -āre, -āvī, -ātum - to call
volātus, -ūs (m.) - flying, flight
volō, -āre, -āvī, -ātum - to fly
~volō, velle, voluī - to wish for; to wish
volucris, -cris (f.) - bird
voluntās, -tātis (f.) - willingness, intention

~vōs - you (pl.)
vōtum, -ī (n.) - vow, oath, prayer
vox, vōcis (f.) - voice
vulgō, āre, -āvī, -ātum - to prostitute
vulgus, -ī (n.) - general public, crowd, masses
~vulnus, -eris (n.) - wound, injury
vultur, -uris (m.) - vulture
vultus, -ūs (m.) - facial expression; face

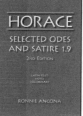

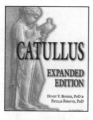